GW00818898

Existential Anthropology

Methodology and History in Anthropology

General Editor: David Parkin, Director of the Institute of Social and Cultural Anthropology, University of Oxford

EXISTENTIAL ANTHROPOLOGY

Events, Exigencies and Effects

Michael Jackson

Berghahn Books
New York • Oxford

First published in 2005 by

Berghahn Books

www.berghahnbooks.com

©2005 Michael Jackson

Library of Congress Cataloging-in-Publication Data

Jackson, Michael, 1940-
    Existential anthropology : events, exigencies and effects / Michael Jackson.
      p. cm.
    ISBN 1-57181-476-0 (acid-free paper)
      1. Philosophical anthropology. 2. Existentialism. I. Title.

BD450.J234 2004
128--dc22   2004053833

British Library Cataloguing in Publication Data

A catalogue record for this book is available from the British Library

Printed in Canada on acid-free paper
ISBN 1-57181-476-0 hardback
ISBN 1-84545-122-8 paperback

CONTENTS

... for several decades now our world has been changing. At the very depths of its hatred, reciprocity reveals itself; even those who enjoy emphasizing their differences must be willing to ignore a fundamental identity. This new disturbance, this modest but stubborn attempt to communicate across the incommunicable, is not the stale and always somewhat stupid desire for an inert and already realized universal; this is what I should prefer to call 'the movement of universalization'. Nothing is possible yet; no agreement is foreseen among the experimental creatures; our universals separate us; they provide the permanent occasion of private massacres. But if one of us, stirred by anxiety, turns back on his singularity *to go beyond it*; if he tries to recognize his solitude in order to escape it, to launch the first bridges, whatever the cost – in a strange, empirical language like the speech invented by the aphasiac – between the islands of the archipelagos; if he replaces our intransigent loves – which are disguised hatreds – by applied preferences; if he tries, in circumstances that are always individual and dated, to ally himself with others whom he scarcely approves of and who do not approve of him, to make the reign of Injustice a little less unjust, then he will force those others to reinvent this same stubborn effort, to ally themselves by the recognition of their diversities.

Jean-Paul Sartre, 'Of Rats and Men', Foreword to André Gorz's *The Traitor* (1989:32–33).

ACKNOWLEDGEMENTS

This book owes much to conversations with Ghassan Hage and Galina Lindquist in 2002, and to my students and colleagues at the Institute of Anthropology, University of Copenhagen, who have so patiently and generously listened to my evolving ideas and provided me with incisive critiques. I would also like to thank Ronda Cooper, Lena Egberg, Joachim Halse, Kassim Kone, Francine Lorimer, Susanne Lundin and Michael Whyte for crucial references, Jan Starcke for his magnanimous bibliographical assistance, and Tine Gammeltoft, Sophie Geisler, Alf Hornborg, Galina Lindquist, David Parkin, Sarah Pike, Tine Tjørnhøj-Thomsen and Susan Reynolds Whyte for invaluable comments on some of the chapters in this book. In Sierra Leone, my fieldwork in 2002 and 2003 would have been impossible but for the friendship and hospitality of the Honourable S.B. Marah, Rose Marah and Noah B. Marah. Several chapters of this book were drafted during my tenure of a Guest Professorship at the Department of Cultural Anthropology and Ethnology, University of Uppsala, in February–March 2003 where Sverker Finnström, Mikael Kurkiala, Inga-Lill Aronsson and Hugo Beach, among others, provided inspiration, support and a home away from home.

Three chapters of this book are revised versions of already-published articles: 'The Exterminating Angel: Reflections on Violence and Intersubjective Reason' (*European Journal of Anthropology*, 39, 2002b: 137–148 [Chapter 3]), 'Biotechnology and the Critique of Globalisation' (*Ethnos*, 67(2), 2002c: 141–154. [Chapter 7]), 'Familiar and Foreign Bodies: a Phenomenological Exploration of the Human-Technology Interface' (*Journal of the Royal Anthropological Institute*, 8(2), 2002d: 333–346 [Chapter 8]). Parts of chapters 4, 9, and 10 have previously appeared, in slightly different form, in my book *In Sierra Leone* (University of Chicago Press, 2004). Grateful acknowledgement is made for permission to reprint these materials.

PREFACE:

THE STRUGGLE FOR BEING

> Ultimately, the focus has to be on what life we lead and what we can and
> cannot do, can or cannot be.
> Amartya Sen, (1988: 16)

With this book I bring to an end a journey I embarked on forty years
ago. Although beginnings are as arbitrary as endings, hindsight per-
suades me that my path was decided by a sense that I did not altogether
belong in the place where I was raised, and by a growing conviction
that in other places, living another life, I might make good what I felt I
lacked and somehow come into my own. The first anthropology book I
ever bought was Malinowski's *Argonauts of the Western Pacific*. It was
not prescribed reading for the first year anthropology course in which I
was enrolled at the University of Auckland, and I picked it up in a book
sale, but Malinowski's closing remarks spoke to me with far more
immediacy that his exhaustive descriptions of the Kula.

> We cannot possibly reach the final Socratic wisdom of knowing ourselves
> if we never leave the narrow confinement of the customs, beliefs and prej-
> udices into which every man is born. Nothing can teach us a better lesson
> in this matter of ultimate importance than the habit of mind which allows
> us to treat the beliefs and values of another man from his point of view.
> (1922: 518)

Without a doubt, this tension between the parochial world that shaped
me early on, and the lifeworlds to which I gravitated in an endeavour
to reshape myself has governed my career in anthropology. It also
explains why I have always seen human existence as a struggle
between contending forces and imperatives.

At times this 'sheer and reeling need to be' (DeLillo 2003: 209) takes the form of a search for oneself, at other times as a search for belonging. At times it consists in working to transform the world into which one is thrown into a world one has a hand in making – to strike a balance between being an actor and being acted upon. At times it entails a struggle to go on living in the face of adversity and loss. At times it is a struggle for being against nothingness – for whatever will make life worth living rather than hopeless, profitless and pointless.

That being is precarious and unstable is obvious from the ontological metaphors with which we typically describe it. Quotidian existence is marked by ups (being high, feeling on top of things,) and downs (being blue, feeling down) – and often compared, in popular thought, to changes in the weather or market oscillations between profit and loss. Allusions are also made to fullness (being full of life) or emptiness (being drained), or the contrast between activity (being on the move, being creative, making something of oneself, going places) and stasis, which is often synonymous with nothingness (being stuck, being trapped, getting nowhere). That one's sense of wellbeing is susceptible to constant change is shown by the way that an affectionate glance, a gesture of recognition or concern, the company of close friends, or an unexpected gift can make one's day, while a cutting remark, a snub, ill-health, the loss of a job, or a falling out with a friend can cast a pall over everything. Although this minutia of everyday life suggests recurring symbolic motifs – the need to *be* recognised, healthy, loved, happy, or free, to *have* security, wealth, an identity, a fulfilling job, a family and friends, and to *do* well in life – it is important to note that being is never an 'either/or' thing, but a 'more or less' question (Hage 2003: 16). Being is always what Jaspers calls 'potential being' (1967: 63–66). Not only is it in continual flux, waxing and waning according to a person's situation, but the very wherewithal for being is, as Bourdieu argues 'unequally distributed' (2000: 241). However, inequality is not wholly politico-economic, as Amartya Sen has eloquently argued. 'You could be *well off*, without being *well*. You could be *well*, without being able to lead the life you *wanted*. You could have got the life you *wanted*, without being *happy*. You could be *happy*, without having much *freedom*. You could have a good deal of *freedom*, without *achieving* much' (1988: 1). Thus, while it is often argued that in today's globalised world, the distribution of infectious diseases and individual pathologies reflect 'social fault lines' and entrenched social inequalities (Farmer 2001: 5), and that education, employment and wellbeing are not shared by everyone in equal measure, it would be facile to reduce the meaning of a person's existence to either such external circumstances or to some inner essence.

The struggle for being may be understood cybernetically – not as a fixed course, but as a course *steered between* a variable environment and the equally variable capacities of persons (Jackson 1998: 18–19). Accordingly, in this work I seek to extend Sartre's insight that our humanness is the outcome of a dynamic *relationship* between circumstances over which we have little control – such as phylogenetic predispositions, our upbringing and our social history – and our capacity to *live* those circumstances in a variety of ways.[1] Obviously, there is double determination involved here. For while it is true that our capacity for being is constrained by external conditions and engrained habits, it is equally true that these limiting conditions are shaped by the ways in which we respond to them, which is why praxis 'is characterized above all by the fact that the qualitatively new appears in it' and 'is a movement which does not run its course in pure identity, the pure reproduction of such as already was there' (Buck Morss 1977: 54, cf. Adorno 1973: 5, Sartre 1968: 91–99).

To escape the reifying and dulling effects of generalisation, some anthropologists have focused on the individual (e.g., Rapport 2003); others on narrative (e.g., Abu-Lughod 1993). My own strategy is to focus on events. Thus, each chapter in this book is centred on a 'critical event' (cf. Das 1995) that broaches this question of being as a relationship between the forces that act upon us and our capacity for bringing the new into being: incidents during the war and postwar in Sierra Leone; the aftermath of the destruction of the World Trade Centre on 11 September 2001; the experience of belonging and being out of place among Aboriginal people in contemporary Australia; cases of organ transplantation, and the interface between humans and machines; instances of ritualisation and the magical use of language in everyday life; episodes of violence and human rights violations; case studies of how people deal with their own suffering and the suffering of others; and finally the kinds of events in which the struggle for being is all but absent, yet in which our being often seems most completely consummated.

Existential Anthropology

A longstanding cliché about existential philosophy is that it is preoccupied with the fate of the individual cast into a world he did not choose, without God-given or natural meanings for existence, yet obliged to assume responsibility for himself and his fellow human beings while creating some sense of the absurd situation in which he finds himself. Defined in this way, existentialism seems to offer nothing to anthropologists whose work takes us into lifeworlds where individuality is often played down, where a person's fate is often decided by forces outside his comprehension and control, where identity is defined less in being than in belonging, where ultimate meaning is associated with God, spirits and the ancestors, where death is never final, and where one's main responsibility is not to oneself but to others. But however being is symbolically expressed, the *question* of being is universal, and constitutes a starting-point in our attempt to explore human lifeworlds as the sites of a perennial struggle for existence – theorising this as a dynamic relationship between the human capacity for life, and the potentialities of any social environment for providing the wherewithal of life. Alluding to this interplay between social and spiritual worlds, the Igbo proverb notes, 'The world is a marketplace and it is subject to bargain' (Uchendu 1965: 15).

Though being and wellbeing are abstract concepts, their value for anthropology lies in their power to translate an infinite number of vernacular and concrete terms, *including* culture, mana, life, individuality, mind and nature. The existential anthropology I want to develop here refuses, however, to reduce existence to any one such category term,[2] or ground it in either subjective or objective realities. Constantly referring human life to culture is no more edifying, in my view, than reducing it to nature or personhood. My argument is not against the meanings people find in *having* a cultural or national identity, or in *being* themselves, or in *doing* their duty – for such notions are what life is ostensively about for many people. Rather, my argument is against our tendency to ontologise such notions, and make them foundational to a *theory* of human being. This is why I reject the idea, so often associated with existentialism, that our humanity consists in our individual will-to-be,[3] a striving for self-realisation or authenticity, for most human action is less a product of intellectual deliberation and conscious choice than a matter of continual, intuitive, and opportunistic changes of course – a 'cybernetic' switching between alternatives that promise more or less satisfactory solutions to the ever-changing situation at hand. For the same reason, I repudiate objectivist notions of existence as adaptation or compliance. Evolutionary biology reminds us that there are 50 million species of life on earth, hence 50 million solutions to the problems of survival. Human societies, though less diverse, may be viewed in the same way. But each is a solution, not only to the problems of adaptation and subsistence, but to the problem of creating viable forms of existence and coexistence. Moreover, human wellbeing involves far more than simple adjustment to a given environment, natural or cultural; it involves endless experimentation in how the given world can be lived *decisively*, on one's own terms.

Moments of Being

The opening pages of Virginia Woolf's *To the Lighthouse* (orig. 1927) brilliantly convey a sense of the *critical* nature of Being.

The novel begins with a mother's promise to her six year-old son, that if the weather is fine tomorrow, and he gets up 'with the lark', the family will go on an excursion to the Lighthouse. Mrs Ramsay's words instantly transfigure her son's mood and vision. Suffused by 'an extraordinary joy', James feels as if the expedition is now bound to take place, and that the 'wonder to which he had looked forward, for years and years it seemed' is, 'after a night's darkness and a day's sail, within touch.' This joy fringes everything he now looks upon, even endowing the refrigerator in the Army and Navy Stores catalogue from which he has been clipping pictures 'with heavenly bliss'. But suddenly his father declares that the weather won't be fine, and James's mood changes instantaneously to despair and anger.

> Had there been an axe handy, a poker, or any weapon that would have gashed a hole in his father's breast and killed him, there and then, James would have seized it. Such were the extremes of emotion that Mr Ramsey excited in his children's breasts by his mere presence; standing, as now, lean as a knife, narrow as the blade of one, grinning sarcastically, not only upon the pleasure of disillusioning his son and casting ridicule upon his wife, who was ten thousand times better in every way than he was (James thought), but also with some secret conceit at his own accuracy of judgement. (Woolf 1977: 9–10)

Yet, no sooner has this mood of disappointment and dashed hopes descended, than James's mother reassures him with the words 'But it may be fine – I expect it will be fine,' and all is well again.

Though this is fiction, and concerned with the flux and subtle shadings of lived experience, it succeeds in giving us a vivid sense of what is at stake at any moment of being, and in introducing us to some of the ways in which existential-phenomenological thought has theorised the question of being.

Being human means, first, that we possess *consciousness* of ourselves and of our world – a consciousness that is, however, unsettled and fluid, oscillating constantly between speech and silence, solitude and sociality, agitation and calm, aimlessness and purposefulness, reflection and habit, joy and sorrow, and embodied and etherealised extremes. Though consciousness is, as Merleau-Ponty famously pointed out, not only a matter of 'I think' but 'I can' (1962: 137), it is also, frequently, a matter of 'I cannot'. To be human is not only to have *intentions* and *purposes*, which one strives to consummate, despite lim-

ited possibilities, finite abilities and scarce resources; it is to be
thwarted, conflicted and thrown by contingency and circumstance.
Another way of making this point is to emphasise that though human
existence is *relational* – a mode of being-in-the-world – it is continually
at *risk*. This implies not only that our being is conditional on our interactions – bodily, linguistic, social and imaginary – with the world in
which we live, but that we are involved in a constant struggle to sustain and augment our being in relation to the being of others, as well
as the nonbeing of the physical and material world, and the ultimate
extinction of being that is death.

The Precariousness of Presence[4]

To argue that the meaning of human existence cannot be reduced to
cultural imperatives any more than it can be reduced to natural forces
such as instincts and appetites, does not mean that we re-centre our
analysis on the human subject. Nor does it imply that one falls back on
the dialectic of internalisation and externalisation that the sociology
of knowledge invoked in its attempt to avoid the simplistic opposition
of the individual and the group, the subjective and the objective. As a
methodological first principle we focus not on relata – whether individuals *or* societies – but on what Hannah Arendt called 'the subjective
in-between' (1958: 183) and on that which comes into being in this
intermediate space of human interest and interaction. Bypassing both
the individual subject and culture as *sui generis* phenomena, we seek to
explore the space of appearances – where that which is *in potentia*
becomes *in presentia* – disclosed, drawn out, brought forth, given presence or embodied.[5]

Object-relations theory is particularly helpful in pursuing this mode
of inquiry. Culture, writes D.W. Winnicott, is 'in fact neither a matter
of inner psychic reality nor a matter of external reality' (1974: 113).
Comparing culture with transitional phenomena and play, Winnicott
goes on to argue that culture is a 'common pool ... into which individuals and groups of people may contribute, and from which we may all
draw *if we have somewhere to put what we find*' (1974: 116, emphasis in
text). This means, for Winnicott, that culture is not some kind of
ready-made, omnipresent composite of habits, meanings and practices
that are located *in* the individual or *in* the environment, but a *potentiality* that is realised and experienced variously in the course of our
interactions with others, as well as our relationships to the everyday
environments and events in which we find ourselves. It therefore bears
a family resemblance to James Gibson's notion of 'affordances'[6] and
Sartre's notion of 'exigences'. According to Sartre – and his view was

shared by Merleau-Ponty (1962: 136–147) – most human action is unreflective, which is to say we do not necessarily form any conscious idea of our intentions before we act. But this absence of conceptualisation does not imply that we are at the mercy of blind *habits*, or that our actions are ruled by *unconscious* drives. Rather, it is as though the world variously 'offered itself', 'appeared' or 'closed itself off' to us as a field of instrumental possibilities (Sartre 1948: 53–58). Conceptualisation, reflection and representation tend to follow *from* our actions; they are seldom scripts or scores that precede it. Beliefs and ideas are thus, more often than not, outcomes of an activity, or retrospective abridgements of it, that help us come to terms with what has already taken place. They haunt but do not govern lived events. Accordingly, theories and stories alike may be seen as selective, imaginative, *post festum* re-workings of reality that make it appear less contingent, and ourselves less insignificant. A theory, as Michael Oakeshott reminds us, is like a recipe. It is not 'an independently generated beginning from which cooking can spring; it is nothing more than an abstract of somebody's knowledge of how to cook; it is the stepchild, not the parent of the activity' (1991: 52).

Our task is thus to explore human being-in-the-world through our ever-changing capacity to create the conditions of viable existence and coexistence in relation to the given potentialities of our environment. Alienation signifies a radical rupture of this relationship between a person's capacities and environmental conditions, resulting in 'the impossibility of making the given into the means to some kind of end worth living for – in perhaps having to abandon all other goals and values in order to maintain the bare minimum of life' (Gorz 1989: 276). Yet hardly a day passes that one is not overwhelmed by the human capacity for love and joy, by what some people accomplish with limited means in a world of scarcity and inequality, and by the ingenuity with which people reimagine and surpass the situations in which they find themselves. At the same time, one is stunned by how easily a life can be lost – in a childhood without love, or in violent situations where people lack the resources to defend themselves – as in the case of the four hundred Samburu and Masai women raped by British soldiers stationed in their district in the northern Highlands of Kenya during the last twenty years. 'All my life, I have not been living the life that is really mine,' said Elizabeth Naeku Mburia, who bore a half-white child after she was raped, and never got to pursue her studies in law, nor marry. Recalling the day in 1983 when her freedom was lost, she said 'I felt pain. I felt shame. I felt my dignity go out of me' (Walter 2003: 2–3). At the same time, one remarks the destructive forces and fantasies that unfold when people invest in a world that gives nothing in return – as when James' longing for the Lighthouse is denied by his insensitive father, or when West African youths take up arms to seize the things they feel they have been unjustly denied.

To understand such violence intersubjectively, one must remember that the principle of reciprocity operates both at the level of being and of having, for being is in all societies invested in and distributed among the *things* which people call their own and with which they identify. What one *has* objectifies who one *is*. The Kuranko notion of *miran* makes this clear. *Mirannu* (pl.) refer both to material possessions – particularly those that contain and protect, such as a house, clothing, water vessels and cooking pots – as well as to personal attributes that give one a sense of self-possession, presence and substantiality of being – such as forceful speech, physical skill and social adroitness. But *miran*, in both senses of the term – material possession and personal disposition – is never a fixed property or attribute. In practice, a person's *miran* may be bolstered by fetishes that symbolically enclose, contain and protect the vital spaces that define his or her being – body, house, village, chiefdom – in exactly the same way that in a consumer society material possessions bolster and define a person's sense of well-being, substantiality and standing. For Kuranko, the notion of a full container is a common metaphor for anyone who is in command of himself and working his utmost to do what is expected of him, to do his duty. But self-possession and morale may be undermined, sapped or lost.[7] Just as a person's property can be stolen, a pot broken and a house fall into disrepair, so a person can lose self-possession and confidence, as when his or her *miran* is 'taken away' by more powerful others (such as autocratic parents, forceful public speakers and powerful bush spirits) whose voice and power 'press down' with great weight, diminishing the *miran* of those in their presence.[8] Then, it is said that 'the container has tipped over and its contents spilled out' – a metaphor for loss of self-control, or for a state of laziness or despair when one has 'let oneself go' (*nyere bila*). Ideally, a balance is struck in which everyone's voice, presence, and property is accorded due recognition in relation to his or her role, age and gender. But some people assert themselves beyond their due station – as in the case of a Big Man who exploits his position to take advantage of an inferior, a senior co-wife who abuses her junior partners, a man whose jealousy overrules his better judgement or a woman whose emotions are not held in check. A kind of intersubjective logic then comes into play, based on the principle of reciprocity, according to which one has the right to counter in kind any action that has the effect of directly nullifying, diminishing, belittling or erasing one's own being, or indirectly doing so by taking away properties that one regards as essential to and as extensions of the being of the other. The Kuranko phrase *ke manni a nyorgo manni* ('something happened, its counterpart then happened') reveals the kinship between the social logic of partnership and the abstract calculus of retaliation.

Since *miran* blurs any hard-and-fast distinction between *having* and *being*, it can be augmented through *taking* the wherewithal of life from others – through theft, witchcraft, abuse and humiliation – or through *giving* such things as respect, food, help and protection that will be returned in equal measure at some later date. At the same time 'real', symbolic, and fantastic calculations enter into people's notions of what constitutes their due, and Kuranko folktales, like folktales throughout the world, with their magical agencies, supernatural intercessories and miraculous transformations, attest to the vital role that wishful thinking and imaginary reworkings of everyday reality play in making everyday life endurable. Yet, as the perceived gap between haves and have-nots widens in today's world, experiences of frustration, resentment and exclusion are exacerbated, leading more and more people to explore vengeful, occult and spiritual avenues to wealth and power (Comaroff and Comaroff 1999, Devisch 1995, 2003, Geschiere 1997, Lindquist 2000,[9] Shaw 2002).

Such thoughts were on my mind in the days after I learned of the death of my friend and onetime field assistant, Noah Marah, in Sierra Leone on 29 January 2003. I had just arrived in Sweden after several weeks in Sierra Leone, and had seen Noah only a few days before. After many vicissitudes, he seemed to be on the threshold of a new beginning. The war in which he had suffered so much, including the partial loss of his sight, was now over. And after several years without work, surviving on handouts from friends, he had, with his elder brother's help, found a job in Kono and now envisaged getting a mining license and hiring young men from his home village of Firawa to prospect for diamonds. When I saw Noah the previous year he had been demoralised and adrift. Now, full of optimism and bonhomie, he joked with me about striking it rich. Our last conversation was a fervent exchange of views on human rights, occasioned by Noah's participation in a training course to become a Justice of the Peace. It was like old times – his casuistry and independence of mind, his confident dismissal of my dissenting views, his wry humour.

For several days after hearing of Noah's death, I could not settle to work. Walking the snow-filled streets of Uppsala, my mind was filled with random recollections of experiences we had shared over a period of thirty three years. I remembered how villagers once saw me as djinn who would favour Noah with wealth and power. I recalled Noah's habit of emphasising blessings over hard work, insisting that his mother had been such a dutiful wife that his father's ancestral blessings were bound to smooth his path through life. But as I remembered the various stories Noah had told me about himself, I began to realise that his entire life had been a search for a mentor, a benefactor, a lucky break, that would change the odds that seemed stacked against him.

The youngest in a family of eight, Noah's acute sense of being 'shut out', as he put it, was, I suppose, a factor in drawing him toward the world of the occult. Yet most of his life he had sought not occult but political power, in part because his beloved father had been such a forceful and respected figure in the colonial Court Messenger Force, in part because his elder brother Sewa – a prominent politician, and man of substance – had become his role model when his father died.

After his father's death in 1957, Noah lived with Sewa for a while. He once described this period as one of domestic servitude. Sweeping, cleaning, fetching wood and water. Virtual slavery. 'When the 1957 elections came round,' Noah said, 'my younger [half-] brother Kaima and I went all over *ferensola* [the Kuranko area] campaigning for S.B. [i.e., Sewa]. I was like his propaganda secretary. In 1962, S.B. again enlisted my support. I was at Magburaka Secondary School at the time, and parliament had been dissolved with the elections about three months away. S.B. sent a telegram, asking me to come and campaign for him. I asked the principal, who said no, so I sent S.B. a telegram saying I could not join him. S.B. then sent a second telegram, ordering me to come. The same thing happened in 1964, when S.B. decided to campaign for the Paramount Chieftaincy in the amalgamated chiefdom of Sa Nieni. I had to leave school to help him, but this time the principal did not allow me to return.

'At the time of the general election in 1967,' Noah went on, 'S.B. was already in parliament. But many of the younger people urged me to run as a candidate for the opposition APC [All People's Congress]. When Sir Albert Margai [the leader of the SLPP, Sierra Leone People's Party, and Prime Minister] heard that I was with the opposition he ordered me to Freetown. The D.O. provided a Fiat lorry to bring me. I can remember leaving Kabala at exactly 4.30 to attend the call of the prime minister. We reached Freetown late at night, and I slept overnight in the lorry. Next morning I was taken to the prime minister's office on the eighth floor of the Administration Building. Mr Kande told the prime minister I had arrived. This could only mean, I thought, that I had been the subject of some discussion. The prime minister told me that he'd heard many reports about my activities. But his displeasure was not the real reason I dropped out of the race because, by then, S.B. had set our mother against me. She began to pester me, crying to me all the time that she would be blamed, and people would mock us if I ran against my brother. She said, "People will laugh at us and say, Oh, these two brothers fighting each other!" You see. So, mindful of all this, I dropped out.

'As it happened, the SLPP lost the 1967 elections, and the APC came to power. From this moment on, my life became very difficult. I was harrassed. At one time I was detained. I had met a man called Babande in the village of Koba, who asked if I could help him find a cure for his sickness. My cousin Dr Osayon Kamara was then at the Kabala hospital. So I told Babande to come to Kabala, and promised I would take him to my cousin. What I did not know was that Babande was a juju man. The APC people in Kabala knew this, and when they found out that I had sponsored Babande's trip from Koba to Kabala they had him arrested, and accused me of hiring him to kill the prime minister, who was then Siaka Stevens, as well as Dr Forna [Minister of Finance] and S.I. Koroma [the deputy prime minister]. The police came to my house that same night and arrested me. I was charged with sorcery. But the case against me failed, and I was discharged. But District Officer Gorvie, and the then Paramount Chief Baruwa Mansaray, decided I should be tried in the Native Court. This time I was fined Le.50. I immediately came to Freetown to hire a lawyer and file an appeal against my conviction. Cyrus Rogers-Wright was willing to help me, but when I told S.B. what I planned to do he ordered me to drop the case. At times, really, I feel very bitter when S.B. tells me I am not serious. People who really know him blame him for what I am. In fact, some people feel I would have been in a better position and been a better person had he not tampered with my destiny. But you know, I hold no grudge against him, except when he makes these remarks about my not being serious. I used to agree with him. I used to say, "You could say I am not serious: if I *were* serious, I wouldn't have gone all out to make *you* what you are today".

S.B. had, as one might expect, a different take on the events that Noah chronicled, pointing out, among other things, that he had urged Noah to finish his secondary schooling, but Noah himself had decided against this; he had also secured Noah his present job in Kono. But it is not objective truth I am concerned with here, but Noah's truth, according to which S.B., rather than being the mentor he sought, had consistently disparaged him. Not only does Noah suffer rejection, but all kinds of misfortune follow from his being associated with his elder brother. Yet, in his view, he was potentially his brother's equal. Had circumstances been otherwise, he could also have become a Big Man.

In his struggle for recognition – a struggle to be 'someone' rather than a nonentity – Noah at first seeks access to secular power. But frustrated in his attempts to become a man of means, Noah is increasingly attracted to what James Fernandez calls 'the occult search for capacity' (1982: 215). In a country where the gap between expectations and opportunity is so great, 'wild' powers such as witchcraft, sorcery, banditry and religious zealotry have become increasingly alluring as avenues to recognition – ways of symbolically compensating for one's sense of exclusion and insignificance. Perhaps the turning point for Noah was when he was arrested and charged with sorcery. Why not become the person that one is accused of being, and turn a stigmatising identification to one's own advantage?

During our last conversation, sitting together in the downstairs parlour at S.B.'s house in Freeetown, the daylight fading, Noah spoke of his occult gifts.

There was a certain Dr Kawa, he said, a senior consultant surgeon at Connaught hospital. Kawa's sister had borne a grudge against her brother from early childhood, jealous of his successes in life and his prestigeous social position.[10] She therefore bewitched him. He began to suffer dizzy spells and blackouts, sometimes during surgery. When several patients died, Kawa was suspended. He became known as Killer Kawa. Noah, who had acquired the powers of an alpha or mori-man, 'cleansed' the doctor. The sister died not long afterward, punished, according to Noah, for her evildoing. Kawa was reinstated, and Noah submitted to an appendectomy and hernia operation under him, confident in the surgeon's skill now that he was free from his sister's baleful influence.

Though Noah's story involves numerous Kuranko cultural motifs – the rivalry between elder and young brother, the marginality of the last-born, the influence of one's mother in mediating the blessings of patrilineal forebears – and refers constantly to the historical and economic circumstances of life in a country characterised by scarce resources and limited opportunity, it allegorises the precariousness of all human existence – the struggle for being in a world where being is mutable and unstable, and where controlling and comprehending the forces that shape one's destiny is an unremitting task.

Second Nature and Second Birth

Pierre Bourdieu's later work provides us with three key concepts for analysing the struggle for Being: habitus, conatus and illusio.[11] Habitus is Bourdieu's way of theorising the ways in which culture comes to be experienced as a kind of 'second nature' (1990a: 56), and the concept is thus reminiscent of Husserl's notion of the 'natural standpoint' (1967: 73) and Schutz's observation that we take our world and worldview largely for-granted (1967: 74). The prevalently unreflective character of human existence covers both phylogenetic and cultural-historical domains. Thus, our biogenetic capacities for language, for sociality and for conceptual thought, as well as the ways in which these capacities are variously realised in different epochs or in different societies all tend to be regarded as 'natural'. A corollary of this is that people in any one society are prone to regard the behaviour of outsiders as 'unnatural' and 'irrational' and thus, by extension, beings to be shunned, isolated or even destroyed. Bourdieu speaks of this as the 'paradox of doxa' – that the *social* order is seldom regarded as the product of human choice, but as an immutable *natural* order – determined by our genetic or ancestral past. Moreover, it is this reification of the social order that lays the groundwork for structural violence, as when an androcentric doxa is imposed on women because it is allegedly reflects an 'ancestral' or 'natural' order of things, or capitalism conflates its enterprise with an allegedly 'natural' human yearning for self-improvement and freedom, though condemns vast numbers of human beings to a life of servility. And yet, the human capacity for creating culture as second nature obviously entails a capacity not only to reproduce what is given, but to reimagine and rework, even negate and confound, the given. In his early work Bourdieu seemed reluctant to address the ways in which 'structuring structures', 'incorporated history' and habitual dispositions contain the seeds of their own contradiction and dépassement, having a potentiality for what D.W. Winnicott calls 'creative apperception' (1974: 76), Sartre calls 'praxis' (1968: 91–100) and Hannah Arendt calls 'natality' – the tendency of all human action not only to conserve the past but to initiate new possibilities (1958: 176–178). Bourdieu's emphasis on habitus as a 'quasi-perfect coincidence between objective tendencies and subjective expectations', producing 'a continuous interlocking of confirmed expectations', is, to some extent, redressed, in his later work, where he explores what he calls 'the margin of freedom', wherein new possibilities are envisaged and struggles takes place 'over the sense of the social world, its meaning and orientation, its present and its future' (2000: 234–235). However, for me, the most compelling insights into the kind of symbolic action that finds expression in, say, Melanesian cargo cults, the migrant's hope of a better life, or the tendency of almost all human beings to affirm life in the face of death, are provided by Hannah Arendt's notion of the vita activa as holding the perennial possibility of 'second birth'.

> With word and deed we insert ourselves into the human world, and this insertion is like a second birth, in which we confirm and take upon ourselves the naked fact of our original physical appearance. This insertion is not forced upon us by necessity, like labor, and it is not prompted by utility, like work. It may be stimulated by the presence of others whose company we may wish to join, but it is never conditioned by them; its impulse springs from the beginning which came into the world when we were born and to

which we respond by beginning something new on our own initiative. To act, in its most general sense, means to take an initiative, to begin (as the Greek word *archein*, 'to begin', 'to lead', and eventually 'to rule', indicates), to set something into motion (which is the original meaning of the Latin *agere*). (Arendt 1958: 176–177)

Natality entails the perpetual reconstruction of one's habitus and one's past, *if not in essence then in appearance, in the way one's world is experienced* – as in religious conversion, falling in love, or recovery from tragic loss. This is why the world is surprisingly new in the eyes of the young, who encounter it for the first time, and why it is 'never what it was' in the jaded view of the old, who have seen it all before. A corollory of Arendt's notion of natality is Bakhtin's notion of the carnivalesque – the 'second world' and 'second life' that carnival festivities and comic spectacles create 'outside officialdom' (Bakhtin 1984a: 5–6). As I will argue in chapter 6, however, the antinomian finds expression not only in formal events such as feasts and rituals, but in the interstices of everyday life, whenever we realise our practical and imaginative capacity to transform the events that befall us into scenarios of our own choosing. Accordingly, the new and the antinomian imply what I have called an 'existential imperative' to convert givenness into choice, and live *the* world as if it were *our own*, (Jackson 1977: 242, 1998: 27–28).

The world is thus something we do not simply live and reproduce in passivity, but actually produce and transform through praxis, creating a sense that life is worth living – a condition of wellbeing that Bourdieu captures in the term conatus. If one's habitus is destroyed – by war, enforced migration, imposed social change, bereavement, debilitating illness, racist humiliation, unemployment or lack of recognition – then the capacities for acting, building and speaking that were developed in one's first and familiar lifeworld are suddenly invalidated, and this may lead to such a loss of confidence, satisfaction and enjoyment that one may feel that life itself no longer has any meaning, and is not worth living. This was the demoralised frame of mind in which I found Noah in early 2002, and this forms of the basis of chapter 2 in this work, in which I explore Aboriginal experiences of marginalisation in contemporary Australia. Bourdieu's argument is that it is at precisely these critical moments, when the expectations that spring from our habitus are no longer reasonable possibilities for us, that our illusio – our interest and investment in life – is shattered. And this profoundly affects our sense of time. Time is no longer experienced as a future we have – a 'forth-coming' Bourdieu calls it (2000: 208–213) – but as an empty and oppressive lack of a future, mixed with a vague longing for the past. This is the time of the refugee camp, of alienated youth, the unemployed, of Noah despairing of his prospects in a country devastated by war, and of many Aboriginal people in contemporary Australia. A present without one's own presence. While habitus defines the field on which a game is played, together with its spoken and unspoken rules, the illusio is our feel for the game, and all those qualities that convince us that it is worth our while to play the game (Bourdieu 1990a: 66–67, 1990b: 195, 1998: 3, 2000: 164–167, 208–216). Habitus as 'embodied history', as a 'durable way of being', an engrained 'disposition', implies the presence of the past in the present as the condition of the possibility of the future. Illusio is that which is actually forthcoming, that which is brought forth, or brought into being, or built in the course of one's present life, as oriented to a possible future – in projects, purposes, interests, hopes, dreams, desires. But nothing is certain, and there is always a discrepancy or tension between objectively given conditions and subjective expectations, between what is on the cards, as it were, and what we hope will happen when we play the hand we have been dealt. Bourdieu often uses an analogy between the social field and a game of chance, and compares our 'social capital' with a gambler's chips or stake. But the structure of the habitus delimits one's social capital, as well as one's confidence or commitment, and thus determines in advance one's chances of winning the game. The more power a person has in the form of such cultural capital as education, wealth, health, talent – or from being born into his or her society rather than coming to it as a foreigner – the greater will be his or her feel for the game, and the greater his or her chances of winning. Marginalised people may have a huge investment in the game (the 'American dream' for example), but their chances of winning may be negligible because they lack the minimum cultural capital that would give them what Bourdieu calls 'preemptive power over the future'. Though the unemployed have time on their hands, time to spare, it is empty time that condemns them to passive waiting, by contrast with the time at the disposal of a businessman, which is valuable time, associated with hectic schedules, intense activity and creative purpose. Though the migrant may have an illusio founded on the hope for a better life in the country to which he or she has migrated, this illusio may prove to be based on unreasonable expectations and false hopes. 'La misère du monde' defines, for Bourdieu, the condition of hopelessness that follows from this widening gap between expectations and chances – this failure of hope.

Luck may be understood as the illusio that dominates the consciousness of those for whom this gap between dream and reality has become impossibly wide – notably the tens of thousands of young men in Africa who have no work, no education, no benefactors, no future. The extent to which one yeilds to magical action and magical thought is a measure of a society's failure to provide a raison d'etre, as well as evidence that the poor are always in the worst position to realistically understand their situation or do anything about it. For them the game of life has become a game of chance, ruled by contingency, though played according to fanciful, opportunistic or occult notions of how luck may be redistributed, fortunes improved, power gained and fate outwitted. But as the logic of the imagination loses touch with the logic of social practice, desperate fantasies and actions are born.[12] This is the subject of chapter 3, where I explore reciprocity and the imaginary of social violence.

Consider the case of Kinshasa, Zaire, for example.

> From the end of 1990 to May 1991 a series of lotteries, popular games of chance, and pyramidal money schemes called *promotions* profoundly destabilized the urban economy. Promising and initially delivering spectacular profits for minimal investment within a very few weeks, these money schemes attracted the whole of the Kinshasa population ... [and] people belonging to virtually every social class gathered their often meager earnings or proceeds from the sale of a refrigerator, jewelry, car, or other personal property, to place them in an investment bureau ... One of the first to establish such a scheme, Bindo Bolembe, acquired the nicknames of Moses, Messiah, and Savior. (Devisch 1995: 605)

When these speculative schemes crashed, the 'bitter frustration of the people led to an imaginary yet vicious mentality of sorcery'(ibid), and many of those duped and ruined by the money schemes turned to pillaging and violence. It is hard to see how this volatile mix of fantastic and violent means of improving one's fortunes may be changed. But one thing is clear: an obsession with violence and with chance diminishes as social integration and knowledge increase. But where, if anywhere, one may ask, in a world where entire populations are now written off as expendable, obsolete and useless, can social integration and knowledge be the prerogative of more than a privileged few?

However, it is important to note that any society, or state, like any family or community, ideally provides what Ghassan Hage (2003) calls 'societal hope' to even the most marginalised persons in the form of education, health care, jobs, job training, voting rights and freedom of speech. Like God for believers, society, for its citizens, 'dispenses, to different degrees, the justifications and reasons for existing' (Bourdieu 1990b: 196). Such a habitus of care inclines people to participate in that society, to trust its institutions, respect its infrastructure and imagine they will find fulfillment in it. But one must also emphasise the ways in which inequality and distinction are determined 'horizontally' – in the prejudices, snobberies and discriminatory gestures with which people stigmatise, ostracise and denigrate others in their everyday lives, thus reinforcing the boundaries that separate those who are deemed to have little worth from those who are extolled and idealised. When any society – family, community or nation – offers no hope, provides no care, and actively blocks certain people from participation in it, these people withdraw their investment and interest from it, and seek an illusio elsewhere. Joining clubs and churches, extolling 'spiritual' over 'material' values, hanging out on street corners, playing games, plugging into music, doing drugs and finding solidarity in crowds are all avenues to re-enchantment, as are games of chance – the lotteries, pyramid schemes, gambling games and high-risk sports that proliferate among those who have been disenfranchised, dispossessed, marginalised and given no hope. In these libidinal and occult economies, working on one's inner feelings or consciousness substitutes for the social field, and desperate passions attach to every calculation. We may include here the illusio of violence, in which people gamble with their own lives, or the lives of others, in seeking the symbolic capital or symbolic power that can no longer be reasonably expected from the society in which they find themselves condemned to live. Thus Ghassan Hage writes of the Palestinian suicide bombers. The 'surreal practice of throwing stones at the coloniser's tanks,' the courage to cop the rubber bullet, to face death in the streets, is a kind of preparation for suicide bombing, in which the individual youth, who lives a hopeless situation, deprived of the power to act, to work, to belong, to make something of himself in the camps, and has no means of armed resistance, has recourse to a heroic self-annihilation in which he gains, however fugitively, the kind of existence (personal status, recognition and honour) he could not possess in life (2003: 131–132).

Toward an Anthropology of Events

Methodologically, it is difficult, if not impossible to produce systematic analyses of the struggle for existence in the way one might produce, for example, analyses of the Darwinian struggle for survival or 'the lineage system' of the Tallensi. The reason is that we can never grasp intellectually all the variables at play in any action or all the repercussions that follow from it, partly because they are so variously and intricately nuanced, and partly because they are embedded in singular biographies as well as social histories. However, it is possible, as the opening passage from *To the Lighthouse* shows, to produce edifying[13] descriptions of what Virginia Woolf called 'moments of being'[14] when we are afforded glimpses into what is at stake for the actors, and how they experience the social field in which they find themselves.

When I did fieldwork on home and belonging in Central Australia, I often had the experience of being in a picaresque novel. Life seemed to take place as a succession of events or happenings, each subtly disjoined from before and after, emergent and framed. Moreover, these events were like Chekhovian slices of life. Something was brought to light in them, something was subtly changed or differently understood. When I came to write *At Home in the World* it seemed only natural to make these episodes, many of which had been journeys, into book chapters – so imparting to the written work something of the shape of lived events. This experience was repeated when my wife and I did fieldwork on Cape York. The rhythm of life with our Aboriginal hosts in the rainforest consisted in comparatively uneventful periods interrupted by explosive events, much as the humid wet season days were punctuated by thunderstorms. Once again, when I began writing up this research, it seemed obvious that I should use these dramatic events to throw into relief the tensions and intentions within this social field.

Nowadays, it is all too easy to forget that many of the classic and enduring works of ethnography are essentially descriptions of single events. Malinowski's epic and detailed account of a Kula expedition, Max Gluckman's account of the opening of the Mulungwana bridge in northern Zululand, Victor Turner's meticulous account of Mukanda, the Ndembu rite of initiation, Lévi-Strauss's narrative of a Nambicuara sorcerer ostensibly carried away from his camp during a thunderstorm, Meyer Fortes poignant study of a Tallensi women coping with destiny, and Clifford Geertz's recounting of a Balinese cock fight.[15] Yet, two of these examples (Turner and Geertz) prove, on closer inspection, to be syntheses or typifications, based on observations of and informants' commentaries on several events. In fact, a great deal of ethnographic writing uses selected details from lived events in order to justify an interpretation, and rarely is an event described so fully or entirely that we, the readers, may see for ourselves the wealth of meanings it contains. Thus, in the examples above, we learn about the socio-political logic of exchange in the Trobriands, social structure in Zululand, lineage relations in a Ndembu vicinage, sacred power among the Nambicuara, fate and freewill among the Tallensi, and status relationships in Bali. But is this all that was at stake for the actors involved? Were these events nothing more than instantiations 'of an existing structure' and exemplifications 'of an extant symbolic or social order', or did they 'reveal substantial areas of normative indeterminacy' (Moore 1987: 729)?

As I see it, an ethnography of events[16] seeks to explore the interplay of the singular and shared, the private and the public, as well as the relationship between personal 'reasons' and impersonal 'causes' in the constitution of events (see Davidson 1980). As such, it approaches everyday life from an existential point of view – as a series of *situations* whose challenges and implications always ramify beyond the socio-cultural (cf. Malkki 1997: 87). Our interest is both in the ways an event gradually or dramatically illuminates what is at stake for those involved, and in the ways it carries ethical and practical implications that far outrun specific individual intentions and awareness. To stress that events tend to take on a life of their own, as I do when discussing the war and postwar in Sierra Leone in chapters 1 and 4, is to empha-sise the currents and cross-currents, eddies and sudden calms that characterise the course of any event, as well as the recurring patterns and precipitating causes.

When I speak of the *sense* of an event, I mean the irreducibility of its meaning. When I speak of the *significance* of an event, I mean its social and ethical ramifications.

Sartre's distinction between *sens* and *signification* (1964) is perti-nent here, though I use these terms somewhat differently than Sartre. For Sartre, signification covers the kinds of denotative meaning with which dictionaries, technical treatises and philosophical essays are concerned, while sense connotes the meanings that literature typically strives for – the shadings, colourings and qualities of lived experience that one can only convey obliquely. But one must be wary here of a romantic phenomenology that would make direct, sensible experience a metaphor for authenticity and, by contrast, characterise conven-tional forms of intelligibility – ideology, theory, narrative – as reifica-tions, falsifications and betrayals of the truth of 'pure experience'. Our task is not to essentialise these terms, labelling them true or false, good or bad, right or wrong, authentic or inauthentic, but to explore the tension and interplay between the modalities of experience they des-ignate. Accordingly, signification may best be understood as a process of transforming lived experiences that are apprehended as 'private', or singularly one's own, into *forms that may be shared*. Sense thereby becomes a term, not for pre-conceptual, raw or unsignified experience, but for experiences in which conventional significations have become charged with such an excess or surfeit of meaning that they seem to overflow and confound those significations. This is the penumbral field that William James called 'the more' – embracing experiences that unsettle, fringe and transgress the boundaries of what is convention-ally focused, thought and expressed (1912: 71). The action of signify-ing, then, is less a matter of assigning determinate meanings as negotiating social meanings – comparing notes, sharing experiences, engaging in conversation, seeing things from various vantage points. While one's sense of an event may be inexpressible and personal, sig-nification mediates connections with other points of view, other perspectives, other people. A common response to distressing events and disturbing experiences is to say that they 'don't make sense'. Murder, wars, violence are 'senseless'. Existence, considered in the abstract, is absurd. But what is implied in these instances is that these experiences defy or elude social significance. They are 'transitory phenomena' (Malkki 1997: 87). They are felt, they are endured, they utterly change our lives, but in so far as they cannot be narrated, explained, systematised or shared, they obey a logic that is not the logic of logicians (Bourdieu 1990a: 86, 2000: 20), and requires that 'we form a new idea of reason' (Merleau-Ponty 1964: 3) – 'a meaning before logic' (Merleau-Ponty 1968: 12–13).

Reason and Reasons for Being

In what I have said so far I have implied that reason should not be made synonymous with the abstract procedures or protocols of what we call science. Reason is a matter of the raisons d'être people ascribe to their actions, the mundane rationales they offer for doing what they do, as well as the rationalisations they provide in defence of what they have done. And so I write, not against reason per se, but against the fetishisation of a logocentric notion of reason, born of the Enlightenment, that has eclipsed our sense of the *variety* of ways in which human beings create viable lives – emotional, bodily, magical, metaphorical, anthropomorphic, practical and narrative. My aim is neither to rank these ways in which people act, speak and think, nor make special claims for any one (since all these modalities of thought and action *may* have useful consequences, just as scientific rationality *may* sometimes have harmful ones); rather, my interest is in showing how they all, to some extent, figure in the human struggle for wellbeing. Accordingly, I set aside epistemological questions concerning the truth or falsity of ways of *representing* events in order to explore the social and ethical entailments of those representations. This methodological relativism is central to my critique of globalisation theory in chapter 7, and my critique of the discourse of human rights in chapters 9 and 10.

My task is to describe an existential anthropology – an anthropology whose object is to understand, through empirical means and expedient comparisons, the eventualities, exigencies and experiences of social Being. To speak of experience is not to constitute this Being solipsistically, but simply acknowledge that while human existence is seldom a matter solely of ourselves, but of our relations with others, *it is grasped only within ourselves*.[17] In seeking to elucidate the *rationales and reasons for being* that are embedded and embodied in the various vernacular idioms, concepts, gestures, actions and imaginings that mediate human relationships, I am sceptical of any notion that the determinants of meaning in human life are to be found either in the structures of the unconscious mind, in conceptual knowledge, or in political and economic infrastructures, local or global. This is not because mind, knowledge, power, or wealth play no part in shaping human experience, but because theoretical reason has so often appropriated these terms for its own ends – making them ontologically foundational to human sociality and history, and subjugating all other provinces of human life to them[18] – that the words have become mere shibboleths. Indeed, rationality has become so thoroughly conflated with discourse concerning the administration of the state, or economic affairs, that it is commonly felt that an anthropology that does not prioritise political economy not only lacks authority but a sense of reality, and risks descending into irrationalism. But irrationality is simply a dirty word that rationalists use to extol their own model of understanding and the interests it serves. That theoretical reason should be so fascinated by the arrangements of the State, and of wealth, is not only because it recognises that the apparatus of the State *also* strives to conjure an illusion of transcendence, but because it finds in the notions of administrative order and control a confirmation and objectification of the very image it has also sought for itself.[19] That anthropologists are attracted to Enlightenment rationality may have less to do with the ostensive aim of understanding the human condition than with a desire to legitimate their authority over others, and their 'expertise'. But, I repeat, to resist this will to power is not to deny analytical reason *tout court* – for much of modern science unquestioningly depends on it – but to critique the uses to which it is often put in the social sciences, and to remind ourselves that other forms of reason, less preoccupied with intellectual certainty and truth, are equally significant in the struggle for life. One thus abjures the way in which statist discourse – whether outside or within the academy – writes off as irrational, nescient, impoverished or ephemeral those forms of life that it cannot grasp or control. Yet it is precisely those forms of human life – transitive, ambiguous, penumbral, elusive, irreducible, intermediate and resistant to what John Dewey (1929) called 'cognitive certification' – that are existentially most imperative to us, and are at stake in the critical moments that define our lives, notably love, mutual recognition, respect, dignity, wellbeing.

An anthropology of events is a strategy for exploring such critical moments. By event I mean a situation, in the existential sense of the term – an occasion, a happening, where something vital is at play and at risk, when something memorable or momentous is undergone, and where questions of right and wrongful conduct are felt to be matters of life and death. Consonant with phenomenology, my object is to enable us to gain 'a close and detailed appreciation of what actually presents itself' rather than simply recognise 'the large outline which a general theory imposes upon events' (Oakeshott 1991: 6).

Notes

1. As Sartre notes, 'the being of human reality is originally not a substance but a lived relation (1956: 575). The capacity to be human will, of course, reflect biological, historical, biographical and cultural factors, and depend on whether a person is a child or an adult, male or female, gay or straight, healthy or sick, rich or poor, alone or with others, in work or out of work, powerful or weak. But as Arthur and Joan Kleinman observe, 'what is at stake' for people cannot be reduced to 'professional sociological categories (roles, sets, status) or psychological terminology (affect, cognition, defense, behavior)' (1996: 171). Though we may define leitmotifs for any social group – honour and shame in circum-Mediterranean societies (Abu-Lughod 1993), *busoga* (physical power, moral strength and social nous) for the Lega (Biebuyck 1973 – a term Biebuyck compares with the Arisotelian concept of *kalokagathia*), whiteness among new Australians (Hage 1998), recognition (Hegel 1971), *egoismos* (manhood) for Cretan men (Herzfeld 1985), *dewa* (spirit) in Sumba (Keane 1997), *machismo* for many impoverished Nicaraguan men (Lancaster 1992), striking it rich among the gold-prospectors of Brazilian Amazonia (Larreta 2002), *ngurra* (land or country) in Central Australia (Myers 1986, *mana* for many Maori New Zealanders, – the force and significance of such 'forms of existence' in the lives of actual individuals will vary from considerable to negligible (Bech 1997: 153–154). 'Life is hard' (*la vida es dura*), as the Spanish phrase has it. But, as Roger Lancaster observes in his masterful study of machismo, danger, and the intimacy of power in Nicaragua, such a maxim 'soaks up a variety of meanings, a range of nuances', so that, depending on context, it may suggest a fatalistic resignation to oppressive conditions, a spirited resistance to power, a celebration of a person's capacity to endure life's hardships, or a dismissive comment on the banality of suffering (1992: xv–xvi).
2. It is not that terms like culture, nature, history, society and mind are fictions; rather that they all too readily entice us into the trap of subverting or eclipsing the events we want to fathom with vocabularies that glibly substitute the complexity of existence for the parsimony of theory (cf. Abu-Lughod 1991, 1993). The result is not illumination, but the consoling illusion that by naming the world we may know it, and bring it under our control. It may well be, as Schiller noted (1934), that many intellectuals not only crave authority for themselves but 'long to escape from themselves, and make appeal to scientific methods to give them extraneous support and to relieve them of their burden of being' (cited in Simon 1998: 348).
3. A person's capacity to speak and to act must not be conflated with the bourgeois notion of agency as individual will, idealised as a form of long-term, strategic action that surmounts obstacles, transcends circumstances, and often realises its dreams, projects and purposes at the expense of others. In many poor societies, for instance, agency is less a matter of transcendence than endurance – less a matter

of freewill than of working within the limits placed on one by birth, role and duty – a stoic acceptance that one's destiny is in the hands of others, and that withstanding hardship and holding one's tongue is often more important than self-expression. A form of fatalism, acquiescence or resignation. This is the counterpoint to heroic acting that Hannah Arendt called suffering, since the reciprocal condition of being a 'who', an actor, is to be a 'what', a being who is acted upon (1958: 190). Similarly, stoic notions of abnegation and acceptance, or zen and yogic notions of agency as a withholding of the ego so that will is freed from conscious effort and desire, and allowed to take effect as an It, not an I, are no less modes of agency than wilful striving.

4. Enrique Rodriguez Larreta uses this phrase in his compelling study of the *garimpeiros* (gold prospectors) of Brazilian Amazonia, whose mineralised bodies and anonymous faces were the subject of Sebastião Salgado's bewitching black and white photographs. In his concluding chapter, which describes the 'bad death' of a 28 year-old gold digger called Indio, Larreta makes the lifeworld of the *garimpeiros* a more general metaphor for the limits of what it means to be human – an existential condition of 'fragility and dependence, in which the intentionality of the subject, his ability to act as a social agent or to control the conditions of existence is seriously limited' (2002: 196). 'With its paranoid component and the terror emerging from the menace of absolute passiveness', Larreta writes, 'Indio's suicide may be understood as an extreme response to the crisis of presence' (2002: 197).

5. In theorising this interplay between latency and patency I am echoing the Warlpiri dialectic between *palka* (embodied presence) and *lawa* (absence/death/latency) (Jackson 1998: 131–133, 139), as well as Merleau-Ponty's use of the gestalt model of perceptual oscillations between figure and ground (1965).

6. James Gibson coined the term 'affordances' in order to shift our focus from the individual perceiver to the *relationship* of complementarity between the perceiver and the environment. 'The affordances of the environment are what it offers the animal, what it provides or furnishes, either for good or ill' (1979: 127).

7. In this respect, *miran* bears a family resemblance to the Latin-American notion of *susto* and the Polynesian notion of *mana*, the loss of which leads to physiological weakening, psychological disturbances, and social death.

8. For example, of autocratic parents it is sometimes said, *an dan miran bo a ma* ('they have taken away the child's *miran*'), and if intimated by a person with commanding presence one might declare, *a yene miran bo ra ma* ('when I saw him my *miran* went out of me').

9. While many societies offer people some reasonable hope of finding fulfilment within them, Galina Lindquist argues that post-Soviet Russia resembles a game most citizens cannot hope to win. While the Western market is controlled by laws that ideally prevent abuse and collapse, and protect investors' interests, the post-Soviet market economy lacks such legal and governmental controls. People find themselves in a world they can neither comprehend or control – where there is no trust, no security, no possibility for fulfilment – a world that is less a game than a minefield, fraught not with risk (for risk implies a controlled environment), but with danger. In this world, alternative channels of agency come into play as means of magically empowering oneself, controlling the future and generating hope. What Galina Lindquist calls the 'magic of business' defines a libidinal or occult economy, characterised less by rational calculation than by passions. As in Sartre's work on magical action (1948), the physical body becomes the main instrument of these passions – a veritable focus of New Age notions of energy fields, amulets, charms, spells, channels and affective ties, relating to romantic love, religious faith and magical transformations that allegedly increase peoples' sense of security, agency and hope.

10. I have heard other versions of this story in which it is Kawa's aunt who is jealous of him, and uses a 'swear' to undermine his position.
11. I am indebted to Ghassan Hage's elucidation of Bourdieu's use of these terms, and allude here to the work he has done, adapting Bourdieu's insights to his own ethnographic projects (1998, 2002).
12. Of unemployed and marginalised people, Bourdieu writes: 'Excluded from the game, dispossessed of the vital illusion of having a function or a mission, of having to be or do something, these people may, in order to escape from the non-time of a life in which nothing happens and where there is nothing to expect, and in order to feel they exist, resort to activities which, like the French *tiercé*, or *totocalcio*, *jogo de bicho* or all the other lotteries of gambling systems of all the *bidonvilles* and *favelas* of the world, offer an escape from the negated time of a life without justification or possible investment, by recreating the temporal vector and reintroducing expectation, for a moment, until the end of the game or Sunday night, in other words finalized time, which in itself is a source of satisfaction' (2002: 222).
13. I borrow the contrasted terms 'systematising' and 'edifying' from Richard Rorty 1979: 360.
14. For Virginia Woolf, these moments betoken 'some real thing behind appearances', and shock us into the realisation 'that behind the cotton wool is hidden a pattern' that connects all human beings (cited in Schulkind 1978: 20–21).
15. Fortes 1987, Geertz 1973, Gluckman 1958, Lévi-Strauss 1963, Malinowski 1922, Turner 1970.
16. Though inspired by work on 'speech events' (Jakobson 1960) and 'speech acts' (Austin 1962, Searle 1969), where the unit of analysis is neither the sentence nor the individual speaker, but intervocal, dialogical interactions, and where language is seen neither as a means of conveying information nor a vehicle for carrying referential meanings (Ahearn 2001: 111) I am wary of the assumption made by many ethnographers of language that the meaning of speech events lies in their cultural value or in the way they work towards a specifically social construction of reality. The 'situated empiricism' outlined by Liisa Malkki (1997) and the 'processual anthropology' advocated by Sally Falk Moore (1987) anticipate the methodology I am proposing here.
17. Sartre makes a similar point. 'Subjectivism means, on the one hand, the freedom of the individual subject and, on the other, that man cannot pass beyond human subjectivity. *It is the latter which is the deeper meaning of existentialism*' (Sartre 1973: 29, emphasis added). Experience is an elusive and problematic word, and given its romantic associations with inwardness, introspection and authenticity, John Dewey was probably right to rue setting such store by it in his *Experience and Nature* (1929). Yet it is impossible to get away from the fact that science derives knowledge from experience (*empeira*), and that human experience is largely socially conditioned (cf. Desjarlais 1996: 71–76).
18. I am thinking of the way lineage theory stressed the corporate and political functions of kinship groups at the expense of other functions, or the way Pierre Bourdieu insists on the term 'symbolic capital' when, as he himself points out, the term is a 'misrecognition' of what is really 'a force, a power or capacity for (actual or potential) exploitation, and therefore recognised as legitimate' (Bourdieu 2000: 242). As Jürgen Habermas has noted, 'Logocentrism means neglecting the complexity of reason effectively operating in the lifeworld, and restricting reason to its cognitive-instrumental dimension (a dimension, we might add, *that has been noticeably privileged and selectively utilized in processes of capitalist modernization*' (1998: 408, emphasis added).
19. Structuralism, of course, deployed a similar strategy, for by claiming privileged insights into the working of the unconscious it could subvert the meanings that subjects consciously assigned to their own thoughts and actions, and arrogate to the intellectual the sole capacity for knowing the truth of the social world.

Chapter 1

THE COURSE OF AN EVENT

Since action acts upon beings who are capable of their own actions,
reaction, apart from being a response, is always a new action that strikes
out on its own and affects others.

Hannah Arendt (1958: 190)

The course of history, like the course of any human life, comprises a
succession of turbulent events interrupted by periods of comparative
calm. It is in these lulls that we take stock of our situation, come to
terms with what has occurred, and begin anew. Accordingly, these are
also the moments when we foreshadow – in the ways we speak, think,
and act – the shape of things to come, which is why ethics is perhaps
more urgently a matter of how we react to circumstances than the
circumstances themselves.

Sartre defines human freedom as our capacity to make ourselves
out of what we are made (Sartre 1969: 45). Hannah Arendt refers to
this generative or initiatory aspect of human action as 'natality'. And
it is this capacity for rebirth – occurring 'against the overwhelming
odds of statistical laws and their probability' and appearing 'in the
guise of a miracle', that redeems us, not simply by freeing us from our
thralldom to the past, but by connecting us with others as co-creators
of a viable social world (Arendt 1958: 178). My work on the politics of
storytelling (Jackson 2002a) was crafted as a set of variations on this
theme, and explored how, in a variety of critical or violent circumstances, the telling of stories enables people to transmute experiences
felt to be theirs alone into forms that can be circulated and shared.
Here, however, my focus is not so much on the relationship between
private and public realms, as on the relationship between events and
what we make of them – in both narrative and interpretive accounts –

Notes for this section can be found on page 14.

and the ways these discursive responses become conditions of the possibility of future events. At the same time, I am interested in how the meanings we give to events eclipse and compromise our memory of them, so that while we go beyond the past in our new imaginings, rationalisations and narrations, engrained habits of thought and action persist, effectively binding us to the past. Important ethical, social and political issues arise here, for in so far as we are slaves to the past, we are not entirely responsible for our own actions, yet in so far as our responses to the events in which we find ourselves embroiled influence events as yet unborn, then we are, to some degree, responsible for the world in which we live. This is the ethical burden of Akira Kurasawa's great film, *Roshomon* – not just that the truth of any event is relative to our vantage point and interests, but that the outcome of any event hinges on how successfully we claim final truth for our own view, and how we relate our own interests to others. In the wake of a violent act, does one decide on revenge or reconciliation? To what extent can parents justifiably plead that they are so shaped by the circumstances of their own childhoods that they are powerless not to repeat past patterns in their relationship with their own children? Can history absolve us? Can new technologies relieve us of the burden of choosing our own fate? Can culture be invoked to explain or excuse our actions? In this chapter I reprise a view I explored at length in *Paths Toward a Clearing* (1989) – namely that the onus is *always* on us to accept responsibility for what we are made, even if it is only to assume this responsibility. As Sartre puts it, freedom may be understood therefore as the 'small movement which makes a totally conditioned social being someone who does not render back completely what his conditioning has given him' (Sartre 1969: 45).

The Roshomon Effect

I begin with an event or, rather, an account of an event – for no event can be disentangled from one's experience of it, or from one's retrospective descriptions and redescriptions. Nor can any one person's account of an event be considered apart from the accounts of others. Let us speak, therefore, of the genealogy of an event, in order to accommodate these various interrelationships.

Three days before I travelled in Sierra Leone on 9 January 2003, I read the following report on the Sierra Leone web.

Election violence in the northern town of Kabala Saturday caused polling officials to flee the town and forced a premature end to Sengbe Chiefdom's efforts to crown a new paramount chief. After the first round of voting,

polling officials said, no candidate had received the requisite 55 percent of
the vote necessary to avoid a runoff. But, according to several reports, the
supporters of Ali Marah claimed their candidate had won a first round vic-
tory and demanded that the staff [of chieftaincy] be handed over immedi-
ately. Supporters of Ali Marah stoned the home of parliamentary leader
S.B. Marah, whom they accused of supporting Alhaji Balansama Marah,
Ali Marah's principal opponent. Glass was broken from the windows, but
S.B. Marah was not injured. The mob also attempted to attack Mohammed
Fasilie Marah, a brother of S.B. Marah, forcing him to flee for his life. S.B.
Marah, reached at his home in Freetown, acknowledged his backing for
Alhaji Balansama Marah, but he insisted it was a private matter on behalf
of a man who had supported him throughout his more than forty years of
political life. 'I am supporting my brother who was supporting me all my
political career,' he told the Sierra Leone web. 'Everybody knows that. I
have been supporting somebody who has been good to me. I want to repay
him in his own coin. Is that a crime?' S.B. Marah decried the political violence directed against him because of his support for another candidate.
'That doesn't mean that they will go and stone my house ... Is that democracy?' (Election Violence 6 January 2003)

S.B. Marah was an old friend and prominent politician whose biography formed the core of a book I was writing at the time. Since I would
be staying with S.B. and his wife Rose in Freetown, this internet report
both disturbed me and aroused my curiosity.

My flight from Brussels reached Freetown via Abidjan, just after
nightfall, and I took the first available helicopter from the airport to the
city. For some reason, however, my bag was put on a later flight, so
though S.B. was at the heliport to meet me we faced a possibly long
wait until the next helicopter arrived. S.B. was with a political colleague who was clearly impatient to get back to the house, where he,
S.B. and others had been discussing 'that Kabala business'. I urged
them to leave and send a car back for me. It was therefore late when I
finally got to S.B's house, greeted Rose, had dinner and went to bed.

In the morning, I found S.B. sitting in the parlour, preoccupied with
visitors and phone calls, so it was Rose who first recounted to me
details of what had happened in Kabala. In Rose's view, S.B. had been
largely responsible for what had befallen him. 'The President had given
strict instructions to all parliamentarians not to interfere in chieftaincy elections', she said, 'but S.B. blundered in'. Rose went on to say
that Ali Marah, a son of the late paramount chief, had spent the war
years in the U.S. and had stayed with her and S.B. when he returned to
Sierra Leone in 2002. He had shown no signs of ill-will toward S.B.,
nor indicated that he had any political ambitions. As for Ali's main
rival in the election – Alhaji Fatmata Balansama Marah, a younger
brother of the late chief – Rose was frankly critical, accusing him of

having squandered the money given at his brother's funeral, and reneguing on his obligation, under the levirate, to take care of his brother's two widows. In Kabala, Rose said, many people regarded Alhaji Balansama as selfish and corrupt, so there was widespread anger when S.B. threw his support behind him. Rose then spoke of S.B.'s second error of judgement. Apparently Ali had claimed that Vice-President Solomon Berewa had given him his support. Upon hearing this, S.B. criticised the Vice-President to his face, without first ascertaining whether or not the report was true. 'Yesterday morning,' Rose said, 'the Vice-President came here and exonerated himself. But the damage is done.' And she confessed her fear that their two sons would not be able to go to Kabala and take up their birthright there – Abu, the house that the mob had destroyed and Chelmanseh, the second house 'near the swamp'. Rose was also critical of S.B.'s expectation that the President would sort things out simply because they were close friends and brothers-in-law (President Ahmad Tejan Kabbah's late wife, Patricia, was Rose's elder sister). 'Even yesterday,' Rose said, 'the President reminded S.B. of the need to be careful what he said, and to whom he said it' – an allusion to a court case eighteen months before in which S.B. had been accused of slapping a police officer on point duty. Although acquitted, S.B. had, it seemed, subsequently bragged about treating the officer as he deserved.

I have said that what matters most is not deciding whether an account of an event is true or false, but how this account echoes half-forgotten events in the past and how it influences what takes place in the future. Every event is thus a make or break moment in which what has been is transmuted into what will be. This was why I was saddened when Rose spoke disparagingly of S.B. or, for that matter, when S.B. later cautioned me against setting too much store by what Rose said.

Next morning, S.B. told me his side of the story by showing me a report he had written concerning the events in Kabala. It was dated 6 January, the day after his house had been attacked, and was addressed to the Inspector-General of Police.

S.B. began his account by describing his arrival in Kabala on 28 December to spend the New Year period with several friends, including members of parliament Hon. Alex Koroma, Hon. Hardy Sheriff, Minister Ibrahim Sesay, Mr Abib Munda, Dalma Sheriff, and a few others including Hon. Chief Kebbie and Hon. Dr. Kamanda. A few days after New Year's day, Kamanda, Kebbie and Koroma left for Freeetown.

'I had to stay behind because I had taken some tools for roadworks, which I had to distribute to my people in the district.

'On the morning of 5 January, between nine and ten, I received information that Ali Marah, a candidate for Sengbe Chiefdom PC election and others were coming to attack my person and burn down my house; this was said in public, so I sent Umaru and Balacun Conteh [two of S.B.'s helpers] to inform the police and tell them that I needed their protection. After fifteen minutes they came to report that the police said they were coming. It took an hour for the police to arrive. From my verandah, I saw a police Land Rover drive toward Ali Marah's place, where a big crowd had gathered singing in Kuranko that Ali has won the election. As soon as the police Land Rover moved away, Minister Ibrahim Sesay, Munda and myself saw the crowd moving towards my house. Just at that moment one or two policemen arrived. One was in plain clothes with a walkie-talkie. The crowd was then busy making road blocks and raining abuses on us. We tried to send a second message to the police, but the whole place was blocked. It was Allie Sheriff who went to UNAMSIL [UN Mission in Sierra Leone] to ask for help since we were not satisfied with the behaviour of the police, due to the way they were handling the situation. The crowd came as close as ten yards from my house and then started stoning my house. They had matchets and clubs which they used to start breaking down the doors and windows of my house, and they were singing and at the same time raining insults on my parents in the forecourt of my house. We were barricaded [in] and the police stood there doing nothing to stop them.

'There was a crowd of about three hundred. Our lives were left to fate as they smashed all the windows of my house. Then the Bangladeshi arrived. They met me at the corner of my house and told me that they were peace makers, but that they would do their best to protect and evacuate me, so I must remain cool, but it took some time to do the security arrangements.

'After they left and went to get more security men, and after my house had been completely damaged, that was the time that the police started throwing tear gas. We were barricaded for four good hours, in the end the place was dark, and the Bangladeshis started making arrangements for our evacuation.'

S.B. concluded his report by listing his material losses – Indian mango trees and cassava plants uprooted, all the windows of the house broken, a satellite dish 'broken to pieces', a large wallet (containing Le. 2,150.000, equal to $US 1,000) stolen, together with two wrist watches (one gold), and S.B.'s sunglasses. The mob also beat to death two cows tethered in his compound (one a gift to the Resident Minister, another that S.B. had purchased for himself). Furthermore, two goats were taken to Ali Marah's house, together with a motocycle (valued at Le 10.7 million, equal to $US 5,000), twenty bundles of corrugated iron sheets, twenty five bags of rice, 1,200 palm oil seedlings, five hundred machetes, wheelbarrows and shovels for roadwork, and some cooking pots – all 'under the very eyes of the police.' Finally, S.B. observed, 'I told Christopher Johns (Regional Commissioner of Police, North) and Chief Police Officer Mustapha that they had seen everything that had been done to me in their presence.'

Since numerous visitors from Kabala were coming and going at this time, I had plenty of opportunities for enlarging my picture of what had happened on 5 January. Balacun Conteh's comments were particularly interesting, if only because he, like Rose, had an axe to grind with S.B. This had became very evident the morning after my arrival in Freetown, when S.B. humiliated Balacun in front of the visitors sitting in the parlour. Balacun had just re-entered the room after carrying two buckets of hot water into S.B.'s bathroom. Convinced that Balacun had spent more time than was necessary in his room, S.B. said, 'I hope you didn't steal anything from my room while you were there.' Balacun did not respond, but later, hurt and indignant, he told Rose that he would quit working for S.B. if he was spoken to in this manner again. (Indeed, he did walk out the following day, after a similar upbraiding). When S.B. left for his parliamentary office that morning – after Balacun had laid out his clothes, helped him dress and put on his shoes, collected his diaries, papers, mobile phone and car keys, and carried his bags to his car – Balacun fetched a deep sigh of relief. 'Thank God,' he said to me, with a wry smile. 'Thank God'.

It was then that I asked Balacun to give me his version of what had happened in Kabala.

That the police had done nothing to prevent the attack on S.B's house, even after Balacun, S.B., and others had phoned them for help, was, in Balacun's opinion, because S.B. had 'smeared' the Chief Police Officer in the days before the election, and because he had not been forgiven for the time he verbally abused and physically assaulted a police officer on traffic duty.

'But why should Ali turn against S.B.?' I asked.

Balacun thought it was a matter of political expediency. Since his main rival was associated with the SLPP – the party in power – Ali decided to throw in his lot with the traditional opposition, the APC. This was also what many ex-combatants had done, still smarting from their defeat in the civil war. The mob was made up of many dissident soldiers and RUF combatants, Balacun said, who were aggrieved at losing the war, or looking for a quick way to enrich or empower themselves. 'We were very frightened,' Balacun added. 'They wanted to kill us. Now they are going around Sengbe, looting and threatening section chiefs.'

That afternoon I asked Noah (S.B.'s younger brother) how he explained Ali's conduct. Rather surprisingly, considering his preoccupation with politics, Noah emphasised Ali's upbringing.

'Ali's father, the late Balansama Marah, was never a strong chief or father,' Noah said, and added that Chief Balansama never demanded that people respect the protocols that governed relations with a chief. 'He was too lenient. He let his children do what they liked. He was kind to a fault. And Ali's eleven years in the U.S. may have set him on the wrong path.'

As to what this 'wrong path' might have been, my friend Sewa Koroma, also known as small S.B, who had been caught up in the Kabala affray, said that Ali probably used drugs, like his cohorts, many of whom were ex-rebels and sobels (renegade soldiers who had fought with the Revolutionary United Front). 'He's also a tool of the APC,' small S.B. added, and he described how he had been spotted by Ali's boys while buying petrol at a Kabala garage. 'Look at the *wutètè* (many) boys coming, those S.B. Marah boys.' Small S.B. jumped into his Suzuki four-wheel drive and drove straight to the police station. The four policemen there said they could not offer him security, and advised him to go to UNAMSIL headquarters. It was there that small S.B. listened in on the radio-telephone conversation between the Bangladeshi field commander and his men at the beseiged house, and heard the police complaining that they were tired and wanting to go home, as well as reports on the mob's attempt to burn a Bangladeshi armoured personnel carrier, and details of the final rescue.

The next fragment of the mosaic that was slowly emerging from the various conversations and accounts of the Kabala incident was a report, written by Christopher E.F. Johns, Regional Commissioner North (Makeni) and addressed to the Inspector-General of Police in Freetown. If S.B. had a contentious relationship with the police, Johns' report made it very clear that the police had their own bones to pick with S.B.

Acting on intelligence reports from Kabala, Johns despatched police reinforcements to the town on 3 January. His report then describes the election on 4 January, in which, of the nine candidates for the Paramount Chieftaincy, Ali Marah received 105 votes, and Alhaji Balansama Marah 91. Under normal circumstances, a second ballot would have been held an hour after the first to decide between the two leading candidates. At 5.30 p.m. Ali Marah, some councillors, the Electoral Commissioner, the Provincial Secretary North, police officers, and representations of UNAMSIL and CIVPOL were all at the courthouse waiting for the runoff to begin. Alhaji Balansama arrived at 7.10 p.m. with some of his councillors and supporters, but when the supporters were told they could not enter the courthouse (*gbare*) they 'started insulting their opponents and throwing stones at the police, thereby rudely dispersing the crowd'. At 7.15 p.m., according to Johns' report, the two Assessor Chiefs summoned the Electoral Commissioner and the Provincial Secretary to a nearby house for urgent discussions. Twenty minutes later they returned to the courthouse and advised Johns that the runoff be postponed for security reasons. One chief even said that he feared for his life. Johns said that he had reinforced the police, so there was no reason for any delay; indeed, he wanted to avoid 'agitating the impatient crowd'. However, the Electoral Commisssioner and Parliamentary Secretary, fearful of the anger of the crowd, fled, taking the ballot papers with them, so at 8.00 p.m Johns was obliged to announce a postponement of the runoff.

Judging that 'the police and UNAMSIL were on top of the situation', Johns then left for his headquarters in Makeni, seventy-five miles to the south.

The next morning, Sunday 5 January, Johns called Kabala for a report. Though informed that everything was calm, he consulted the LUC 'G' Mr M. Kamara. On the strength of what he heard, he decided to return to Kabala, where he arrived at 3.07 p.m. Hearing of the attack on S.B. Marah's house, he went immediately to the scene. 'I saw over three hundred people armed with sticks, stones and branches shouting at the top of their voices, demanding the 'head' of Hon. S.B. Marah and the chieftaincy 'staff'. The group was a blend of men, women, youths (male and female) and children. I noticed a lot of damage had been done to the house. I was able to talk to the crowd and the situation was partially brought under control.'

Johns observed that people were converging on the house from all directions. Because it had no protective walls or fences around it, policing was very difficult. However, he noted, the Bangladeshi troops under the command of Col M.H. Saladhudin, and RSLAF troops under the command of Bambett Seven, 'were on standby'.

On learning that S.B. and his family were 'held up in the house', and after conferring with Colonel Saladhudin, Johns said that he then entered the house to talk to S.B. 'We convinced him to move out to safety, but he was not ready to go, instead insisting in having his belongings with him. After much talking he agreed to leave. At about 20.30 hours we were finally able to get the crowd off the road. At about 21.00 hours Hon. S.B. Marah and family were smuggled out of his house in a convoy to the headquarters of Bambett Seven, where final arrangements were made for his movement to Makeni. SLP 294 was provided for him with a police driver OSD 4700 and one guard. I led the way to Makeni.'

Johns' report concluded with an account of the journey back to Makeni – how S.B. ordered a halt at Fadugu where he 'said a lot of bad things about the police' and then later, at Police Headquarters in Makeni, where S.B. and the Resident Minister North 'hauled invectives at the police', threatening the police driver who had driven them down from Kabala with 'a lesson he will never forget.' In his final 'comments', Johns noted: 'I have observed that the Hon. S.B. Marah and the

Minister are in the habit of provoking the police and subjecting us to a lot of ridicule and embarrassment in the eyes of the public. Even where we went all out to rescue him and his family from possible death, instead of saying thanks, it was molestation.'

I will return to this theme of 'ridicule and embarrassment', but for the moment let us consider one further account of events in Kabala, given by S.B. in the course of a telephone conversation with the Inspector General of Police, Keith Biddle, on 11 January.

S.B. was clearly determined to use this conversation to rebut several of the assertions Christopher Johns had made in his report. 'I am the target of misinformation,' S.B. began. 'I've seen the report by Christopher Johns. Quite honestly, I was not alone in Kabala. There were other important people there. Moreover, whenever I am in Kabala I never step out of my house. I stay there. But one thing I do – I've got a musical instrument (an amplifier and sound system) that the kids love. I try to arrive in Kabala in time to play music, so the kids can dance. And before I go to Kabala I always inform the police. It was alleged I didn't notify them, but in fact I did – for security – even though I've never feared for my safety in Kabala. But I wanted security in case the kids quarrelled at the dance.

'On the day of the election I was never in the court *gbare*. I was in my house. I heard the results of the election there. Ali and his followers declared no need for a second ballot because they had won a majority in the first. Ali accused me of being responsible for the stone-throwing at the court *gbare*. But nobody can accuse me of interfering in the election. I favoured Alhaji Balansama because this man was in Fadugu when I was a teacher there many years ago. He used to bring me bread. He supported me all out in the 1956 election. He later went to Kono to mine for diamonds. He would often assist me with money. During the war he provided food for the CDF [Civil Defence Force]. He was SLPP chairman. He is progressive. He has houses in Freetown that he built with his own money from diamond mining, yet he returned to farming. I gave Alhaji Balansama money because I owed him as a human being. Is it a crime to support someone? If I've broken the law, let God be the judge of that.

'Someone came and told me that Ali had announced his intention of attacking me, killing me, and burning my house. I sent for the police. They said they would come. They took an hour – and only after going to Ali's house first, which was two hundred yards away from mine. I could see the crowd.[1]

'Ali's people blocked the road a hundred yards from my house. The man I sent to the police told me that the police were unwilling to interfere. I got a message to the Bangladeshis. They came and explained they were only peacekeepers. The police came two hours later.'

After giving details of how the cows were beaten and killed, and his property looted, S.B. described the worsening situation inside his house.

'Stones were thrown. They even tried to burn a Bangladeshi armed vehicle. We had to move from one end of the house to the other as windows were broken and doors were smashed. I had some extra doors, and we used these to barricade the broken windows. In the evening the army came. 'We could not come until the police requested it,' they said. We were told to gather our luggage in the parlour. The Bangladeshis took videos of the damage. Then we were taken to the Bangladeshi barracks. The first and only time I saw Christopher Johns was at the end of the day, as we were about to leave Kabala. I talked to him in the Bangadeshi compound for the first time.

'Believe me, Keith, if you had been there you would not have thought I would come out of it alive. It was a sad spectacle for me to be molested like that. I can be difficult at times. I am difficult to people who try to get things without working. That's what I am down on. Even the public sometimes. That's the trouble with this country – people trying to get things without working for them.

'Even this morning there have been reports from Kabala of Ali's people beating people up, terrorising them. Everyone is scared now.

'As for the police, they say that I removed their CPO from office, but even this CPO, when he left school he came to me; I sent him to college, helped him, advised him not to drink or quarrel. And Christopher Johns, I helped him get back into the police force after he was jailed by the NPRC [the military junta, National Provisional Ruling Council, that seized power in 1997] in Makeni. I don't know why the police are holding grudges against me. I am not anti-police. I'm against people who don't work hard. And I want justice done. Because Alhaji Balansama's supporters are really scared now. Ali's people are beating people up, saying they must be for Ali Marah.

'I am grateful to you for listening to me, because I have been made the culprit in this business. People have given you the wrong picture, Keith.'

In the days that followed, S.B. urged whoever had been witness to the events in Kabala to make statements to the police. He even sent a somewhat reluctant Alhaji Balansama down town to do this, phoning Freetown police headquarters to say he was on his way. It was S.B.'s hope that these depositions would lead to charges being laid against Ali Marah, and that the runoff would be delayed until a police investigation had been completed. He therefore urged Alhaji Balansama not to be intimidated by his opposition, but cultivate support, make friends, and confirm old alliances in preparation for the second ballot.

Such hopes were soon dashed. The President ordered a thorough and immediate investigation, the outcome of which was that S.B. was cleared of any wrongdoing, and the runoff went ahead as scheduled on 24 January. S.B. confessed that he was mystified as to why the President should make this decision. In any event, a few days before the runoff, Alhaji Balansama decided that he had no support, in part because of the widespread intimidation of local chiefs, and he withdrew his candidacy. His box was nonetheless included, and he received five votes. Ali got 148 and was declared the winner. For S.B. it was 'all wrong'. Alhaji had been chairman of the SLPP for many years, had spent millions of his own money during the war, buying food for the army and CDF; he was owed this position.

'Will you make your peace with Ali now?' I asked.

'I'll never work with him,' S.B. said, despite the President's decree that Ali must apologise to S.B. or the staff of chieftancy would not be handed over to him. S.B. considered this idea 'childish and insulting' and was annoyed that the President should ask this of him. 'I couldn't do this,' he said. 'I would betray all Kuranko. Ali insulted my mother, my family. He destroyed my house, my property. How could I accept an apology?' So when the moment came for S.B. to hand over the staff of chieftaincy to Ali Marah, he abruptly told the new chief 'get out of my sight'.

Events and Aftereffects

Events quickly and imperceptibly blur into and become stories. In S.B.'s telephone lobbying, and in the numerous discussions that went on every morning and throughout the weekend in S.B.'s parlour, during which the Kabala affray was recalled, recounted and analysed, and declarations made as to what ought to be done to resolve the issues arising from it, I could observe this transmutation of what *had* happened into what people now thought *should* happen. Clearly, this social hermeneutics – which included formal reports as well as anecdotal accounts – involved the transformation of a lived reality, with manifold viewpoints and ambiguous meaning, into a discursive reality that was both ethically conclusive and consensual. After ten days, the event was no longer remembered as it had been lived, but as it had been reworked and recounted in the process of making sense of it and creating an account that spoke to the interests of those whose fates had been most deeply affected by it. In the same way, secondary elaboration occludes our memory of our dreams, photographs impair our ability to recollect the events or persons whose images they have captured, and fieldnotes erase the immediacy of a lived moment, rendering it in a form that already anticipates purposes that belong to another place, another time. This is why the causes of an event are almost impossible to disentangle from the rationalisations, stories and interpretations that are born of it, and why we so readily, though fallaciously, claim that our *post festum* conclusions may be treated as primary causes. The multiple points of view, the ethical ambiguity, the conflicting opinions that characterised the actual events in Kabala on 5 January 2003, were reshaped and simplified in each account rendered, until there was only one truth, one reason, one cause, one reasonable outcome.

Any event discloses both a will toward the future and the sedimented will of the past. Any event may therefore be seen as an epiphany – a window, as it were, onto previous events that are all but forgotten, and possible events that are already being anticipated or prepared. Let us first consider the past in the present.

During the period when the events in Kabala dominated almost every discussion among visitors to S.B.'s house in Freetown, I often had a sense of déja vu. What happened in Kabala was not only a repercussion of previous events (S.B.'s assault of a police officer, his alleged 'smearing' of the Chief Police Officer in Kabala, his abuse of a police driver in Fadugu), but a replay of the past. For instance, one of the agitators in the crowd at Kabala was a son of A.B. Magba Koroma, whom the 23-year-old S.B. had defeated for the seat of Koinadugu South in 1957, following his first political campaign. Informants told me that the humiliation of this defeat had never been forgotten or forgiven by the older man – an ex-serviceman and close associate of Albert Margai. There were also memories of APC thugs during the years of Siaka Stevens' autocratic rule – the same intimidation of voters with the police standing by and doing nothing – not to mention the violence of dissident soldiers and rebellious youth in the recent civil war. 'It's like the APC period all over again,' Balacun remarked, only a few days after a report appeared in a local paper on the problem of restructuring and reforming the Sierra Leone Army. 'Many soldiers after their training go "awol"', *Concord Times* reporter Regina Thomas observed, 'and go in search of money as they had been used to attacking civilians during the war.' It seems, she concluded, that 'as the adage goes, 'money nor go lef hin black han biyen' ('money would not leave its black hand behind')' (Thomas 2003: 5). One may call this the *politics of resentment*.

The second theme here is the conflict between different modes of authority. Though S.B.'s authority derived from both his political and heriditary positions – as Leader of the House of Parliament and member of the ruling house of Barawa Chiefdom – he was still subject to the law of the land. It was this law, in the police view, that S.B. continually flouted. But, invoking customary Kuranko notions of work and duty (the Kuranko word *wale* covers both), S.B.'s argument was that the police had a duty to serve, work for and obey senior parliamentarians. Understandably the police saw this as putting oneself above the law, and they complained of the 'ridicule and embarrassment' they had suffered from S.B.'s behaviour. This conflict of wills – between constitutional and civil law on the one hand, and the *politics of influence* on the other – discloses a state that is not so much 'failed' as ineffective. Competing networks and alliances, based on friendship, kinship, provenance, party membership and commercial interest tend to determine the nature of truth and the course of events.

Third, events as 'abstract particulars' must be related to the singular subjects who both shape and suffer events. This is to say that any event discloses biographies as well as histories. This was borne home to me in Noah's comments on Ali's upbringing, in S.B.'s reasons for supporting Alhaji Balansama (both S.B. and the SLPP were indebted to Balansama for what he had given them over many years of loyal service), and in S.B.'s remarks about Christopher Johns (having helped him in the past, he was owed loyalty now) and the Chief Police Officer (who owed S.B. for similar reasons). It was also evident in Balacun's personal reasons for criticising S.B. (though well-educated and deserving of respect, he was obliged to do menial work for a Big Man who treated him like a slave), as well as in Rose's resentfulness. One may speak here of a *politics of reciprocity*, not only because these relationships involve conflicting views as to what is 'owed' or 'due' between men of different rank, or a husband and wife, but because understanding these relationships requires a knowledge of both lifestories and social histories. From this point of view, one may see the competing accounts of what happened in Kabala as allegories of the vexed relationship that exists in Sierra Leone between Big Men and 'small boys', between those in power and those who feel excluded from power. The competing claims of the candidates and their supporters during the Sengbe elections disclose the deep rift between a 'traditional' gerontocratic order, with all its symbolic privileges, and a generation of young men and women who demand equality, inclusion and respect in terms of modernist conceptions of social justice. S.B. Marah and Alhaji Balansama represent the old order, Ali and the recently elected Diang Chief, also educated in the U.S., though now, by all accounts, struggling to reconcile the 'traditional' expectations of town chiefs and elders with his own libertarian philosophy, represent the new. That so many ex-combatants threw their weight behind Ali suggests that the root causes of the civil war still find expression in a simmering desire among many of those on the margins of power to assert their right to break with a history of what they see as corrupt, arrogant and unjust title holders, at both local and national levels, and assume a vital role in determining the destiny of the nation.

The Curse of the Empirical Present

To say that an event is irreducible is simply to acknowledge that one can never trace out all the antecedent conditions and causes that determined its advent or appearance, and to stress that the meaning of any event is relative to one's point of view, and related to the stories and other events that it entails. As Hannah Arendt puts it, 'the story that an act starts is composed of its consequent deeds and sufferings' and these 'are boundless, because action, though it may proceed from nowhere, so to speak, acts in a medium where every reaction becomes a chain reaction and where every process is the cause of new processes' (1958: 190). These caveats do not mean, as Bourdieu suggests, that one is perversely ahistorical and antigenetic (2000: 147); rather, that one is mindful that what endures historically is not lived experience but its residues, its byproducts, its sediments. As Adorno observes, 'Just as no earlier experience is real that has not been loosed by involuntary remembrance from the deathly fixity of its isolated existence, so conversely, no memory is guaranteed, existent in itself, indifferent to the future of him who harbours it; nothing past is proof, through its translation into mere imagination, against the curse of the empirical present' (1978: 166). To speak of irreducibility is also to acknowledge that one can never predict the outcome of the events that befall us, which is why one can only hope (as with the event whose various facets and implications I have sketched above) that history will not repeat itself in cycles borne of escalating resentment, estrangement and retaliative action. For there is always the possibility, as in any mystery story, that factors will emerge and come into play of which one has no inkling, and that these unforeseen factors will free the future from the impress of the past. It is in this sense that every event opens up an ethical space in which new directions become possible, difficult though it may be to see how one can grasp and act upon them. Paraphrasing Paul Feyerabend (2000: 28), 'The trick is,' not so much 'to *present* events which dissolve the circumstances that made them happen' but to *create* them.

Note

1. One informant, present at the court *gbare*, told me that Christopher Johns told Ali Marah, 'Don't let things get out of hand'.

Chapter 2

THE SPACE OF APPEARANCES

It is hard to defy the wisdom of the tribe, the wisdom that values the lives
of its members above all others. It will always be unpopular – it will
always be deemed inappropriate – to say that the lives of the members of
the other tribe are as valuable as one's own.
Susan Sontag (2003)

In the aftermath of the destruction of the World Trade Center in lower
Manhattan on 11 September 2001, almost everyone in New York City
suffered the numbing shock of bereavement. At the same time, countless others, thousands of miles away, and in various countries around
the globe, experienced a similar reaction. In this chapter I broach the
question as to how is it possible for one to mourn the deaths of
strangers as though they were friends, and to mourn the destruction of
a place as though it were a person. Far-reaching issues of comparison
are entailed here, concerning the ways in which we bridge the gap
between ourselves and others, and the parallels that might be drawn
between the American trauma of 9/11 and the trauma so many
indigenous and displaced peoples have suffered in wars of conquest
and colonisation.

Ground Zero

When the Twin Towers collapsed in a cloud of toxic dust on 11 September 2001, many people felt that they had lost not only a *public*
landmark – a familiar part of their *material* environment – but a vital
and intimate part of their *personal* lives – something as ontologically
essential to their identity as family and friends. As Simon Schama

---

Notes for this section can be found on page 32.

wrote on the first anniversary of the event, 'a gaping, blackened ground zero had opened inside every New Yorker (and everyone who had, through the catastrophe, become a New Yorker)' (2002: 1). Like the bereaved everywhere, people searched desperately for answers. And each person, in his or her own way, struggled to repair the broken web of his or her lifeworld – calling family long-distance, e-mailing friends, rekindling old relationships, reaffirming old ties, attending teach-ins, obsessively watching CNN for news, standing together in solidarity and silence, and, through the exchange of anecdotes and stories, reclaiming a sense of shared certainties and meanings.

Not only did 9/11 bring home to us the extent to which the public sphere is internalised and experienced as part of one's private world, as imperative to an individual's wellbeing as nourishment, recognition and love; it was a shocking reminder that for some people – whom we label terrorists – the public space of America is perceived to be an alien, domineering and minatory power that is to be resisted, extirpated and destroyed. As Germany's chief prosecutor observed on the opening day of the trial of Mounir al-Motassadeq, a 28-year-old Moroccan member of the Hamburg cell, all the conspirators 'shared the same religious convictions, an Islamic lifestyle, *a feeling of being out of place in unfamiliar cultural surroundings*' (Hooper 2002: 1, emphasis added). In attacking an icon of this foreign space, this monumental statement of capitalist transcendence and excess (de Certeau 1984: 91–93), this infidel power, the 'terrorists' sought simultaneously to destroy its omnipotence and acquire symbolic presence for themselves as martyrs.

It is this duplexity of power that compels my interest here, for the *same* space in which many people consummate their sense of belonging and objectify their sense of identity is, for others, a space of dysappearance in which they feel so ostracised, oppressed and insignificant that they will believe that its defacement or destruction will somehow redress the balance of power that they, and their own, imagine they have lost.

The Fusion of Eigenwelt, Mitwelt and Umwelt[1]

Phenomenologically, 9/11 was nothing new for North America. The catastrophe had precedents in the experience of African-American slaves, stripped of their heritage and their humanity, and in the destruction of native American communities and the alienation of indigenous lands. Indeed, the aftershock of 9/11 palls in comparison with the tragedies that unfold, somewhere in the third world, every day. After an earthquake in northern Algeria in May 2003, that left more than 1000 dead, a survivor, Mohammed Khalfallah, declared 'If it's not terrorism, it's floods, if it's not floods, it's earthquakes' (Tremlett and Bendern 2003: 2). In a moving account of the forced resettlement of people following the construction of the Zimapán Dam in Mexico, Inga-Lill Aronsson describes the pain and loss people suffered when a landscape deeply embued with symbols of identity and belonging was gradually destroyed. As mountains were razed, explosions filled the air with dust, houses fell into ruin and fruit trees died, the displaced peasants returned to their old places 'to desperately search for signs to help them understand what was happening around them' (2002: 108). As the natural and cultural landscape deteriorated before their eyes, many succumbed to mental and physical health problems, speaking of the *dolor* ('pain') of seeing *their* lifeworld 'sacrificed' for 'light/electricity in other places' (*para luz en otro lugares*) (ibid: 109). A similar poignancy informs Maja Povrzanovic's 1997 account of Dubrovnic under siege, when the city itself – 'the most beautiful place in the world' – suddenly became a no-go zone, a place of terror and of death. As this familiar, personified place that people knew and trusted became uninhabitable, they themselves became isolated, cut-off and bereaved. To reconnect with the city they had lost then became synonymous with life itself.

> A man from Cilipi, a village close to Dubrovnik, took his two 80-year-old aunts to Dubrovnik in the first days of the occupation of Dubrovnik region. They remained in exile for one day: 'Our love for the house and for the animals dragged us back. We couldn't stay there, we returned'. (Povrzanovic 1997: 156)

This phenomenological fusion of personal identity and physical environment is, of course, not a product of contemplation but a byproduct of our everyday relationships – sensible, corporeal and imaginative – with and within the built environments we inhabit. As Heidegger observed, being takes the form of building and dwelling (1975b: 145–161), making the intersubjective bond between ourselves and the world an ineluctable outcome of the habitual patterns of our practiced life in a familiar place. In exactly the same way as tools and material possessions come to embody something of ourselves as a result of the work we put into making and using them, so public buildings, familiar streets, neighbourhoods, parks and squares become invested with the vitality and experiences of we who dwell and work in them. This objective world not only becomes endowed with, and animated by, our subjectivity; it becomes the primary source of the images and tropes whereby we identify and think about ourselves. At the same time, we come to feel that we incorporate and depend on the existence of the people and places with which we habitually interact. What befalls these things, befalls us.

Another point is crucial here. When the routines that connect us to a place are disrupted, or when we can no longer trust or manage the macrocosm in which we locate ourselves, we are thrown. Typically, we retreat into a microcosm that we *can* trust and manage. And so, when a city is bombed we seek refuge in our homes, or with those we can trust, laying up provisions as though for a long siege, and desist from travelling out into the open space of the world. Public life becomes untenable. The day after the 9/11 disaster 'America's most populous city resembled a ghost town in some neighbourhoods, as commuters stayed home, businesses and schools were shuttered and events were cancelled' (Usborne 2001a: 4), while government offices, law courts, entertainment complexes 'all seemed uncertain whether it was appropriate, or safe, or tasteful to reopen for business as usual' (Cornwall 2001: 7). Few people flew, and even a month on, United Airlines would report 'a load factor' (percentage of seats filled) down from 72.3 per cent in the month until 10 September to just 53 per cent. A desire for protection and enclosure was ubiquitous.[2]

'Instability is a permanent factor now,' wrote Andrew Marshall. 'Fear is the dominant emotion... We will have to learn to live, once more, with that sense of insecurity: looking above us, not for missiles, but for ... something.

'The end of the Berlin Wall was supposed to be the end of a restriction that stood in the way of human interchange. Now, we want those walls back. We want to block off the flow of refugees and asylum- seekers from east of what was once the Wall. In Israel there is talk of building walls to block off Jew from Arab.

'There is a rising movement to limit trade. America wants a shield against the rest of the world'. (Marshall 2001: 11)

There are many people in the world for whom this stands as a fair description of the way things are day after day. In making their life-worlds the focus of this chapter, I move from the violence of 9/11 to the 'structural violence' and 'violences of everyday life' (Kleinman 2000) that seldom makes news headlines yet the effects of which are identical. And I try to elucidate how the public realm is experienced by these people as they struggle to preserve their humanity against the corrosive power of a dominant culture and find their freedom within the limits that are imposed upon them.

Knowing Your Place

Public space, Hannah Arendt observed (1958), is the space of appearance. It is where a people's dominant ethos of self is decided, normalised and regulated. Whether a city square, plaza or piazza, or a public monument, building or landmark, or simply the landscape in which one makes one's livelihood, this is where we consummate our identity as something more than a random aggregate of individuals; this is where we objectify ourselves as a community, a civilization, a nation. But the same processes that bring forth that which is deemed normative or ideal, involve forms of censorship, denial, stigma and sequestration that determine what is abnormal or abominable. The cities that arose with industrialisation were full of strangers, lacking common codes of public behaviour. Gradually, however, the public spaces of these cities were dominated and 'domesticated' by the bourgeosie, whose unspoken and spoken rules of conduct came to define the norm, whether of comportment, costume, headdress, hairstyle, cosmetic appearance, adornment, greetings, speech or appearance. Subalterns and strangers carried with them the taint of an alien habitus, and had 'no place' in the public spaces of these cities. As Richard Sennett has shown, the monumental public squares that were constructed in European cities in the early eighteenth century were 'not designed with a lingering, congregating crowd in mind' and great effort was put into eliminating 'stalls, bands of acrobats, and other forms of street trade' from them (1977: 54). In time, homosexuals, prostitutes, the insane, beggars and, to some extent the elderly and the infirm, were made to disappear from public space in the same way that androcentrism assigned women to the domus, and in time to come, apartheid would ban blacks from the American or South African polis, which was symbolically white. Whether the normative is symbolically defined in terms of gender, sexuality, age, health or physical appearance, it entails a symbolic violence that denies 'public, visible existence' (Bourdieu 2001: 119) to the counter-normative, while producing a discourse around phobias that are at once the conditions of that violence and its inevitable consequences. That the *social* category to be ostracised should be identified with *bodily* functions that must be kept hidden, is a reminder of the intimate symbolic links that universally exist between public space, publicity, masculine power, racial supremacy and ideal appearances (Arendt 1958: 72–73; Jackson 1989: 121).

One of the lasting impressions many people have of visiting Australia for the first time is the abject and self-abnegating way in which many Aboriginal people behave in public space. So fraught is public space for many Aboriginals that they will often venture into it only when drunk. The likelihood of attracting aggressive stares, verbal abuse or pitying glances is so high, that one may speak here of cultural agoraphobia – a dread of the space that is 'owned' by the other, and on which the other has inscribed his existence as author (de Certeau

1984: 31), even though one has, legally, every right to enter it. At the same time, a schismogenic situation arises in which whites become equally fearful of Aboriginal spaces – such as the Redfern 'ghetto' in Sydney, and rural reserves and settlements – with the ironic and tragic consequence that mutual avoidance actually engenders racist fears, feeds wild fantasies and entrenches social prejudice.

While white anxieties have historical precedents in the fear of the unknown that haunts all colonial expansionism, the guarded attitude of Aboriginals toward 'white' space is, to some extent, grounded in a habitus that makes it inappropriate to encroach upon the space of others unless one is invited or requested to do so. Thus, visitors wait some distance away from a host's camp, eyes averted, saying nothing, until contact is invited (von Sturmer 1981). But in urban Australia this avoidance behaviour also springs from bitter experience of racial abuse (Aboriginals are 'uncivilised' *myals*, who belong in the 'bush'), and from feeling that one lacks the social skills that would enable one to confidently enter the white habitus. Public spaces thus confront one as an enemy might – foreign, forbidding and minatory – and people complain, 'I don't feel comfortable going there. It's not our place. I don't feel I belong'. Moreover, the space of the other is like the gaze of someone who has greater power than oneself; it fills one with a diffuse sense of shame. As Sartre puts it, such 'shame is not a feeling of being this or that guilty object but in general of being an object; that is, of *recognising myself* in this degraded, fixed, and dependent being which I am for the other' (1956: 288, emphasis in text).

In June 1990, my wife and I were returning to Lajamanu, a Warlpiri community in the northern Tanami desert, after spending several days at an Aboriginal festival at Barunga. After picking up the various people who had come from Lajamanu with us, we headed toward the town of Katherine. It was late in the day, and everyone agreed that we should camp overnight in Katherine rather than drive the remaining three hundred kilometers in the dark. Warlpiri people usually camped in a truck depot near the centre of town, but we found the gates locked. As for the cheap hostels where Aboriginals often stayed, there were either no vacancies or there were too many drunks, or no one had money for a room. After driving around for half an hour, I noticed signs indicating a caravan park, and suggested we camp there. In Aboriginal Australia, such directness is considered socially crass, and most communication is circumlocutory, using conditional phrases, studied silences, pregnant pauses, and indirect speech in order to avoid giving the impression that any one person is determining the course of events for others. But I was weary, and when no one demurred, I followed the signs for about seven kilometers, and came to what resembled an immense park or golf course, with eucalyptus saplings everywhere, well-watered turf and a breeze-block reception building. I paid sixty-five dollars, and drove to a place well away from the parked caravans and the astonished, curious, though not reproving gaze of the white campers sitting on their folding chairs, at their folding tables, eating dinner in the dusk.

A few days before, when we arrived at Barunga, we had located the Lajamanu 'mob' near the creek beyond the softball oval. After we had lit fires, spread out our bedding and brewed tea, we wandered toward the sound stage where an Aboriginal band was playing pounding, driving rock music and singing of freedom and pride in Aboriginal culture. Now, by contrast, as I parked the Toyota in the camping ground, everyone was silent, solemn and hesitant. No one made a move to spread out the swags, collect firewood or light a fire. Old Japanangka sat on the ground with his boomerangs. The Nakamarra sisters – Beryl and Pompidiya – sat apart, and began playing cards. Japanangka's wife looked sheepishly at the ground. It was suddenly very clear to me that this camping ground was, for these people, a camp in name only. It wasn't just because there were no shade trees and no firewood; it was because this was, as Liddy said a little later as we drove away, a '*kardiya* (whitefella) place'.

That night we finally found a camping spot at a place called Morrow's Farm – owned by retired missionaries – where Aboriginal people were welcomed and made to feel at home. And as we laid out our swags there, built our fire and cooked food, people said how good it was to have gotten away from the drunken fighting at Barunga, and 'that *kardiya* place'. Clearly '*kardiya*', in this context, had less to do with whites per se, than with places one felt one did not belong. And it was then that I recalled all the rubbish dumps, truck depots, riverbanks, riverbeds and patches of wasteland where Aboriginals camped in 'white' Australia. The only places they could make their own – and then, only because they were, for white Australians, safely out of sight and out of mind. That night, as Japanangka sang himself to sleep with songs of the emu dreaming, I tried to ignore the whining outback singer at the nearby Historic Springvale Homestead, singing 'Tie Me Kangaroo Down, Sport', as part of an advertised 'Aussie Dinner and Show Including Aboriginal Corroboree'. The irony was compounded next day as we drove away, and I read the sign on a lamp post announcing *1988 Territory Tidy Town Winner. Best Tourist Facility.*

Here is another anecdote from the same fieldwork period.

I had been camping near The Granites goldmine with Zack Jakamarra – a senior custodian of the site, well versed in the watijarra (two men) and janangpa (possum) dreamings there. I had punctured three Toyota tyres on mulga stakes, and Zack insisted we had the right to ask the mining company to repair them for us. Driving along the fenceline

that separated the 'sacred site' of Purrkiji from the area being mined,
I observed several signs that read *Aboriginal Sacred Site. Keep Out.*
When we came to a padlocked gate, Zack climbed down from the Toyota and opened it 'yapa (Aboriginal) way' by unbolting it and lifting it
bodily from its hinges. 'This our country,' he declared, after I had driven through the gap, and he had replaced the gate and got back in the
vehicle. 'We boss here.'

But as we drove into the mine complex itself, past rows of modular
offices and living quarters, with eucalypts planted around them, and
here and there rusted relics from the old days – the skeletal chassis and
cab of a truck, bits of machinery – Zack became withdrawn, and
hardly spoke. Yet he was still adamant that we could get our tyres
repaired at the mine workshop. First, however, we had to locate the
mine office.

Zack went in ahead of me. He was clearly nervous, but eager to tell
the mine manager who he was and explain our business at The Granites. The office was air-conditioned. In his bare feet, frayed bell-bottoms and grubby windcheater, Zack looked as incongruous as I felt. It
was hard to guess what the manager made of us, but he took pains to
show us the greatest courtesy. As for Zack, his manner was an odd
mixture of bravado and deference. After forthrightly announcing that
he was a traditional owner of The Granites, he stood cap in hand, so to
speak, waiting for the mine manager to respond.

The manager asked Zack if he remembered Gordon Chapman, the
son of Colin Chapman who headed the company that owned The
Granites' leases in the 1930s when Zack worked there. Apparently
Gordon Chapman was dying of cancer in Darwin.

Zack seemed not to understand. He was looking increasingly nervous.
He shifted his feet, before suddenly declaring, 'Right. We going now!'

Though the manager had been polite, and had ordered a clerk to
accompany us to the workshop and get our tyres repaired, Zack's confidence seemed to have evaporated in the few minutes we had been in
the mine office, and it only returned when he guided me back to the
fenced-off area that he called 'proper Purrkiji'. We parked the Toyota
and went ahead on foot. Zack was again animated and voluble, pointing out the stacked boulders where the watijarra – dreamtime heroes
who had travelled from Manjamanja on the Lander river, hunting bush
turkey (jipardu) – had climbed up and looked about for their quarry one
last time before flying home. He then led me around the base of an
immense heap of rust-red boulders to where a snake had come from
Kunajarayi (Mt Nicker), far to the south, in the Dreaming and camped
some distance away, eyeing the local women. He showed me the rock it
plunged under, and the soakage where it emerged on the other side, and
the spot where a local janangpa (possum) snake fought and killed it.

Zack pointed out the main janangpa camp, not far away – the main hill of Purrkiji. He then drew my attention to the women's camp (jilimi) – marked now by a pile of boulders to the south – and the men's camp, a similar pile to the north. Finally, scrambling down into the cool, shaded waterhole where the snake had descended, Zack gleefully picked some of the wild tobacco growing there, and filled our billy with fresh water. 'Proper Purrkiji water, this one,' he said, his old self again.

Objectively speaking, a limit is a line one cannot readily cross – a physical barrier like a river or a mountain range, an international frontier, a traffic regulation, the law of the land. But seen phenomenologically, a limit suggests a limit to what I can endure without losing my sense of who I am, without compromising my humanity. A limit is thus a threshold, comparable with the threshold of a person's tolerance for pain. One may speak of this threshold in objective terms ('I don't think I could live in New Zealand, so remote from Europe'; 'I am uncomfortable unless the thermostat is set at seventy degrees fahrenheit), but in truth it can never be exactly determined, since so many subjective factors enter into its definition from moment to moment, or context to context. What remains constant, however, is a sense of existential risk – a rubicon that separates situations in which one feels relatively confident and in control, and situations in which one feels ignorant, out of place, lost for words and unable to cope. It is not, therefore, primarily a risk of physical harm or of breaking the law that keeps one from crossing the threshold from familiar to unfamiliar circumstances, but a dread of losing one's basic ontological security, one's existential footing, and of finding oneself ill-equipped to deal with, or even comprehend, the new situation. This loss of what it means to be 'at home in the world' is suggested by the anecdotes I have recounted above, and was vividly illustrated the day my wife and I drove Ringer Japanangka to Katherine hospital where he had to spend several days while medical tests were carried out.

A few days before, I had been sitting under a bough shade at Lajamanu with Ringer and some other men when Ringer suddenly lost consciousness and toppled over. The men immediately moved as one, helping Ringer sit up, holding him steady. Everyone laid his hands on Ringer's body or head, containing the life-spirit which had, for a moment, gone out of him.

When we left Ringer at Katherine hospital, he looked forlorn and lost. Garbed in a green hospital gown, he sat cross-legged on the bed as if sitting on the ground back home, clutching his two boomerangs, wondering where to stash them. I helped him slip them under the mattress where he could easily find them, while his wife filled a pitcher of water and placed it on his bedside table. I could only guess what thoughts were going through his mind, but I knew enough about how disoriented and fearful Aboriginal people felt in hospitals – foreign spaces where bizarre, life-threatening things occurred, and where one was separated from kith and kin – to imagine what Ringer felt.[3]

Perhaps one should draw a distinction between *being* ostracised and *feeling* ostracised. The habitus of the hospital, or the Katherine camping-ground, or The Granites mining complex, made Aboriginal people uncomfortable, not because anyone was unkind or unaccommodating, but because the habitus was foreign to them. Because the white habitus is the dominant habitus in contemporary Australia, Aboriginal people find themselves on the defensive, aware that they cannot enter this world on their own terms, and deeply ambivalent about their ability to compete or cope in it, despite the prevailing pluralist ethos to which most Australians pay lip service.

In October 1993, my wife Francine and I accompanied Mabel and McGinty – the Aboriginal couple with whom we were living near Ayton, on southeast Cape York – to an outstation at Port Stewart, an old pastoral lease, on Queen Charlotte's Bay. It was here that McGinty had spent his early childhood, and the meeting at Port Stewart was concerned with a claim by the Lawa Lawa people, under Queensland land rights legislation, to their traditional land. It was an emotional homecoming for McGinty. In 1954, when he was nine, a station boss rode into his parents' camp and demanded their son. McGinty's parents were powerless to say no, knowing that if they did so the station boss would have them arrested by the local police and sent to the notorious Aboriginal 'reserve' on Palm Island.

'Couldn't your parents have hidden you?' I asked.

'We weren't game to go and hide in the scrub,' McGinty replied.

McGinty became, in effect, a slave. He recalled crying all the time, homesick for his mother and father.

'Was there no one you could turn to, who could take care of you?' I asked.

'I tried, but ...'

McGinty then spoke of an old Aboriginal man, whose surname was Bassini, who later took him under his wing. 'But it was a hard life. By the time I was eleven or twelve I was breaking in horses'. Nor did McGinty ever seriously entertain the thought of escaping from Lilyfield station. 'Couldn't go far anyway. Get beaten, taken back. Nowhere to go anyway.'

As we talked, McGinty reflected, with characteristic understatement, on things that had never crossed his mind when he was a child – the unfairness of the way Aboriginal people were treated, the whippings and verbal abuse from white bosses, the loss of contact with kith and kin. 'We had to work with bosses, you know, station owners. We had to. If we had to go anywhere we had to get permission from the

Police. Sometimes they'd say yes. Sometimes they'd say no. We had to stay in the same place, except Christmas when they let you visit your mum and dad for a few days.'

'How do you feel now, coming back?' I asked.

McGinty said he'd got permission from the Lilyfield station owner and come back two years ago. 'There was nothing here, only wild pigs, and that made me real sad, you know. I left my country a long time ago.'

That evening, after making camp, McGinty and I walked down to the river mouth. Mullet were jumping, and there were shoals of herring in the shallows, which, as a boy, McGinty netted for bait. When they were kids, McGinty told me, they would walk the entire length of the beach, eating turtle eggs, fishing, camping, moving on, but always keeping an eye open for the Police, and fleeing into the scrub when they appeared.

Although McGinty felt at home at Port Stewart, his wife Mabel felt uncomfortable and disoriented. Not only had the trip to Port Stewart made her impatient to reclaim her own land on the Bloomfield River, she felt out of place and marginalised among McGinty's kin. Lethargic and homesick, she bemoaned her lot, wondering why the hosts were not bringing firewood or food to her camp, grumbling about the absence of shade trees, and a sore foot. Her increasing sense of insecurity reached a climax on the way home, as we crossed the bridge over the Hann river. Hearing the beep-beep of a car horn, but failing to realise this was not an Aboriginal way of signalling for attention, I stopped the Toyota and drove back, thinking someone might be in trouble. As I approached the bridge, the snout of a Land Rover in dark camouflage colouring emerged ominously from the scrub. Mabel ducked her head immediately. After days of being in a place where she had no voice, no say, no rights, no presence, no recognition, this was the last straw.

Clearly, Mabel's habitus was what Francine Lorimer has called 'a land identity' (2003a). Moving from this habitus was traumatic for her – a replay or reminder of the historical trauma her people suffered when forcibly removed from their land and crowded into the Mission settlement of Wujal Wujal. As Francine Lorimer has demonstrated in compelling detail, everyday movements around and on land that Mabel considered her own – visiting kin, fishing and hunting – sustained this sense of 'land identity', this habitus that gave her a sense of being someone, of having presence. And the same was true of Mabel's daughter Adelaide.

It was not surprising, therefore, that when Adelaide went to school she experienced the school environment in the same way as her mother had experienced the environment of Port Stewart and the settlement of Wujal Wujal. It was foreign and forbidding, and radically challenged her sense of self. Again, like Zack at The Granites mine, this was not necessarily because of anything anyone said or did *to* her, but because the habitus itself was inimical to her sense of who she was. Though this sense of estrangement could be alleviated by the presence of a cousin in the same class, or exacerbated by an unkind word from a white classmate, it sprang mostly from the otherness of the lived environment – its implicit rules and strict routines, its physical organisation, its disciplines, its book-based learning. That the schools were sited on places to which the Aboriginal children's parents had claims, born of their movements on, their knowledge of, and their use of the land, only exacerbated this sense of contradiction between the habitus that had shaped their 'land identity' and the habitus of the white world (Lorimer 2003).

On 14 December 1993, Francine and I, together with Mabel, McGinty, Adelaide, Mabel's sister Lizzie and her son Louie, and granddaughter Cheyanne, travelled to Cairns. Only a day before, we had all visited the site of an old sugar plantation and mill (now reclaimed by the rainforest) that had operated a hundred years ago just north of Ayton. Walking along the forest trails, Mabel was in her element, pointing out tidal creeks where she had gathered mussels and mud clams as a girl, places she had camped with her family, noting which fruits were edible and which were inedible, which were ripe and which were not. She seemed rejuvenated and energised, and when a scrub hen nest was located atop the old concrete and brick foundations of the sugar mill, she, Lizzie, Francine and Adelaide went to work digging down through the mound of earth and black humus to where, hopefully, a cache of eggs would be found. Though Mabel was usually taciturn and withdrawn, reluctant or unable to respond to Francine's questions, she was now voluble and enthusiastic. The reason? Her knowledge of this country was now grounded, embodied, and at hand – in the hallucinogenic fungi she told us not to pick, trample, or eat lest this bring storms, the fungi growing on a fallen log that glowed in the dark and could be used to light one's way at night, or the wild cherries that were now almost ripe. This habitus was in her very body, as she moved easily through the familiar rainforest, showing us the charcoal and clam shells of an old camp, or locating the place where we could safely ford the tidal creek.

When we got to Cairns it was as though we had passed through a looking-glass. At the site of the old sugar mill, people had seemed at home; now they seemed to feel insecure, conspicuous and out of place. Louie suggested we eat at McDonald's. But Mabel insisted we buy takeout food and eat at one of the concrete tables along the foreshore. As I took everyone's orders, Louie's voice fell to a furtive whisper and his mother stood awkwardly in the doorway as if impatient to leave.

Again, there was no apartheid here, no laws prohibiting *bama* from the tourist restaurants along the Esplanade, but Mabel and her family moved as if every glance was a menace, every place a source of hidden danger. Even when we settled down to our meal, Louie remained preoccupied with the police, wondering if we would be moved on, or forced to sit in the park, while Lizzie fretted about where they would stay that night. When Louie and Adelaide sighted two pelicans out in the bay, or an unusual fern among the familiar palms along the Esplanade, or talked of a place at the Pier where you could see turtles and wild life, I thought for a moment they were relaxing into the adventure of our trip to Cairns, but then it crossed my mind that they might be expressing a desire for the one habitus where they felt they belonged, though even these benign allusions were oblique proofs of their sense of alienation.

I also found myself musing on the fact that when Francine and I had visited this very place as tourists six years ago, we had noticed the *bama* sitting in the parks and wondered how we might cross the invisible line into their world – something we did, finally, though not without trepidation, by climbing aboard a bus whose destination was the Aboriginal settlement of Yarraba.

It sometimes seemed to me that the only way *bama* could transform 'white' space from a no-go zone into a space where they felt they also had a right to be was by getting drunk. For it was only through some such altered state of consciousness that one acquired the 'dutch' courage and self-assertiveness required to raise one's voice, speak one's mind, or look whites in the eye. But people got drunk and ran amok in their own communities too, and unruly behaviour at home could prove as problematic for family and friends as it could in the 'white' world, where it confirmed the worst suspicions of local whites and the police, and often brought about the very exclusion one imagined one might overcome.[4]

Consider, the following incident, for example, during our fieldwork at Wujal Wujal.

When Cockroach took offence at Bob's spectacles, got hold of a shotgun, and blew Bob's brains out while he was sitting with some *bama* friends playing a hand of cards, we all suffered the repercussions. Cockroach was a whitefella, a fugitive from the south who'd been living on an island in the river for several months; Bob, also white, whom everyone called 'that old man', was married to McGinty's sister, Winnie. Poor bugger, with his torn bell-bottoms and bare feet, his straw hair, blonde eyebrows and sun-blistered face, always so abashed and self-effacing, I now wish I had gotten to know him better. He was buried in Sydney by his sister, his only living kin. As for Cockroach, the cops came and took him back to New South Wales as well.

Bereft, and with six grandchildren to take care of, Winnie came to live with McGinty and Mabel on the outstation. Her arrival could not have been more ill-timed, for almost immediately McGinty's niece turned up with her white boyfriend, Darren, and their two kids, and also settled in. McGinty resented Darren's braggart and self-centred manner – his endless stories of outwitting cops, ripping people off, getting something for nothing. Nor could he and Mabel abide the way Darren would bluster into their camp without asking, 'cutting in' on conversations that were none of his business, 'talking freely'. At first McGinty tried to make light of these intrusions. 'I bin watching him. He can't understand. Might be too hard for him.' But then the hints of irony disappeared. '*Bama* way', explained McGinty, 'father-in-law and son-in-law don't sit together like that. Darren should have more respect.' When he asked his niece to help her boyfriend understand the protocols of *bama* kinship, Christine simply shrugged and said that if Darren didn't talk 'he'd just sit there like a stuffed monkey'.

A few days later, McGinty and Mabel did what they always did when the tensions and demands of an overcrowded camp became intolerable; they decamped to the beach. Francine and I, also needing a break and fresh supplies, decided it would be an opportune moment for us to go to Cairns.

Winnie and her oldest granddaughter, Wilma, came with us. Though only ten, Wilma was her grandmother's intelligence and conscience, and seemed able to intuit or anticipate every eventuality. On the way to Cairns she explained that her grandmother shouldn't have been drunk when Bob was at Wujal, as if to imply that if Winnie had taken better care of 'that old man' Bob would not have been killed.

When we reached Cairns, Winnie wanted to locate her daughter, Lulu, who had just been released from jail for knifing her boyfriend. 'Where Lulu?' she sang out to the *bama* in the parks we passed. Wilma tried to hurry her grandmother along, breaking into Winnie's conversation with some *bama* along the waterfront to remind her that we were double-parked in the middle of a busy street and needed to get to our hotel. 'Come on! We can't stop here. We gotta go *now.*' When we finally did drop Winnie and Wilma off at the house where they were going to stay, Wilma made sure she had our hotel address and telephone number so that we could rendezvous later, and she could call us for a 'loan'.

The following morning I ran into Lulu and her new boyfriend, Tom, in the railway park. Lulu was wearing a grunge shirt over leopard-skin tights. Tom sported a beard, and was wearing a baseball cap and thongs.

'We killing time,' Lulu explained. She and Tom had gone to Winnie's house that morning to pick up their things, but 'the place stank, like someone dead in there'. Winnie told Lulu that all their possessions had been taken away and dumped. Lulu's and Tom's things included.

'I read about you in the newspaper,' I said.

Lulu had a clipping in her pocket, and was proud to have had 'her story' published. And her nights in custody awaiting trial hadn't been all that bad, she said. 'When the men got together they really liked to see us. Food was good. You could watch T.V.' Now that she had a new boyfriend, everyone said how well she looked.

The article in the *Cairns Post* was headlined 'Probation for Knife-Wielding Park Drinker'.

A mother of six who chased after a man on the Esplanade in Cairns while wielding a knife was yesterday placed on probation for 18 months.

Doris Lulu Kulla Kulla, 31, of Wujal Wujal, pleaded guilty in Cairns District Court yesterday to going armed in public in a manner causing fear on May 12.

Crown prosecutor Carl Heaton told the court Kulla Kulla had repeatedly swung a 15 cm knife at her former de facto in an incident on the Esplanade that day.

He said even when a police patrol arrived and the man ran to officers for help, Kulla Kulla had continued to lunge at the man with the knife ...

John Harrison, for Kulla Kulla, said his client had been on the Esplanade drinking earlier that day when the man accused her of selling herself on the street and they had an argument.

They had been throwing insults at each other during the day, including the man telling Kulla Kulla she was a dead woman if she went with another man. (Scott 1994: 21)

'You mustta been really wild,' I said. 'I'm glad I wasn't down on the Esplanade when you were running around with that knife!'

Lulu laughed. 'Too much,' she said – putting her fist in her mouth to mime drinking – 'and fightin'. Then she asked if there would be room in our Toyota for her and Tom when we went back to Wujal.

'We can squeeze you in,' I said.

I walked to the Pier. I wanted to locate the wildlife show that Wilma had told me about as we drove down to Cairns.

Taking a shortcut, I entered the lobby of the Radisson Hotel.

The lobby was a plastic and plaster rainforest. Although real water trickled through it, splashing gently over real stones, and real goldfish swam in the pool beneath the waterfall, the forest was a replica of the real thing. Plaster cassowaries, tree kangaroos, frogs and turtles inhabited the simulated foliage. Stuffed snakes, crocodiles and opossums lurked beneath plaster trees that had been festooned with plastic lianas and epiphytes. And strolling through this artificial wilderness, without any apparent awareness of it, were immaculately dressed Japanese tourists, their bodies smelling of soap and shampoo, their skin as polished as porcelain. Other tourists were sitting at tables, discussing plans with travel agents for trips to the reef or rainforest. Still others were setting off, sun-hatted, into the Pier to shop. So different was this world to the Bruegelesque world I had just left that it made me reflect on the itinerant, vagrant, improvised routines that governed our everyday life in the field, and echoed an older nomadism: the perennial search for food and booze, of carousing, loitering, waiting in parks, pubs, parking lots, railway yards, cheap digs and doss houses, of fights, of splitting up and coming back together. And I thought back to the trip we had made to the old sugar mill north of Ayton, the decaying ruins reclaimed by the rainforest, the women digging for scrub hen eggs, Mabel warning us about the hallucinogenic mushrooms along the path, the danger of falling bloodwood branches, the death adders under the dry leaves.

Next day Wilma phoned. Her grandmother was ready to go home. We picked them up at Ozanam House. They'd slept there their first night in Cairns, and slept rough the second in the corner of a nearby playing field. It was warm, Wilma assured us: 'We weren't cold.'

As soon as they'd clambered up into the back of the Toyota, we drove off in search of Lulu and Tom at the Fountain. But Wilma was impatient to get going. 'We can't drive round lookin for them two, we gotta go,' she said.

But we found Lulu, who climbed in beside us, and we continued on our way, cruising the streets in search of Tom.

As we passed the old wharfside pubs where _bama_ loitered in the parking lots or ambled up and down the street, Winnie began to get impatient. 'That fuckin Tom, I bin see im there waitin for you. I gotta get home to my little girls. Tell im to hurry up.'

'We can't find im,' Lulu said aimlessly.

Tom no longer seemed to matter. Someone's money was due today, so the park mob would have some food.

Lulu clutched her bottle of VB bitter, her eyes heavy, words slurred. 'I might stay, eh?'

Making Comparisons

The foregoing anecdotes from my fieldwork in Aboriginal Australia are ways of allegorising the situation in which many people find themselves in modern states and within the global economy – thrown to the margins, without presence or power, limited in their capacity to participate, and recognised only as objects of pity, compassion or contempt. But to allegorise is to compare, to see one situation from the vantage point of another, and it is this methodology that I now want to explore.

For phenomenologists, the central question of social science is how one can enter or grasp the experience of another. This implies that understanding is a *social* rather than a purely *intellectual* activity. By this I mean not only that the process of understanding is dialogical, but that the 'knowledge' that emerges from our interactions in the field are to be evaluated less in terms of epistemological criteria than in terms of the practical, ethical, social and aesthetic demands of the world *we both share* (cf. Whitehead 1947: 226; James 1978: 30–40; Dewey 1980: 136–138; Rorty 1982: 203–208).

Theorising is practically synonymous with generalising – a rhetorical strategy for going beyond the local, the immediate and the particular, in order to say something about the 'human' or 'global' condition. But a lot of the generalising that goes on in the social sciences reflects 'a view from afar', in which the observer strives to distance himself and his vocabulary from the lifeworld he seeks to understand, thus giving the impression that the observer and the observed occupy discrete, if not essentially different, positions in the world. By contrast, I favour a comparative method that does not privilege 'our' viewpoint over the viewpoint of the 'other', but places them both on a similar footing. This demands that one find something in one's own experience that is analogous to, or approximates, the experience of the other, and may thereby bridge the gap between the two. But it also demands that we compare the actor's viewpoint with the viewpoints of others who are also involved in the same event or situation. Contrary to a naïve phenomenology, that supposes that every actor is in possession of the 'true' meanings of her or his acts, I follow Husserl (1973, 1: 114) in arguing that we are, to a considerable extent, blind spots ('nullpoints') to ourselves. As Sartre puts it, 'lived experience is always simultaneously present from itself and absent from itself' (1974: 42). Accordingly, our understanding of the world cannot arise from reflection, it must pass through a medium external to ourselves, such as language. And it must go through others, it must involve some kind of inter-experience.

Clearly the kind of comparitive method I am suggesting here is very different from the kind of comparison that Edmund Leach dismissed as 'butterfly collecting', which involves placing phenomena in taxonomic categories and classes, typecasting or labelling them as matrilineal or patrilineal, oral or literate, traditional or modern, etc. (1966: 1–27). But I also eschew the kind of comparison Leach and Lévi-Strauss preferred, in which 'particular phenomenon' are integrated into 'a larger whole' through successive generalisations (Lévi-Strauss 1964: 85; Leach 1966: 2–3). Rather than a taxonomic or algebraic method for making sense of data, comparison may be construed as a matter of putting oneself in the place of the other. This does not mean that one can transcend the limits of one's own habitual ways of seeing the world, nor that one may see the world from the other person's point of view. It simply means that we go some way toward *overcoming our estrangement from others, finding some common ground, and working out ways in which coexistence is possible in a divided world.* Human sociality is thus no longer simply the object of our understanding, but the very method whereby we achieve it.

Though the epistemological tradition privileges modes of signification that involve getting 'beneath' or 'above' events, my interest is in modes of signification that involve what Merleau-Ponty (1964) called 'lateral displacement' and Hannah Arendt (1982b) spoke of as the 'visiting imagination' – in which *our* understanding is born of seeing an event from *elsewhere* – in the light of other events, from another person's vantage point, or from inhabiting an unfamiliar lifeworld. This is what Edward Said urges when he says that it is never enough to chronicle a particular nation's suffering; one must 'universalize the crisis' by comparing and affiliating the situation of one people with that of others (1994: 44). And this is what Marshall Sahlins accomplishes in his perpicacious essay on 9/11 in which he recounts a chapter from the Peloponesian War (2002: 95–103). But understanding is also conditional on our capacity for being open to otherness, which is why good anthropology depends less on one's mastery of new interpretive vocabularies than on one's ability to sustain interaction and conversation with others, in their place, on their terms, under troubling and trying circumstances. However, to 'train one's imagination to go visiting' (Arendt 1982b: 42), or participate in 'the conversation of mankind' (Oakeshott 1991: 490), or 'dream up new vocabularies' (Rorty 1989: 27–28), or engage in thinking that 'points beyond itself' (Adorno 1998: 293) remain empty gestures, a mere rhetoric of humanism, unless we can, in practice, achieve through direct, face to face, encounters with others those changed perspectives that make a difference to the way it is possible to see, think, and act in the world.

Notes

1. Existential analysis distinguishes three modes of being-in-the-world: *eigenwelt* (the mode of being in relation to oneself), *mitwelt* (the mode of being in relation with others), and *umwelt* (the mode of being in relation to one's biological or physical environment).

2. Similar consequences followed the anthrax scares – 'Deadly Spores, Crazy Scares: a World on the Edge of Panic' (Usborne 2001b: 3) – when public space again became a place of risk, inclining many people to stay at home, to seal themselves off from the world. This scenario was replayed in early 2003 with the outbreak of the SARS epidemic in southern China.

3. Some of the most critical events in the lives of cultural strangers are visits to doctors or hospitals. Not only does the medical practitioner not recognise one's symptoms (often dismissing them as psychosomatic or as superstitions), but the treatments themselves may be thought to cause illness. At the same time, hospitalisation may isolate a person from the support of kith and kin, and be experienced as social death. This is why, despite the best medical care in the (Western) world, refugees often feel that they are receiving no real care at all. Among the Hmong of Laos, the commonest cause of illness is soul loss – the separation of a life-soul from the body through anger, grief, fear, curiosity or wanderlust (Fadiman 1997: 10). Accustomed to shamanistic healing, Hmong who came to the U.S. as refugees were shocked by the medical procedures and protocols they encountered – treating the body without mentioning the soul, drawing blood (the body contains a finite amount of it), administering anesthesia (this leads the soul to wander), surgery (cutting the body or cutting out parts of the visceral body creates imbalances, and prevents reincarnation) (ibid: 33). Recourse to 'traditional' practices may, in such cases, be interpreted less as signs of 'ignorance' than as ways in which people attempt to re-establish ontological security. Thus, in Kabala, northern Sierra Leone, I often observed that young mothers would sometimes *not* take prescriptions written for their sick babies to the hospital dispensary, but mulch the paper and drink the concoction, much as one would wash Koranic suras from a slate and drink the 'writing' in order to effect a cure. The familiar procedure gave confidence in a way that the 'foreign' procedure would not.

4. Drunkenness and substance abuse in Aboriginal settlements frequently leads to fighting, and to the defacement or destruction of public property. I often wondered whether this vandalism sprang from a desire to destroy the organised and alienating space of the other that has been imposed on one, as cage or container, since human beings readily neglect or destroy that which they have had no hand in building, that which they did not decide. Hence the rampant vandalism in Europe's council estates, America's projects, and Australia's refugee camps and Aboriginal settlements.

Chapter 3

VIOLENCE AND
INTERSUBJECTIVE REASON

The real structures are intersubjective.
– René Girard (1965: 34–35)

Recalling the impact made on him by Roman Jakobson's 1942–43 New York lectures on structural linguistics, Claude Lévi-Strauss speaks of the importance of prioritising relations over relata. 'Instead of being led astray by a multiplicity of terms', he writes, 'one should consider the simplest and most intelligible relationships uniting them' (1985: 139). His notion of the atom of kinship (1963), and his critique of totemism (1964) brilliantly exemplify this insight. But while I am in complete agreement with this methodological first principle of structuralism, I am not convinced that one can understand relationships between persons or events by approaching them as relationships among 'terms', for the simple reason that the 'terms' whereby any relationship or event is explained *or* represented are not necessarily the terms on which the relationship or event is actually lived. For example, that systems of classificatory kinship blur the differences between a person's many mothers, sisters, and brothers does not erase the phenomenological distinctions between 'real' and 'classificatory' kin, any more than structure determines sentiment. Understanding involves exploring the *indeterminate* relationship between experience and episteme, process and product, and not assuming an *isomorphic* relationship between them.

It is for this reason I have turned to an exploration of the structures of intersubjectivity,[1] endeavouring to elucidate the logic that informs everyday patterns of social interaction and inter-experience (Jackson

---

1998). My assumption is that the elementary forms of intersubjective reason have their origins in the pre-reflective, protolinguistic, sensuous, and embodied patterns of the human infant's relationship with its mother – an ebb and flow of synchronised, rhythmic movements and noise-making, of touching, smiling, looking, holding, clutching and playing. But at every stage and moment of our lives, our interactions with others involve what Merleau-Ponty called a *logos endiathetos* (a meaning before logic) – a 'wild' *logos* of carnality, emotion and sensation that the mind does not constitute yet informs the way we think (1968: 169, 12–13). Unlike Lévi-Strauss and R.D. Laing, who argue that modes of intersubjective reasoning and rationalisation *may* be analysed with, as well as distilled into abstract logico-mathematical terms (Laing 1970: Preface, Lévi-Strauss 1990: 635–637), I regard these modes of configuring and refiguring our experience of social relations as very different from the 'deductions from axiomatic or self-evident statements, subsumptions of particular occurences under general rules, or techniques of spinning out consistent chains of conclusions' (Arendt 1958: 171) that we usually think of as rational or logical thought.[2]

Intersubjectivity is universally experienced in terms of relations of reciprocity. For the Kuranko of Northern Sierra Leone this is captured in the phrase *nyendan bin to kile, a wa ta an segi*, meaning that when you walk along a path through the *nyendan* grass (used for thatching) it bends before you; but when you return along the path, the grass bends back the other way. Thus, greetings, goodwill and goods and services move to and fro within a community, keeping the paths open, as Kuranko say, keeping relationships alive. However, the inescapable ambiguity of exchange, that makes it so difficult to agree on whether a gift has been returned, respect shown, honour satisfied, words heeded or justice done, means that the human mind is a site of endless internal bargaining, calculation and rationalisation. 'I've done everything for you; why don't you do something for me for a change?'... 'If I offer this red goat to the ancestors surely they will favour me with their blessings?'... 'I've had so much good fortune in my life, it's about time I gave something back.'... 'You've had all the luck; isn't it about time *I* got a break?'[3]

In as much as these modes of intersubjective reasoning do not conform to the logic of logicians, they may be compared with Bourdieu's 'logic of practice' (1990a: 86–92), except that Bourdieu studiously avoids examining the subjective dimensions of practical reason. Intersubjective reason is also very different from the reason that Lévi-Strauss identifies with the binary logic of the unconscious mind. As for Lévi-Strauss's well-known dismissal of lived experience as epiphenomenal, I follow Sartre and Merleau-Ponty in making *le vécu* my primary focus in exploring the reasoning that people consciously adduce when explaining and justifying their actions, or when manipulating and imagining their relationships with others. And where Lévi-Strauss argues that 'true reality is never the most obvious of realities, and that its nature is already apparent in the care which it takes to evade our detection' (1973: 57), I take the view that reality is elusive *not because it lies beneath the surface, but because it is, so to speak, right under our noses* – a point that Husserl (1975, 1: 114) made when he noted that the lived body always constitutes a 'nullpoint' in one's own lifeworld (cf. Drew Leder's notion of the 'absent body' 1990: 13). To apprehend the intersubjective life in which we are immersed, we not only need theoretical models that are constructed outside the empirical field, then brought to bear upon it; we need to examine the metaphors, images, stories and things that human beings everywhere deploy as 'objective correlatives' of the give and take of their quotidian relationships with others. The ways in which we arrange and organise words and things thus provide us with rough analogues of the patterns of intersubjective experience which we are seldom in a position to *directly* apprehend.

This phenomenological method is not, therefore, a means of plumbing the depths of the unconscious, but a way of shedding light on the ways in which intersubjectivity reveals itself in the ways we arrange and play with objects, images, ideas, words and others – as well as the reasons and justifications we give, in the form of stories and ethical statements, for making such arrangements.

Consider techniques of weaving, binding and knotting – humanity's oldest tools and oldest metaphors[4] – and the following ethnographic example of how an analogy drawn between social relations and bound objects enables the field of intersubjectivity to be first objectified, then managed. Among the Önge (lit. people) of the Little Andaman Islands, the word *eranabeti* (lit. anger) closely approximates our word 'violence'. In anger, blood is shed, things get thrown about and broken, and people run away into the forest. Anyone or anything that bears the brunt of such destructive action becomes, according to Önge reasoning, both 'light' and 'other' (Radcliffe-Brown 1964: 48–50; Pandya n.d). To restore 'weight' to an intersubjective world that has been shattered by anger, Önge reverse the actions that led to things being broken and people being driven away. They gather up smashed baskets and reweave them. Damaged outriggers are reattached. Arrow heads are rebound. The intersubjective logic here is clear: in repairing valued objects by relashing, retying or reweaving the fibre cords that hold them together, people are rebinding the ties that hold their community together.[5] Since objects stand for subjects, and since these objects are social objects, cooperative action on those objects transforms intersubjective experience. In this way, the community repairs and reverses the violent events that have befallen it.

The first part of this chapter explores this logic of reversal. I then turn to a reappraisal of Mauss's and Levi-Strauss's classic works on reciprocity, arguing that reversal is a form of counteraction, comparable to the return of a gift or the taking of revenge. In the third part of the chapter I focus on the logic of revenge and the phenomenon of scapegoating. I then conclude with some comments on the possibility of resolving grievances through peaceful rather than violent means.

The Intersubjective Logic of Reversal

Among the Gogo – Bantu pastoralists who live in the dry central region of Tanzania – calamities such as drought, barrenness in women, crop failure and cattle disease are all spoken of as reversals of the ideal state of things (*mbeho*), and necessitate ritual redress. But where the Önge of the Little Andamans repair broken objects as a way of inducing changes in their intersubjective experience, redressive action among the Gogo involves the reversal of gender roles. 'For a set period of time, a certain number of married women, acting in concert, dress like men and ceremonially carry out male tasks performed in 'normal' circumstances exclusively by men, or even 'prohibited' (*mwiko*) to women' (Rigby 1968: 159). While the men sit idly at home, the women aggressively take spears, sticks and machetes, tie their cloths in male fashion, and daub themselves with soot, red ochre, ashes and white clay. Then, actively assuming control of the herding of the cattle, and singing lewd songs, they 'dance away' the forces that have contaminated the land, moving steadily in a westerly direction until they reach a water-pan or swamp where they 'throw down' the bad ritual state (*ibeho*).

How can we understand the intersubjective reasoning here?

Of a period marked by such disasters as drought, crop pests and disease, the Gogo say 'the years have turned about.' Specifically, the rain-bearing winds from the east and south have been occluded by parching winds from the west and north. Since east is symbolically male and west is female, this ecological reversal is open to translation into social terms. 'The complementary opposition between the sexes as social categories now provides the "model" for the *manipulation* of ritual symbols to attain a desired end. That end is a "re-reversal" of time and a return to the previous ritual state and events (*mbeho swanu*)'. To accomplish this reversal in space-time, the reversal of men's and women's roles presents itself as an obvious 'model for symbolic action' (Rigby 1968: 172). 'The final act of "throwing away" the *ibeho* over the western boundary (*mimbi yomwezi*) of the area involved is also directly linked with the general series of symbolic oppositions. Its symbolic meaning therefore lies primarily in the positional and operational contexts. The west is associated with death, darkness, sorcery and evil spirits. It is the way in which the wind (*mbeho*) blows. You cannot "throw" sickness or contamination away to the east, for the wind will blow it back again' (Rigby 1968: 173–174).

As in ritual, so in fantasy. When things go amiss in human life, people often imagine that if only they could return to a prior state all would be well. Myths of eternal return, of a golden age, of Eden, of the noble savage or childhood innocence, and the psychoanalytic quest for the roots of adult unhappiness in early childhood are all variations on this theme, as are reversionary cults in colonised societies. Indeed, Franz Fanon's argument for decolonisation as a form of inversion in which 'the last shall be the first and the first last' (1968: 30) found its violent apotheosis in Christopher Gbenye's exhortations in the Congo in 1964 that history had to be reversed if the new order was to arise. He thus ordered the execution of everyone who was literate or had worked for the Belgians, declaring 'We must destroy what existed before, we must start again at zero with an ignorant mass'. Like Pol Pot in Cambodia a generation later: French colonial rule and modernity had allegedly polluted Kymer culture; by purging 'foreign' elements, the Kymer Rouge sought to purify the social body – a foretaste of the 'ethnic cleansing' that would sweep through Yugoslavia and Rwanda in the 1990s, and a powerful reminder of Bakhtin's incisive comments on destruction as a necessary prelude to regeneration: 'To degrade is to bury, to sow, and to kill simultaneously, in order to bring forth something more and better ... Degradation digs a bodily grave for a new birth' (Bakhtin 1984a: 21).

But what makes a state 'degraded', 'polluted' or 'bad'?

Badness is the result of a breakdown in the reciprocity that should ideally obtain between senior and junior persons – parent and child, elder and younger sibling, ruler and subject, coloniser and colonised, rich and poor. When a ruler fails to protect his subjects, a father fails to provide for his children, or an underling fails to give respect or show gratitude, the moral order collapses, often with fatal consequences. Referring to Maori thought on this matter, Marcel Mauss (1954) clarified the intersubjective logic that is implicit here. Gifts give life. But everything that is given is imbued with the spirit of the giver – or, as we might say, embodies a memory of the giver – and this spirit longs to return to whence the gift originally came. So gifts oblige us not only to receive them, but to pass them on, and return them. For Maori, not to give, not to receive, or not to return gifts brings ill-health, disaster or death (*mate*) – in which cases the breath, wind or life-sustaining power (*hau ora*) that imbues the gift is said to have become inverted or turned aside (*hau whitia*) (Sahlins 1972: 161; Salmond 2000: 40). Failures of reciprocity, real or imagined, are thus experienced as reversals in the life-affirming order of social life. And against this movement toward entropy and death, ritual re-reversals of the order of things are required.

This is the theme of countless folktales (Jackson 1998: 62–65). It is also the theme of Luis Buñuel's great film, *The Exterminating Angel* (1962) with all its famous repetitions and replays. The film begins with a group of affluent Spanish urbanites returning one night from the theatre to the lavishly-appointed home of their host. After dinner, they adjourn to the living-room for drinks. But when one of them makes to leave the room, he comes up against an invisible wall. Bewildered and not wanting to make a fool of himself, he says nothing, and rejoins the others. But it isn't long before everyone realises that he or she is trapped. As the night wears on, and the guests' civilised masks begin to slip, a virgin among them suddenly sees a way out of their bind. She announces that everyone should go back to where he or she was at the beginning of the evening; this will break the spell, and release them from the room. So they return to the positions in which they were sitting or standing hours earlier, and by reversing time are freed.

Buñuel's film suggests a link between the reversal of time and the inversion of a unjust social order. A socialist, living in exile in Mexico, Buñuel regarded the wealth of the church and aristocracy as a kind of blasphemy. Inequality was a form of social violence, in which the privileges of a few condemned the poor to nothingness. Although in Buñuel's eyes, his film simply explores 'a group of people who couldn't do what they wanted to – leave a room' (1985: 239–240), and this fascination with frustrated desire is indeed a recurring theme in Buñuel's movies, in his unsparing depiction of the wealthy as they succumb to their physical ailments and reveal their psychological weaknesses, Buñuel touches on an impossibility that is deeper than the impossibility of satisfying a simple desire – namely, the impossibility of maintaining the cultivated facades with which the wealthy create the illusion of moral superiority.

But when we consider exactly what we imagine we may return to in order to create a better, or happier, or more equitable state of affairs, there is no end to the possibilities. 'If time were like a passage of music', writes Joyce Johnson, alluding to her unhappy marriage to Jack Kerouac, 'you could keep going back to it till you got it right' (Johnson 1983: 237). Other people ask themselves what might have happened had the course of their lives been different, had they made a different choice at a crucial moment, or taken another turning, taking Robert Frost's 'road less travelled by'. Our inner lives are replete with such vain conjectures and second guessing. But always at the back of our reasoning is a sense of what John Rawls calls 'justice as fairness' (1971: 14–15) – a sense that the things that make life worth living are scarce, and that we have either received more than our fair share, and should therefore, as some celebrities say, 'give something back', or, as is more often the case, that we have for some obscure reason missed out on or been wrongly deprived of our due. This sense that the good should somehow balance the bad no doubt has its origins in early childhood. 'I being nice to you but you not being nice to me,' my six year old daughter complains to her mother. And on another occasion, after the scrupulously equal distribution of candies: 'Not fair, Josh (her brother) got more than me.'

As Ghassan Hage suggests (1998: 20), scarcity implies both material and existential values – values that are often interchanged and confused, as when a person who feels that he has not been loved or properly recognised steals things as a way of making good his sense of loss, or a person claims material compensation for having suffered a loss of his or her spiritual or cultural heritage – as in the case of the Australia's 'stolen generation'. Although such attempts to reclaim, by direct or indirect means, something a person regards as rightfully his, and wrongly taken from him, does not necessarily entail violence, this kind of intersubjective reasoning often lies behind racist brutality. In Burnley Wood – an impoverished white working-class estate in the north of England, and the scene of race riots in July 2001, many whites complain: 'They (i.e., Asians) get more than we get, allegedly because the council has been intimated by them (Vasagar 2001: 12). In fact, like the candies my wife gave to our children, southwest Burnley Wood, which is mainly white, has received exactly the same amount of investment as the Asian areas have (£4 million). The source of the suspicion that one is not being treated fairly, that fate or the powers that be are in conspiracy against one, is not objective but intersubjective – the cumulative outcome of a felt lack of recognition, of material equality, of power, and of knowledge in one's relations to others. Consider this example from Protestant north Belfast. Kate Riley is 53. She left school at 15 to work as a spinner is Belfast's linen mills. Her husband was murdered by the IRA in 1974. 'They want our houses. They took my husband's life 20-odd years ago and I've worked since then for this house. Now they want to take my home away from me. If we don't stand up now, where will the Catholics take over next ...' Kate's partner, Hugh, added: 'Why should we be pushed out to take care of their breeding?' Kate clinched the argument. 'Those Catholics have got more than they ever dreamed of. How would you like it in England if the Indians and Pakistanis came along and told you not to fly the Union Jack?' (O'Kane 2001: 1–2).

Violence is the implementation of this logic of reversal. It is governed by the desperate and magical conviction that by turning back the clock, reversing the sequence of events that comprise one's national history or personal biography, nothingness will yield to being. One will somehow make good what one has lost, repair what has been broken, and forget the tragedy that has befallen one.

Reciprocity and Violence

When Marcel Mauss invoked the Maori spirit (*hau*) of the gift to eluci-date the threefold character of reciprocity (1954: 8–12), he glossed over the fact that the Maori word for reciprocity – appropriately a palindrome, *utu* – refers *both* to the gift-giving that sustains social sol-idarity *and* to the violent acts of seizure, revenge and repossession that are provoked when one party denies or diminishes the integrity (*mana*) of another.

Analytically speaking, violence is not an expression of animal or pathological forces that lie 'outside' our humanity; it is an aspect of our humanity itself. Rather than dismiss it as antisocial behaviour, we must approach it as a social phenomenon whose conditions of possi-bility inhere in the 'three obligations of reciprocity – giving, receiving, repaying' (Mauss 1954: 37) – which together define the most elemen-tary form of intersubjectivity.

The logic of reciprocity governs relations with those one loves as well as those one hates, and provides a rationale for both the giving and taking of life. Thus, while gift-giving is an interminable process, compelled by the felt inequality of what is given and received in any single exchange, 'violence' is similarly cyclical, sustained by the impos-sibility of both parties ever deciding unambiguously when a score has been settled, when wrongs have been righted, when debts have been paid, and losses made good.

Although reciprocity frequently invokes notions of quantity ('I owe you one'... 'I am in your debt' ...'Now we are even'), it also rests on qualitative notions that cannot be easily substantivised ('You have saved my life; how can I ever repay you?'... 'Nothing you do will ever make up for the suffering you have caused me'). In a powerful essay on the anthropology of pain, Veena Das provides a telling example of this switching between quantitative and qualitative signs. Beginning with Nietzsche's notion (1996: 46) of reciprocity as a relationship between creditor and debtor, and the corollary that a debtor forfeits his right over his possessions – *including his body* – because of the injury he has caused his creditor, Das points out that under conditions of violence entire groups reclaim the debts they believe they are owed by other groups (e.g., Hindu-Muslim) not by seizing a 'material equivalent' of the debt, but by inflicting pain on the 'most precious possession' of the debtor. Often as not, women's bodies are the site of these acts of viola-tion, torture and seizure (Das 1995: 185–186).

Because, as Mauss put it, 'things have values which are emotional as well as material' (1954: 63), two incommensurable notions of value are always at play in any exchange – the first involving the strict calculation of determinate values, the second involving elusive moral values (Mauss's 'spiritual matter') such as rightness, fair play and justice.[6] Another way of making this point is to say that all exchange involves a continual struggle to give, claim or redistribute some scarce and elusive *existential* good – such as recognition,[7] love, humanity, happiness, voice, power, presence, honour or dignity – *whose value is incalculable*. And it is precisely this ambiguity that makes it impossible to reduce intersubjective reason to a form of logico-mathematical reason – for while the latter works with precise concepts abstracted from material, bodily and affective contexts, the logic of intersubjectivity never escapes the impress and imprecision of our lived relationships with others.

Although quantitative and qualitative measures of fairness are often irreconcilable, three ideal types of reciprocity may be distinguished, each implying a different mode of intersubjectivity.

'Balanced reciprocity' (see Sahlins 1968) covers interactions in which an ethos of fair dealing or fair play is at work. On either side of this median, however, lie two extreme positions that I will characterise as all-giving (Sahlins' 'generalised reciprocity') and all-taking (Sahlins' 'negative reciprocity'). In the case of generalised reciprocity, the line between self and other is so blurred by empathy, codependency and physical intimacy that one could not conceive of life without the other. The trust between mother and child exemplifies this modality, as may the bond between a patriot and the motherland or fatherland. At the other extreme, self and other are so sundered and polarised that the very condition of the being of one is the annihilation of the other. The absolute antipathy, paranoid fantasies and ethnic divisions that underwrite genocidal violence provide an obvious example.

In my view, *all* these modalities of intersubjective reasoning are steeped in an awareness that one's humanity is simultaneously shared and singular.

That is to say that our humanness consists both in our identity *with* others and our differences *from* them. Identity connotes both *idem* (being identical, the same) and *ipse* (being self in contrast to other) (Ricoeur 1992: 2–3, 116) or, as Hannah Arendt puts it, a sense that human plurality implies both equality and distinction (1958: 175). For Arendt, however, human distinction does not automatically imply otherness. Although all human beings are distinctive, she argues, they are not absolutely other, for they interact and communicate with one another, sharing vague assumptions of common humanity. To make a person other, one arrogates will, choice, judgement and affect entirely to oneself, and makes of the other a mere object of one's actions, one's judgement, one's compassion or one's hate.

This transformation of distinction into otherness, of another subject into a mere object is the precondition of the possibility of violence. Sameness is played down – 'sacrificed' we might say – and difference played up until a polar opposition is made between self and not-self. But, I repeat, violence is not inspired by otherness as such, which is why we are rarely violent toward things we do not think of as part of our human world. Violence is the extreme form of the desire to make other through the systematic suppression of everything that is manifestly shared or the same.[8]

In his ethnography of a Mexican secondary school (*secundaria*), Bradley Levinson shows that an ethos of equality obtained among the students – an expectation that class, gender and ethnicity should not debar people from participating in and benefitting equally from their society. But distinctions were inevitable. Interviewed six or seven years after leaving school, Socorro recalled happy times, before reflecting on the superior fortunes of two of his old friends. 'You know, it does make me sad to know they've become something and I'm not anything. Well, in the end, everyone has their own fate, no?' When Levinson asked Socorro to elaborate on what he meant by 'being something', Socorro replied: 'I'm referring to what they'll have one day, I mean a degree, in other words to be someone more. I don't feel less than them, but with the simple fact of their having a degree, I don't know, it's already something more, let's say it counts for something more. But that's just the way things are. I have to be [considered] something too, you know' (Levinson 2001: 256). Arguably, if Socorro ever came to see things less fatalistically, felt more desperately his inferior lot, and or adopted a more revolutionary notion of how equality might be achieved, mere distinction might become radical otherness, and fatalism give way to violence. After all, this is the very transition that is made a thousand times over every day in countries that condemn vast numbers of their citizenry to inequality.[9] It is, however, because no act of othering can entirely eradicate an awareness of sameness or equality (there but for grace of God go I), that racist and nationalist extremism is less a strategy for the creation of absolute difference than desperate action for the elimination of sameness. It is the persistent ambiguity – that the other remains, despite all one's efforts to deny his or her humanity – ritual, conceptual, or military, a mirror of oneself – that also shapes the logic of scapegoating, for the scapegoat is neither a complete stranger nor a kinsman, but someone who is simultaneously of one's own world and foreign to it. This is why people select for sacrifice a 'domestic' animal that is deemed 'close' to humans (Girard 1977: 2–3), for the 'sacrificial process requires not only the complete separation of the sacrificed victim from those beings for whom the victim is a substitute *but also a similarity between both parties'* (ibid: 39, emphasis added). In sacrificing a surrogate victim, people imagine that their community will be purified and reborn, for the *life* of this community is thought to be contingent on the *death* of the designated other (ibid: 254–255).

Violence and the Scapegoat

One of the most ontologically primitive ways of dealing with anxiety and distress is to reimagine one's inner pain as an external object – something that can be removed, and got rid of – as easily as one divests clothes, cuts hair, or removes a thorn from one's side. The latin *obicere*, which gives us our term 'objectify' means literally 'to throw away'. But it is obviously self-defeating to objectify one's inner pain by blaming or dumping on someone one loves, for this simply moves the pain to another quarter of one's own intimate lifeworld. We therefore seek another who, though familiar, is foreign, and though one of us can also be said to be not of us. In other words, intersubjective logic dictates that in as much as I need the scapegoat to carry something away that presently pains and oppresses me from within, then this other that I will drive out into the wilderness and ostracise must be in some sense part and parcel of my own world.

If the paradigmatic scapegoats of Europe have been the gypsy and the jew, the scapegoat in West Africa has been the witch. As a neighbour, wife or mother, she is one of us. But in other ways she has never ceased to be a stranger. She retains ties of loyalty with her own people, and harbours intentions we cannot divine. She is the enemy within. And so, when epidemic illness oppresses our village, or we suffer reverses in our fortunes, and see these afflictions as coming from elsewhere, who better to carry our troubles away than one among us whose origins or essence we can readily interpret as alien? So some poor soul is pressured to confess to having visited our misfortunes upon us before being buried alive in no-man's land, deemed to be 'not a person' (Jackson 1989). Francine Lorimer has recently shown how spectral images of the European witch as rank outsider become fused with anxieties about immigrants in the ritual burning of a witch's effigy at the June festival of Sankt Hans in contemporary Denmark. At stake, she notes, is 'an anxiety concerning the uncontrollable agency of the Other' (2003b: 123).

Scapegoating does not, therefore, assume an a priori ontological difference between self and other; rather, it is a strategy in which some distinctive trait in the other's appearance, situation or behaviour is foregrounded and stigmatised – as bestial, antisocial or inhuman – while everything that makes the other resemble us is backgrounded, eclipsed and denied.

Violence is commonest within families or communities. It is an expression of nearness, not distance. This is no less true of scapegoating. The scapegoat is an intimate stranger – someone who is simultaneously of us and not of us. When the scapegoat is, so to speak, sent up in smoke, or sent packing to where we have decided he or she properly belongs, we simply reverse the sequence of events whereby he or she came to be among us in the first place. The rationale for this ritual reversal is that we are redressing a wrong, taking what we are owed, restoring a just balance. During the late 1970s and early 1980s, Hutu refugees in camps in western Tanzania, worked tirelessly on a mythico-history that would rationalise these kinds of retaliative actions (Malkki 1995: 52–104). Cosmological in scale, these mythico-histories reimagined the crucial events whereby Hutu had lost their homelands, and envisaged how this loss might be made good. According to the mythic version of events, Hutu were the original and autochthonous inhabitants of Rwanda, but the Tutsi, migrating from the north at a later date, had usurped Hutu power through stealth and trickery. This involved a negation of reciprocity. The Hutu allowed the Tutsi pastoralists to graze their cattle on their land. In return, the Tutsi gave dung to the Hutu to make their fruit trees grow, milk to make their children stronger, and cows. But before long, the Hutu were beholden to the Tutsi, and obliged to work for them. Thus Hutu (which in folk etymologies means 'servant' or 'slave') lost their autonomy. Though they regained it for a while under Belgian rule, Independence restored Tutsi fortunes. They blocked Hutu advancements through education, and in 1972, determined to tip the demographic and social balance further in their own favour, Tutsi massacred Hutu and forced tens of thousands into exile.

In both fantasies of violence and acts of violence, the focus on the scapegoat becomes so intense that one is unable to reconsider whether or not the object of one's hate is the actual cause of one's misfortune. This brings me back to my earlier discussion of objectification. For in violence, we no longer deploy *things* as 'objective correlatives' of our subjective thoughts and feelings, but *persons*. And in so far as violence is a form of false consciousness in which the external symbols of our inner discontent are given a facticity and fixity that allows no revision, we fall prey to the belief that in ridding ourselves of those symbols we will somehow cleanse our lives of their baleful influence. Blaming, scapegoating, ostracising and genocide are all logical expressions of a form of intersubjective reasoning in which others are treated as objects that stand for what we find inimical in ourselves or our own lifeworlds. Instead of throwing things into swamps, or dancing away a bad state of affairs, as the Gogo do, violence involves throwing away or sacrificing the lives of people that we have come to regard as things.

Redemption and the Transformation of Time

It is all very well saying that if we are to break cycles of violence we must break our discursive habit of dialectic negation – transforming difference into alterity so that others embody what we cannot abide in ourselves. And it all very well exhorting sworn enemies to enter into dialogue and recover, through face-to-face contact, a sense of shared humanity. But if, as I have argued in this chapter, human reasoning is inescapably steeped in our experience of social relations, how can we think about what is amiss in our lives without blaming others? To what extent is it possible to invoke cause without anthropomorphising it – to speak of *what* oppresses us rather than *who*? And in so far as the logic of reversal leads to recrimination and revenge, does human intersubjectivity contain within itself the germ of reconciliation?

Replacing the notion of reversal with the notion of renewal, Hannah Arendt uses the concept of natality to provide a creative answer to these questions. Against the Heideggerian view that human existence is an inescapable movement toward death, Arendt places her emphasis on the perennial possibility of rebirth. In the miracle of birth is encapsulated the imminent possibility of changing the world, of making a new beginning, and of freeing ourselves from our thralldom to the past (Arendt 1958: 247). Even revolution, she writes, is 'the experience of man's faculty to begin something new' (1963: 27). But if natality is to radically transform our relationship to time, it must offer more than returns to the past for reckoning or revenge; it must offer us the promise of a future. This promise is linked to forgiveness.

> The possible redemption from the predicament of irreversibility – of being unable to undo what one has done though one did not, and could not, have known what one was doing – is the faculty of forgiving. The remedy for unpredictability, for the chaotic uncertainty of the future, is contained in the faculty to make and keep promises. The two faculties belong together in so far as one of them, forgiving, serves to undo the deeds of the past, whose 'sins' hang like Damocles' sword over every new generation; and the other, binding oneself through promises, serves to set up in the ocean of uncertainty, which the future is by definition, islands of security without which not even continuity, let alone durability of any kind, would be possible in the relationships between men. (Arendt 1958: 237)

Forgiving is not necessarily a forgetting, though many traumatised individuals endeavour to forget what they cannot forgive. Nor is the focus of forgiving on one's oppressor; rather it is on the conditions under which one's own life, and the lives of those to whom one is most closely bound, can be released from the oppressor's grasp. Unlike revenge, punishment, or 'repressed memory', which tend to reenact and perpetuate the original trespass, enslaving one to it for as long as one lives, forgiveness conserves a memory of the original outrage while releasing one from it. It is in this sense that forgiveness redeems one's life and refuses the oppressor the power to determine it. But, as Arendt points out, the power of forgiving and promising does not consist in these acts alone, but in the ways in which these acts involve others. Both depend on plurality, she writes, 'on the presence and acting of others, for no one can forgive himself and no one can feel bound by a promise made only to himself; forgiving and promising enacted in solitude or isolation remain without reality and can signify no more than a role played before one's self' (1958: 237).

As active refusals to replay events of the past, forgiving and promising imply a repositioning of oneself in an imaginary future community that can, so to speak, annul history. It is this hope that informed the hearings of the Truth and Reconciliation Commission in South Africa, and that is invoked after every epoch of terror. But Arendt's views on how human beings may redeem the past by committing themselves collectively to the building of brave new futures entail modes of *spatial* repositioning as well as optimistic projection. Here, Arendt's notion of renewing our understanding through the exercise of a 'visiting imagination' (Disch 1994: 158) is crucial.

For Aristotle, homelessness was one of the blessings of the philosopher's way of life (Arendt 1971: 199–200), and in his *Protreptikos* he celebrates the life of the mind (*bios theoretikos*) as the life of a stranger (*bios xenikos*). The intellectual life is best pursued nowhere, doing nothing; it can only be hindered by a preoccupation with particulars, and with local allegiances. True thought, he observed, requires neither tools nor places for their work, for 'wherever in the whole world one sets one's thought to work, it is surrounded on all sides by the presence of truth' (Aristotle 1952: 34). I share Hannah Arendt's view that thought cannot free itself from the practical, physical and sensible immediacies of our worldly existence, and imagine she might have shared Merleau-Ponty's view that philosophy is not a matter of rising above the mundane, but of a 'lateral displacement' (1964: 119) that enables one to critically reconsider one's views from another vantage point. Rather than a 'nowhere' outside of time and circumstance, one seeks an 'elsewhere' *within* the world. For an ethnographer, this elsewhere is some other society; for the historian some other time.

Anthropologists call this 'stranger value'. While insiders may find it difficult to see the world from any point of view other than their own, a visitor may try out a plurality of perspectives without any personal loss of status or identity, because he is already marked as marginal, stateless and indeterminate. This 'visiting imagination' of the outsider implies neither an objective standpoint (he does not seek disinterestedness or distance from the other), nor an empathic one (he is not interested in losing himself in the other); it is, rather, a way of putting himself in the place of another, a way of destabilising habitual patterns of thinking by thinking his own thoughts in the place of somebody else. The result is neither a detached knowledge of another's world nor an empathic blending with another's worldview. Rather it yields a story that switches from one point of view to another without prioritising any one, yet unsettles in the mind of anyone who reads or hears the story not only his certainties *but his belief in the possibility of certainty.* The *impartial* understanding attained through storytelling is linked, therefore, to the doubts that arise from displacement. It is neither a matter of seeing the world from some privileged 'nowhere', nor of aligning oneself with any particular person or group of persons on the sentimental grounds that they are in sole possession of the truth, but of interleaving a multiplicity of particular points of view in a way that calls into question *all* claims for privileged understanding. No matter how abhorrent the view of the other, it represents a logical possibility for one's self. It is in this sense that the difference between self and other is always conditional upon our social interactions, and not predetermined by some genetic, cultural or moral essence.

When the WTC was destroyed on 11 September, a shocked eye-witness commented: 'This is the sort of thing I thought only happened elsewhere'. This comment immediately reminded me of the David Rousset line with which Hannah Arendt prefaces Part Three of *The Origins of Totalitarianism* – 'Normal men do not know that everything is possible' (Arendt 1967: 303). But it is this very 'normal' ignorance that makes it imperative that we do everything in our power to deconstruct, both in practice and discourse, the 'abnormal' distance that we believe to exist between ourselves and others, and between 'here' and 'there', and so reclaim a deeper understanding of the ways in which everyone is a part of the same human condition.

Notes

1. I take it as axiomatic that (a) the social is *lived* as a network of reciprocal relationships among subjects, that is to say intersubjectively, and that (b) intersubjectivity and reciprocity embrace both identity and difference, as well as life-affirming and life-denying extremes (Jackson 1998: 4).
2. It is, however, often the case that people strive to retrospectively rationalise events according to such calculations (Schutz and Luckmann 1989: 57–65 on 'rational action'), and I envisage the possibility of demonstrating that the conditions of the possibility of such abstract operations as addition, multiplication, division, subtraction lie in the elementary forms of intersubjective experience.
3. A.R. Luria and Margaret Donaldson suggest that a child's ability to handle logical propositions is improved when these are embedded in a story. But whether the intersubjective logic of narrative sequencing and character interaction is the same as logico-mathematical reasoning is another matter. Jerome Bruner points out that a child's storytelling is motivated less by a 'push toward logical coherence' than 'a need to "get the story right": who did what to whom where, was it the "real" and steady thing or a rogue happening, and how do I feel about it' (1990: 92) – i.e., driven by a need to restore his or her sense of agency and of fair play in the face of overwhelming events.
4. In societies throughout the world human intersubjectivity is made analogous with bonds, networks, ropes, knots, skeins and woven cloth. Even anthropologists have had recourse to these images in their models of social relations. The reason may be that spinning and weaving are so closely associated with clothing – itself a core image of social identity and social role, as in the cognate terms costume and custom. That these same metaphors are commonly used of luck or fate suggests the intimate link between a person's destiny in life and his or her primary relationships with parents and close kin. Kinship, like fate, connotes givenness and necessity, rather than choice – that which is binding or bound. But as I have already remarked, relations of primary intersubjectivity tend to be projected and reified as *external* relations, involving fates or divinities. In Homer, for instance, fortune is 'a cord or bond fastened upon a man by the powers above' (Onians 1951: 331). 'At birth the gods or fates spin the strands of weal or woe which a man must endure in the course of his life' as invisible threads (ibid: 336). And man is bound to die. Comparable images appear in Norse mythology, where the gods are called 'the Binders' and the Norns spin, weave, and bind the fates of men at birth (ibid: 381). For the Anglo-Saxons, too, fate was woven, while pain, age, and affliction were spoken of as bonds (ibid: 357).
5. Gregory Bateson's notion of the 'double-bind' (1973) and R.D. Laing's 'knots' (1971) are good examples of this imagery, and D.W. Winnicott has published perceptive accounts of how a child will play out the 'ebb and flow' of his or her relationship with the mother by attaching and detaching, tying and retying, a piece of string (Winnicott 1974: 22,50; cf. Freud's famous example of the *fort-da* game 1957: 18,14–16).
6. Bourdieu's notion of 'symbolic capital' covers this same field of rare, incalculable, and 'priceless things' – of 'fair words' or smiles, handshakes, shrugs, compliments or attention, challenges or insults, honour or honours, powers or pleasures, gossip or scientific information, distinction or distinctions, etc.' (1977: 178).
7. Francis Fukuyama emphasises Hegel's 'need for recognition' (Hegel 1971) in arguing against the reductionist view that economic life is driven chiefly by 'rational desire' for material gain (Fukuyama 1992).

8. As a pathology it bears comparison with fetishisation in the Freudian sense of the word. A conspicuous part (skin colour, mannerism, mode of dress) is made definitive of the whole.

9. Such a transformation from difference to otherness can occur literally overnight, and Michael Herzfeld's comments on events in Cyprus and Crete recall more recent events in Rwanda, the former Yugoslavia and Indonesia. 'On both islands, over long periods, Greek-speaking Christians and Muslims lived side by side, separated by their respective religions but conjoined in certain ritual practices of local significance and by ties of reciprocity that would be enacted in dramatic public displays on special occasions such as feast-days. Yet virtually the entire Muslim population of Crete was shipped off to Asia Minor in 1924, while the current hardening of "ethnic" lines between "Greeks" and "Turks" on Cyprus further illustrates the transformation of identities into ethnicity and thence into nationality – a progression that has brought little but disruption and death to the local communities and transmuted local norms of feuding into national "causes"' (Herzfeld 1997: 80–81).

Chapter 4

CUSTOM AND CONFLICT IN SIERRA LEONE: AN ESSAY ON ANARCHY

> Time does not always flow according to a line ... nor according to a plan
> but, rather, according to an extraordinary complex mixture, as though it
> reflected stopping points, ruptures, deep wells, chimneys or thunderous
> acceleration, rendings, gaps – all sown at random, at least in a visible
> disorder. Thus the development of history truly resembles what chaos
> theory describes.
> Michel Serres (1995: 57)

Anthropological studies of the recent war in Sierra Leone have tended
to focus on the causes or preconditions of the conflict. While some
emphasise longstanding, local-level patterns of structural violence,
exclusion, secrecy, struggle and suspicion that periodically erupt into
open conflict, even in 'times of peace' (Ferme 2001a: 1), others place
less emphasis on indigenous culture as such, and see the war as a
'product of [a] protracted, post-colonial crisis of patrimonialism,' trig-
gered by global politico-economic changes in the 1980s that sharply
reduced resources available for redistribution (Richards 1996: xviii).
While not denying the value of these perspectives, my own interest is
less in tracing the specific origins of the conflict than in exploring some
of the ways in which a constellation of elements – historical, politico-
economic, sociocultural, symbolic and imaginary – was variously
combined and permuted in the lived experience of Sierra Leoneans
over several generations, and found expression, in the early 1990s, in
internecine war. Rather than explain the war in terms of determinate

Notes for this section can be found on page 72.

trajectories or objective conditions – cultural, historical, economic or political – my aim is to disclose what was at play, what was at stake, in the lifeworlds of those who actually experienced this war as combatants or as victims. At the same time, I want to explore the ways in which this war, like any other, outstripped the sociocultural conditions under which it emerged and the political rationale with which it began, running its course like a storm or a fever. As Allen Feldman notes, chronic violence characteristically 'detaches itself from initial contexts and becomes the condition of its own reproduction' (1991: 20), which is why changes in the conditions that produce violence do not necessarily end it. While the rebellion in Sierra Leone refers us back to the lifeworlds in which it was, as it were, prepared, it clearly took on a life and logic of its own. There is, however, another reason for not reducing the meaning of the war to antecedent conditions. That the lives of countless Sierra Leoneans have been terribly and irreversibly changed by this war is itself an argument against reducing effects to causes or, for that matter, against the disinterested language of orthodox social science.

I begin this chapter with a young Kuranko man's account of 'his' war. On the basis of Sewa's insights and observations, I proceed to explore the politics of the body and the nature of anarchy, focusing on some of the symbolic forms common to both ritualised and armed rebellion. Finally, I consider the critical interplay of expectation and disappointment, inequality and *ressentiment*, that have been recurring motifs in colonial and post-colonial Sierra Leone.

Sewa's Story

In January 2002, just before the war was declared officially over, I returned to Sierra Leone after more than ten years away, and travelled to Koinadugu district, where I had carried out fieldwork intermittently between 1969 and 1986. During my time in Kabala, a young Kuranko man, Sewa Bockari Koroma, recounted his harrowing experiences in November 1994 when a brigade of the Revolutionary United Front (RUF) overran the town. After the success of the Tamaboros[1] in repelling the RUF from Kono and forcing them back to their base in Kailahun, the National Provisional Ruling Council (NPRC) became uneasy, for their sole justification for staying in power lay in their own ability to destroy the RUF. They accordingly dissolved the Tamaboro, who they now described as a 'rogue army', and sent Komba Kambo back to Koinadugu. It is very likely that when the RUF sacked Kabala in November 1994, it did so in complicity with the Sierra Leone military. Travelling over mountainous terrain and avoiding roads, an RUF force of about seventy youths walked 110 miles in seven days, from Kalmaro, northeast of Magburaka, and entered Kabala with some of the government troops that locals had seen pass through the town in uniform only three days before. One of the objectives of this raid was to punish the town that had given birth to the Tamaboros, which explains why certain houses were targeted for destruction and why Dembaso Samura, one of the Tamaboro 'field marshals', was stabbed and beaten to death. The town was subsequently invaded several more times, and many houses pillaged and burned.

I saw the destruction through Sewa's eyes, as we sauntered along dusty lanes that had once been thoroughfares, past rows of derelict houses, and through unfamiliar neighbourhoods. So many refugees had poured into Kabala during the war that the town had expanded almost beyond recognition. But we were soon trudging up the rutted road toward the roundabout, and then past the mosque into the main street. Opposite the market there was a poster advertising a Nigerian movie. *Okuzu Massacre* The Robbers Revenge. 'On the 19th of July my entire family and twenty two others were killed. Who is responsible? The Governor, the Igwe, the Robbers, or the Gods?'

'What do you think?' I asked Sewa.

'You can rent a video if you want,' he said. And sure enough, a few doors away we found the Kaku Video Centre, with *Evil Forest* – The Lord Vindicates for hire. And *Jungle Rats*. 'A war of betrayal and deceit. The fight to the finish.'

'I would have thought,' I said, 'that people were sick and tired of this kind of violence.'

'Sometimes you have to remember,' Sewa said. And as we headed along along the road toward the Catholic school, he told me his story.

He had come to Kabala from Freetown to spend some time with his mother Tina and his father, Sheku Magba Koroma II, who was the Paramount Chief of Diang. I had known Chief Magba well, and had done fieldwork in Kondembaia, the main town of the chiefdom. Both Tina and her husband had taken refuge in Kabala in 1994, though they were not staying in the same house. 'At about 4.00 in the afternoon of 7 November 1994,' Sewa said, 'we heard gunfire. People were running about in a panic, saying that the rebels had entered the town. I was with my cousin Sheku. We went to my dad and said, "People are saying that the rebels are here." My father said, "No, it is the Tamaboros." But the rebels had entered the town on foot, without vehicles, using cross-country paths rather than roads. By nightfall, many houses were on fire, and my father was asking us, "What shall we do, what shall we do?" Sheku and I wanted to get away from the house, but there were rebels moving down the street, so we stayed inside and locked the door. About 8 o'clock the rebels banged on the door. They shouted, "If you don't open up we'll set fire to the house and you'll burn." I quickly threw my father's staff (of chieftaincy) under the bed. Then they smashed the door. The rebels saw my father's briefcase. It was filled with money and gold dust.[2] They shouted, "Whose is this?" I said I didn't know who it belonged to. I told them that we had taken shelter in the house when the shooting began. The rebels said, "If you had nothing to hide, why did you run away?"'

As the rebels moved on down the street, Sewa and Sheku found themselves face to face with two young men their own age, armed with AK-47s. The one who gave orders was called Kujé. His sidekick was called Abu. 'Fortunately,' Sewa said, 'they believed my story, and did not suspect that the old Pa was my father, let alone a Paramount Chief. Had they known the truth they would have killed him. But I think they were afraid of us. Only two of them against the two of us. They were thinking we might overpower them and take their weapons.

'Kujé said, "Now we'll kill you," and he shot Sheku in the stomach. As Sheku died, I pleaded with them. "Don't kill me," I said. "I'm going to come with you. I want to come with you."

'They ordered me to pack a bag, and to make up a headload of food. Then we headed off the way the rebels had come, along the path to Kamadugu Sukurela. We spent that night in Kamadugu Sukurela, which the rebels had already burned and looted on their way to Kabala. I was one of many captives. One of the girls was Fanta Konté, who was Miss Koinadugu. Next day we went on to Singbian. We arrived there at nightfall. The Town Crier was in the process of announcing that the RUF had entered Kabala. He was blind. He did not realise that these same rebels had just entered his village. "So you're telling everyone that we are evil?" the rebels asked. And they shot him dead. Next morning we left for Dalako, near Lake Sonfon. We reached there at about 4.00 in the afternoon.

'When the rebels said they wanted food, I told them that there was a cassava garden behind the house, and that I would prepare cassava for them. They trusted me now. I had been helping them talk to the other captives, especially the girls, who were afraid for their lives. So they let me go to the garden alone. It was then that I made my escape. I had dreamed about it the night before. And because I believe that dreams presage real events, I had already decided to escape that day.[3] I made my way to Yara where I met the townchief and some hunters. They were very happy to see me and to hear that my father was alive. One of the hunters then escorted me back to Kondembaia.

'Three years passed,' Sewa said, 'before the captured girls emerged from the bush. They told me that the rebels claimed to have shot me when I tried to escape. Everyone believed I was dead, like my cousin Sheku.'

One remark of Sewa's about the RUF – among whom there were undoubtedly many renegade soldiers – particularly intrigued me. The rebels, he had said, were all young men. Many were only boys. They smoked a lot of cannabis, which made them 'wild.' And their leader, whose name was Mohammed, and hailed from Makeni, wore a red beret, and a red bandana around his neck. His companions praised him constantly. And he did not carry a gun, only a knife, and was at all times surrounded by his bodyguard.

What interested me was this odd mix of bravado and vulnerability. Surely Sewa was right when he suggested that the rebels shot Sheku because they felt threatened by the pair of them, that they killed Sheku in order to break Sewa's spirit and to reduce the danger of taking two friends prisoner together. Perhaps, too, I thought, they felt vulnerable – so far from their homes (they had come from Kailahun in the south), afraid of the Tamaboros, who possessed magical medicines to ward off bullets or kill their enemies, and the powers of shapeshifting and witchcraft – *their* way of dealing with their terror.

Unless one has been caught up in a war and experienced the terror that comes of knowing that hundreds of heavily-armed individuals are bent on one's annihilation, it is hard to realise that most violence is not primarily motivated by evil, greed, lust, ideology or aggression. Strange as it may seem, most violence is defensive. As William James observed, fear 'is a reaction aroused by the same objects that arouse ferocity' which is why we 'both fear, and wish to kill, anything that may kill us' (1950: 415). This is why violence is so often motivated by the fear that if one does not kill one will be killed. Either by the enemy or by one's own superiors. Against this constant anxiety, and the acute sense of fear and vulnerability that accompanies it, one conjures an illusion of power – torching buildings, shooting unarmed civilians, firing rocket grenades, smoking cannabis, shouting orders, chanting slogans, seeing oneself as Rambo, taunting and abusing the individuals one has taken captive. But all this display of might – this weaponry,[4] these medicines and armulets, this noise, these incantations, both political and magical, these Hollywood images, these drug-induced fugues, these rituals of brotherhood and solidarity – simply reveal the depth of one's own impotence and fear. This is Hannah Arendt's great insight – that while military power consolidates itself in numbers, and in coordinated, automatic forms of mass movement, terrorism seeks power in implements, and is driven not by might but its absence (1969: 24–26).[5] And so it is that in the auto-da-fé, with explosions and bomb blasts, fire, noise and mayhem, that the terrorist, like a child, finds his apotheosis, achieving the recognition, presence, voice and potency he has been denied in the real world.

Like any other animal, human beings will fight to the death when threatened or cornered, but as a species we are perhaps alone in imagining that our survival depends on such elusive properties as recognition, love, identity, national honour, prestige, freedom and wealth. Only we will feel that our very existence is endangered when our name is taken in vain, our pride is hurt, our freedom is threatened, our reputation impugned, our voice ignored, our loyalty betrayed. No other animal will fight tooth and nail, not only to see that such symbolic losses are made good, but that those who have allegedly taken these things from us are themselves subject to all the torment, degradation and loss that we have suffered at their hands. This is why violators seldom admit to guilt. For they believe they were fully justified in their excesses; they were only taking back what was rightfully theirs, preserving their civilisation, defending their rights, upholding their honour, regaining their freedom, and of course, obeying orders from above.

It is never easy – seeing images of bewildered refugees on a Kosovo road; looking at an old photograph of a column of men, women and children, some with hands held above their hands, others clutching small suitcases, herded along a smoke-darkened Warsaw street to oblivion; or interviewing villagers in Sierra Leone who have had their limbs amputated by machetes – to believe that in the eyes of their tormentors they were part of a single, monstrous entity bent on their annihilation. When I asked Leba Keita, a young man I met in Kabala, why the RUF mutilated and killed so many innocent people, he thought for a moment and said: 'They used to say the government was not paying any attention to them.' When I asked Patrick Koroma, whose father was a famed storyteller with whom I had worked in the past, the same question, he recalled one man from Kondembaia who had had both his hands cut off. The rebels wrote a note to the President, saying 'We rebels did this', and they stuffed the note in the man's shirt pocket and told him to go to the President. 'You used those hands to vote for him,' they said. 'Now he is bringing in all these ECOMOG soldiers to fight against us. Encouraging the CDF to kill us. Go to the President and ask him to give you another hand.'

The Politics of the Body

Though warfare may be justified in terms of political ideology and waged on the basis of military strategy, it is clearly *lived* in more immediate terms, as a visceral, emotional and chaotic reality that often defies thought.[6] Analytically, this poses something of a dilemma, for how do we evaluate, let alone integrate, such diverse approaches to the phenomenon of war? More precisely, how are we to understand the relationship between the logic underlying the Clausewitzian notion of war as 'the continuation of policy by other means' (1982) and the logic that governs the lived experience of violence?

Generally speaking, both logics reflect the imperatives of reciprocity. As I have argued in chapter 3, breakdowns of reciprocity, either real or imagined, tend to be experienced as reversals in the life-affirming order of social life. Against this movement toward entropy and death, ritualised re-reversals of the order of things occur or are contrived. Thus, violence generally takes the form of retribution or payback, driven by the need to reclaim something one imagines to have been wrongfully taken, and that is now owed. One's very existence is felt to depend on making good this loss – a legacy stolen, a promise broken, a loved one murdered, a dream betrayed, one's honour impugned.[7] In the politics of peace, indemnification is sought according to a strict calculation – political, legal and ethical – of what has been taken and what is owed in return. In the politics of war, however, the existential damages are felt to be so deep and degrading that material indemnification is seldom considered adequate. The injured party demands satisfaction, and this, as Nietzsche observed, commonly involves punishment inflicted on the debtor's body – by branding, amputation, rape, and mutilation. The logic of this kind of exchange, Nietzsche goes on to say, rests on the fact that, 'instead of a direct compensation for the damage done (i.e. instead of money, land, possessions of whatever sort), a sort of pleasure is conceded to the creditor as a form of repayment and recompense – the pleasure of being able to vent his power without a second thought on someone who is powerless, the enjoyment '*de faire le mal pour le plaisir de le faire*', the pleasure of violation (1996: 46).[8] Sadly, one finds little difficulty in finding evidence for Nietzsche's unusual insight, whether in the medicalised brutalities to which the Nazi doctors submitted the inmates of the death camps, in the stylised processes of dehumanisation, disfigurement and dismemberment during the genocide in Rwanda, or the RUF practice in Sierra Leone of cutting off people's hands because they had, allegedly, voted in the wrong way.

I hope to have made it clear that the wartime atmosphere of fear and peril (doubtless exacerbated among the RUF by their knowledge that the local Tamaboro – who possessed powerful protective medicines and techniques of sorcery – might counterattack at any moment), as well as the escalating acts of vengeance that increasingly characterised the conflict *were self-generating phenomena* that largely eclipsed the grievances and ideologies that orginally precipitated armed rebellion in Sierra Leone. Indeed, by the mid 1990s political motives had paled into insignificance, despite the RUF leadership's insistence that the sole reason for waging war was to liberate the country from oppression and corruption. When I asked Sewa if he had seen any evidence of political ideology when the RUF invaded Kabala, he referred to a certain Mr Lawrence, a high school graduate and slightly older man, who was second in command. But none of the other rebels explained their actions in political terms, he said. My former field assistant, Noah Marah, made the same observation. When he was abducted by rebels at Lunsar in 1996, he asked his captors what they were fighting for. They said, 'Pappy (Foday Sankoh) has money for us'. They had been promised money if they won the war. 'However,' Noah said, 'they had no political agenda, no political motives'. Noah's son Kaima said the same thing. The ones he knew that joined the RUF saw it as a way of getting money. They went to Kono where the RUF controlled the diamond mining. Others, Kaima added, had grievances, and he mentioned young men who had been cut out of their father's inheritance, and had a bone to pick with their older brothers. Another young man called Unisa Mansaray, a young electronic journalist, recently returned from a BBC training course in London made a similar point. When the rebels and their Junta allies fought their way into Freetown on 6 January 1999, some came to Unisa's parent's house where he was staying. They were kids that Unisa had known at school, with old scores to settle, imagined slights, trivial grievances – pretexts really, Unisa said, for the deeper grudge they bore against a government that had betrayed their dreams. When they shouted his name, ordering him to come out of the house, Unisa leaped from the second floor balcony and fled. But his grandparents and parents, trapped inside the house, were shot and killed.

Although longstanding grievances played a part in the killings, they may, of course, have been rationalisations rather than motives. And the same question hangs over the recurring reason the rebels gave in the late 1990s for the atrocities they committed, namely that they were avenging themselves against the government that had funded and encouraged the militias to destroy them. If I place these rationales in brackets, it is not because they lack explanatory value but because they blind us, to some extent, to the ways in which barbaric acts are products neither of reason nor of unreason, but of disorder itself.

The Nature of Anarchy

In his study of peasant insurgency in colonial India, Ranajit Guha notes that ritualised modalities of resisting or defying politically constituted authority often have precedents in everyday social life (1987: 12), and he cites as an example the calendrical rituals of rebellion and role reversal that anthropologists have studied in great detail, in India, Africa and elsewhere. These simulated and temporary inversions of the social order – such as the Medieval Feast of Fools and the Lord of Misrule, the Shrove Tuesday carnival, the Nomkubulwana ceremonies of the Zulu, the Teyyam festival in Malabar, and the celebration of Holi rite – may, Guha observes, become models for the permanent violation of social hierarchies, a 'real turning of things upside down'(ibid: 36).[9] A similar observation was made by Max Gluckman in one of his talks on the BBC's 'Third Programme' in 1955: 'The rebellion principle I have outlined for Africa does seem to pull together rules of succession, the law of treason, and other customs, *and to explain to some extent the results of civil wars*' (1956: 48, emphasis added).

One of the first people with whom I spoke about the war was a young baggage handler at Lungi airport who I met within minutes of my arrival in the country. When I asked Isa how the war had affected his life, he told me that his brother had been abducted by rebels while travelling from Kenema to visit their father in 1996. Though he managed to escape, he came home with a bullet in his knee, which now caused him great pain and prevented him from working. '*During the war, everyone was alone,*' Isa said. '*Everyone had to fend for himself. There was no order*'.

This lack of order was, nonetheless, not wholly chaotic. Rather, it seemed in many ways to be a carnivalesque reversal or inversion of the normal order of things.

Sewa's comments on this phenomenon will serve as a starting point for elucidating the cultural precedents for this 'grotesque realism' (Bakhtin 1984a) in which life is 'turned inside out' (Bakhtin 1984b: 122). I asked Sewa why the rebels sometimes wore comic-book masks, women's underwear, or wigs, carried children's toys, and adopted nicknames like Black Jesus and Captain Blood. 'When I was taken captive in Kabala,' Sewa answered, 'there was one rebel who called himself Born Naked, and went about without a stitch of clothing. Another was called Arab. He dressed in a djellaba and keffiyeh, like a sheikh. And then there was Albila'u, which means "dangerous thing" in Mandingo, and Kill-Man-No-Law, because there was no law in existence that could prevent the RUF from doing whatever they liked to you. They dressed up,' Sewa added, '*because no laws or rules applied to them; it was to show that they could do anything*'. This echoes a telling remark by an ex-SLA combatant who participated in the 1994 Kabala attack: 'I liked the army,' he said, 'because we could do anything we liked to do. When some civilian had something I liked, I just took it without him doing anything to me. We used to rape women. Anything I wanted to do [I did]. I was free' (Peters and Richards 1998: 93).

In all human societies, order and disorder are mutually entailed. Image creates counter-image, in the same way that figure becomes ground, and ground becomes figure in those ambiguous and illusory images from first-year psychology textbooks. As Bakhtin has argued, carnival is an apposite word for this 'working out, in a concretely sensuous, half-real and half-play-acted form, [of] a *new mode of interrelationship between individuals*, counterposed to the all-powerful socio-hierarchical relationships of noncarnival life' (1984: 123, emphasis in text).

Among the Dogon of Mali, the figure of Yourougou is associated with extravagance, disorder and oracular truth, while its opposite, Nommo, represents reason and social order (Calame-Griaule 1965). For the neighbouring Bambara, a similar contrast is posited between Nyalé – who was created first and signifies 'swarming life,' exuberance and uncontrolled power – and Faro, or Ndomadyiri, who was created next and signifies equilibrium and restraint (Zahan 1974: 15). For the Kuranko, the contrast between bush and town signifies the same extremes. Because the bush is a source of vital and regenerative energy, the village must open itself up perennially to it. Hunters venture into the bush at night, braving real and imagined dangers in their search for meat. Farmers clear-fell the forest in order to grow the upland rice that is the staple of life. And initiation rites – which take place in the bush, and have as their ostensible goal the disciplining and channelling of the unruly energies of children so that after a symbolic death they are brought back to life as moral adults – simultaneously open up the possibility of intense individuation because they encourage each initiate 'to live the 'found' world as though it were of his or own making' (Jackson and Karp 1990: 29). Accordingly, though all these transgressions in space and breaks with routine are necessary for the renewal of life, they also imperil the collectivity.

Whenever the boundary between town and bush (or their symbolic analogues – day/night, domestic/wild) is crossed, disorder and confusion momentarily reign. Walking through the forest at night, one does not speak, for fear that a djinn might steal one's name and use it for bedevilment. During initiations, people fall prey to similar anxieties, and consult diviners to see how they may safeguard themselves from witches, who, it is said, can leave their bodies and go forth in the shape of night animals. At such times, parents often send their children to the homes of medicine masters, so that they will be protected from the nefarious powers that are abroad, while others redouble the protection of their bodies and houses with magical medicines. And day in and day out, role reversals and masquerades give outward expression to this inner disquiet and uncertainty – a consequence, informants would tell me, of the normal order of things being momentarily in abeyance.

I used to devote a lot of thought to this relationship between ourselves and our environments, trying to understand why our consciousness, composure and self-control are so easily disturbed when the routines and rhythms of ordinary space-time are suspended. I became particularly interested in how we cope with such disconcerting experiences by literally taking upon ourselves – incorporating, internalising – the disorder that lies about us, before playing it back to the surrounding world, as it were, in the form of feigned madness, possession, abusive speech, role reversal and ritual inversion.[10] In doing this, we do more than mimic the chaos that has besieged us; we master it, for it is no longer something that has befallen us from without but something we have decided from within. So, during Kuranko initiations, women don the clothing of hunters, act aggressively toward men, or pretend to be soldiers, marching up and down with fake rifles, while one woman, known as the mad Kamban or Sewulan, dressed in a man's clothes, dances clumsily with distracted gestures and deadpan expression, occasionally chasing away men and children with the switch she holds in her hand (Jackson 1977: 181–217).

Disorder is probably the wrong word for what is occuring here. More accurately, we should speak topologically – of the reordering and recombination of roles, images, behaviours, language and routines, and of what Bourdieu calls 'the practical transference of incorporated, quasi-postural schemes' (1977: 116). Thus, in initiation the passage of human life from birth and death is played in reverse. When neophytes are symbolically killed and reborn, a natural course of events gives way to a culturally contrived sequence, creating the impression that men have mastery over life and death. This entire process – in which the older generation tames the raw and unruly energies of the young, and so brings into being a new, vital, but tractable generation of adults – is played out as a journey into the bush, where the power of the wild is tapped and domesticated before being brought back to the village.

Metaphors that compare initiation to death and rebirth, combat to hunting, social subservience to slavery,[11] or armed rebellion to initiation, simply disclose these transfers of imagery and behaviour that are spontaneously and continually occuring within a social field (*metapherein* = 'to transfer'). Thus, armed rebellion and revolution spring from the same imperitive of rebirth that underlies such rites of passage as birth, initiation, and death. But these correspondences may be *consciously* seized upon, as when the RUF leadership invoked initiation rites to justify its revolutionary method of preparing young boys in bush camps for the violent, but necessary, cleansing of corrupt towns, under such codenames as Operation Pay Yourself and Operation No Living Thing.[12] For many of the kids who went to the bush and joined the RUF, this desire for initiatory rebirth as men of power (purified of the taint of childhood) may have been stronger than their commitment to the RUF cause. Certainly, their sense of impunity, of which Sewa spoke, was reminiscent of the license enjoyed by neophytes. And

the abduction of children by the RUF, and their adoption by rebel leaders – who were regarded as fathers, and called Pappy or Pa – recalls the
initiatory seizure of children, whose ties with their parents are symbolically severed so that they can be reborn, in the bush, as men. This
idea that war – like initiation, or play, or an adventure – is a moment
out of time, spatially separated from the moral world, may also help
explain why many combatants today anticipate a remorse free return
to civilian life. But the analogy between rebellion and initiation can be
pushed too far. For in initiation, as in play, the ritualised disordering of
the mundane world, with its dramatic negation of hierarchy and distinction, is but a profane prelude to its symbolic reintegration – a reaffirming of the bonds that make a community viable. Initation is a
drama of restoration, not radical change – which is why rebirth is its
central metaphor. In war, by contrast, disorder breeds disorder, and
death is the dominant image.[13] War is playing with fire, or 'playing for
keeps' – a phrase we used as children, when playing marbles, to declare
that gains and losses would henceforth be irreversible. In playing for
keeps, one's honour, one's pride, one's possessions, one's manhood,
one's life are on the line. One stakes everything. Winner takes all. That
is why coping with terror, bolstering one's courage, surviving to fight
another day, consume one's waking hours and pervade one's dreams,
and why any attempt to drop out of the game, or escape, is to invite
immediate punishment, which in the RUF meant mutilation or death.

What is at Stake

So many factors were in play, or at stake, in the Sierra Leone war, that
it would be foolhardy to try and identify a hierarchy either of goals or
of motives. It would be equally impossible to ascertain the relative
importance of indigenous cultural factors, of history, and of national
or global politics in determining the character and course of the war.
This indeterminacy is of the essence, and in what follows I want to
explore the histories and lifeworlds in which the war was, as it were, a
violent and transitory variation on a theme that had been part and
parcel of Sierra Leonean life since the advent of colonialism. I am
speaking here of the question as to what constitutes viable existence –
social, moral, as well as personal – and how the wherewithal for this
existential viability can be accessed and controlled.

Typically, the existential values on which human beings set greatest
store – freedom, dignity, respect, honour – defy definition. They are, as
Mauss put it, 'values which are emotional as well as material' (1954:
63). This implies that two incommensurable notions of value are
always at play in any human encounter – the first involving a strict cal-

culation of determinate values, the second involving elusive moral values (Mauss's 'spiritual matter') such as rightness, fair play, and justice.[14] Another way of making this point is to say that all exchange involves a continual struggle to give, claim or redistribute some scarce and elusive *existential* good – such as recognition, love, humanity, happiness, voice, power, presence, honour or dignity – *whose value is incalculable.*

Consider, for example, the Kuranko notions of luck (*hariya*) and blessings (*duwe*). Connoting both charismatic and material power, the distribution of *duwe* seldom conforms to an individual's estimation of what is his or her rightful due (Jackson 2002a: 42). Accordingly, it is the subject of perplexed deliberation – though much of this deliberation takes place within the individual imagination – as a kind of intense soul searching and as fantasies of reversed fortunes and revenge. These inner monologues are, of course, difficult for an ethnographer to access, and difficult also to discuss. Facts of experience though they are, they exist in the space between people, or comprise a penumbral domain lying elusively beyond the field of visible social practices. Much as Kuranko seek such things as *baraka* (blessedness), *miran* (charisma), *yugi* (temperament) and *fisa mantiye* (status), these phenomena overflow the boundaries of what can be said, measured or objectified. In many ways, we are speaking here of what Bourdieu calls the illusio – all those things in which we place our hope, or discover a sense of purpose, or consummate our sense of well-being – all those 'well-founded illusions' (1990a: 195) without which we feel our lives to be unjustly diminished, and for which we will give our lives or take the lives of others.

Concepts like *duwe* are well-nigh universal, and though they often resist exact definition and may be dismissed as illusory, they can rule our lives. Thus, *duwe* bears a family resemblance to the Rom notion of *baxt* (luck/destiny), the Melanesian concept of *kago* (cargo), the migrant's vision of pastures of plenty or of a gold mountain, the adventurer's dream of El Dorado or Shangri-la, the exile's longing for the promised land, and oppressed peoples' yearning for freedom or independence. It goes without saying that all such existential values promise more than they can deliver. Yet their very scarcity increases our desire for them, and strengthens their hold on our imaginations. People will often harbour resentments against those who seem to possess more than their fair share of luck, willingly risk everything to gain more of it, and readily fall prey to thinking that their own ill-fortune can be attributed to their own moral failing or to the machinations of others. Among the Kuranko, these emotions are nowhere more intense than among children who share the same father but have different mothers. Known as *fadenye*, (father-child-ship), sibling rivalry has its genesis in the qualitatively different relationships between co-wives and their husband (Jackson 1977: 149–161). If the child of one wife prospers while the child of another suffers, incriminations and envy often follow. But the notion of *fadenye* has wider connotations, for in a country like Sierra Leone, oppressed by acute scarcity and entrenched inequalities, fantasies of improving one's fortunes through supernatural means are as common as anxieties about losing them through witchcraft.

When I lived in northern Sierra Leone, I often heard rumours of a fabulous town somewhere in the hazy savannah regions to the north-east, known as Musudugu – town or place of women. No men lived there, and the women of the town were famed for their skills in divination, medicine and sorcery. Traders and travellers told of great wealth bestowed on men who had found favour with the women of the town, though none could confirm whether this place was identical with the town of Mousadougou which lies in the Konyor country at the edge of the forests that border Ivory Coast and Liberia.

If these myths of Musudugu taught me anything, it was that the imagined wellsprings of a person's fate and fortune easily elude his or her grasp. This is the penumbral domain of what William James calls 'appreciations', since these elusive goods 'form an ambiguous sphere of being, belonging with emotion on the one hand, and having an objective 'value' on the other, yet seeming not quite inner nor quite outer' (1912: 34). 'These fields of experience,' he observes, 'have no more definite boundaries than have our fields of view. Both are fringed forever by a more that continuously develops, and that continuously supercedes them as life proceeds' (ibid: 71). Yet for all its mercurial, distant, and indefinable character, this field of vital being obsesses us.

As long ago as 1824, when the first white man entered Kuranko country, people's desire for things from the outside world was so great that Major Alexander Gordon Laing reported on it in detail. The female praise-singers (*jelimusu*) 'sang of the white man,' he wrote, 'who had come to their town; of the houseful of money which he had; such cloth, such beads, such fine things had never been seen in Kooranko before; if their husbands were men, and wished to see their wives well dressed, they ought to take some of the money from the white men' (Laing 1825: 186–187). Echoing the praise-singer's words, the Barawa Chief Marin Tamba, alias Sewa – who incidentally would be the first of his lineage to embrace Islam, presumably because it also promised access to the bounty of the outside world – sang of Free-town, which he called Saralon, and of houses a mile in length filled with much more money than Laing possessed, money they might receive if they left Laing unmolested, for 'whoever wants to see a snake's tail must not strike it on the head'. In Sengbe, people sang the same refrain. Chief Balansama declared the road from his country open, so that Kuranko and Sankaran men with gold, ivory, camwood and kola might travel to the salt water with the white man. And in token of his earnestness, Balansama ordered his brother, as well as his son Denka, to go with Laing to the coast. (ibid: 433).

Though there is no suggestion, in Laing's account, of a link between wealth and knowledge, Kuranko were undoubtedly aware of it.

One rainy afternoon, many years ago, in the course of an aimless conversation with a group of Kuranko elders, I was asked if I thought of them as my kinsmen. Assuming they meant this literally, I said no. The old men reproached me, asking was I not aware that Africans and Europeans had the same ancestral parents, and that our forefathers were brothers. Adama and Hawa had three sons, they said. The eldest became the ancestor of the whites, the second the ancestor of the Arabs, the third the ancestor of the blacks. The first two sons inherited literacy and the knowledge of books, while the last-born son, the ancestor of the blacks, inherited nothing. When I asked why this should be so, one of the elders said, 'If you uproot a groundnut and inspect the root, isn't it always the case that some of the nuts are bad and some good?'

The myth, I would later discover, was widespread and very old. Winwood Reade (1873: 424) heard a version of it in northern Sierra Leone in the early 1870s. When God made the world He created a black man and a white man. He offered to the black man his choice of two things: gold and a covered calabash. The black man took the gold, and the white man got the calabash in which a book was contained; and this book has made white men powerful and wise, and the lords of the earth (see also Jackson 1998: 108–124).

This mystique of literacy was the subject of my initial Kuranko fieldwork. What struck me, talking to Kabala Secondary School students, or reading their responses to my questionnaires and TAT protocols, was the poignantly impossible gulf between their dreams and their reality. Though most were the children of farmers, they showed their disdain for farming in the zeal with which they laundered their uniforms, washed their bodies, manicured their fingernails, and at one time, wore white gloves on their hands. Thirty years have passed, but as I leaf through the tattered stacks of paper that I have lugged around the world for so long in the vague hope that I might one day find a use for them, I read of ambitions to become a doctor, a teacher, an engineer, 'to help my people', 'to help my parents', 'to help my country', and wonder what became of these dreamers when they left school and found their hopes dashed. Sixteen year-old Marie Kandeh for example, who wrote: 'As we all know that education today is the key of life, anyone who does not try to be educated will just be like a slave.' Or twelve year old Daimba Koroma: 'I want to be a doctor to free people from death.' Another thing arrested me as I read through my old notes, was the clandestine care with which many students used magical medicines, either to tie the hands of a superior student or to protect themselves from such attack.[15] It brought to mind a story that my friend Rose Marah once confided to me. Her brother was the top student of his year. The day after sitting his Cambridge Entrance exams in 1956, he attended a celebration party at which he fell desperately ill. He died the following day. One day later, his best friend also died. Autopsies revealed that both both boys had been killed with a traditional poison, and though suspicion immediately fell on a fellow student who had made no bones about his dislike of Rose's brother, nothing was ever proved. Rose's parents died four years after the death of their son. 'They never got over it,' Rose said. 'They died of broken hearts.'

Expectations and Reality

Almost invariably, acts of violence are prepared over a long period of time, often in the subconscious, as an aggrieved individual licks his wounds, composes his self-justifying story, and contemplates revenge for the injury he feels he has suffered. Though violence appears to be an eruption of irrational or primitive impulses, a bolt from the blue, its rationale and its necessity have usually been long contemplated. This is why it is impossible to assign any one cause to an episode of violence, though defining moments there may be, last straws as we say, which are invoked in retrospect to justify the recourse to action.

At some time or another, we all find ourselves struggling to reconcile the gap between expectation and reality – to explain the sense of disappointment and unfairness that oppresses us whenever wishful thinking comes up against limited opportunity. Sometimes we say the fault lies in the nature of things; it is fate, and we must accept it. Sometimes we blame ourselves. Much of the time, however, we blame others. According to a Kuranko adage, the *lenke* tree – a species of acacia, whose pods explode in the heat, scattering seeds far and wide – does not benefit the ground directly beneath it. I have heard the adage used when a person is complaining of the way an older brother or Big Man has given favours to friends and strangers, rather than look after the welfare of his own immediate kin. In a country like Sierra Leone, where popular expectations continue to be raised by the global media, despite diminishing local resources and opportunities, men of means and influence are the focus of both adulation and resentment. Indeed, as Rosalind Shaw has so persuasively argued, fantasies of having one's essence drained, stolen or 'eaten', and access to symbolic capital blocked, by men of power are endemic in

Sierra Leone (1997, 2002) where inequality is often explained as a result of 'economic witchcraft'.

Perhaps it was different in the past. An older generation sought only to conserve the social order, not to transform it. One's horizons of expectation were delimited by what one knew from past experience, not what one imagined the future might hold. Colonialism changed all this, so that nowadays young men, looking beyond the village, face confusion – a nation in name only, summarily carved out of the continent by colonial powers, a place whose centre had never held and whose infrastructure is as fragmented as it is surreal – a modern highway that runs eighty miles through the middle of nowhere, a fleet of unused ambulances rusting away in a city yard, a school without teachers, a clinic without pharmaceuticals, a petrol station with no petrol. Young men drift into opportunism and fantasy as orphans sometimes do, hoping for some fantastic change of fortune, of a second chance in a another country, or a powerful benefactor or political leader who will guide them out of the wilderness.

There is no one word for what these young men crave. Perhaps power comes closest, if we allow that the word covers a vast array of imperatives, any one of which an individual may consider vital to his very existence – manhood, wealth, work, education, status, strength, renown – though it eludes his grasp.

But what of the village? Was this not also a source of power?

In the villages, life is a matter of reciprocity – the expectation that what you give in the course of your life will somehow be given back, and that whatever you receive will be shared. You respect your elders, parents and rulers; in return they protect you and see to your welfare. To the lineage from which you take a wife, you give bridewealth in return. And you offer guests food and lodging on the understanding that they will do you no harm.

Lapses in these everyday protocols of give and take are the concern of Kuranko stories, where, like stories everywhere, all problems are happily resolved in the end. An exploitative chief is overthrown, a jealous co-wife punished, a duplicitous guest unmasked, a liar hoist by his own petard, a recalcitrant bride reconciled with her lot. Everyone gets his due, or his just desserts. But for many young men, there is no natural justice. For them, the time-honoured roles of gender and of age, together with hereditary chieftaincy, cult associations and labour collectives, are no longer binding or viable. The dreams of the village are no longer their dreams.

As for the new sources of power that preoccupy them – diamonds, commerce, education, Islam and the military – these seem to belong to a world apart, where justice is subject to no known laws.

Even if you landed a job, you were often paid sporadically or not at all, and then, like everyone else would have to fend for yourself, or be driven into desperate schemes. My old friend Noah spent a lot of his time playing draughts. Sometimes I thought of that board of painted squares, with bottle top counters, as an image of his world. The tried and tested moves, the gambles one might take. A person could have, as we say, more than his share of good luck, just as another could suffer unfair setbacks – as though singled out by some cosmic power for Jobian punishment. 'Haven't we endured enough,' people would say. 'Don't we deserve a break?'

In the villages I used to meet young men who had returned from the diamond districts of Kono. Having heard so many stories of sudden riches, they were baffled as to why luck should desert them while smiling on others. Mohammed Fofona – 'the man who could turn into an elephant' – had joined the army as a young man (Jackson 1989: 108–111). He saw it as a kind of initiation. 'The army gave you discipline, made you a man, made you feel a real force,' he said. 'In those days, a soldier was like a white man in the villages; he commanded great respect.' After a few years in the military, Mohammed drifted south into the diamond districts. But things did not pan out, and as he became more and more dissatisfied with his lot, he lambasted the bribery, bias, exploitation and croneyism he saw in the government, and began to dream of radical political change.

Others imagined that Islam might provide the answer to their prayers. In the dry season of 1979 one of my nearest neighbours was a young man called Abdulai Sisay. After many fruitless months digging and panning for diamonds in the alluvial fields of Kono, he returned home bewildered and disappointed. My hands are empty, he told me. Some years before, he had consulted a Koranic diviner who had given him good advice. He had then gone to Kono and made enough money to fund his elder brother's pilgrimage to Mecca. Now the same diviner told him that his run of bad luck was about to end, and advised that he should sacrifice a sheep to Allah and share the meat among his neighbours. But even after dutifully taking the diviner's advice, Abdulai was nagged by doubts, and desperate for further insights into the cause of his fluctuating fortunes.

For years I observed these anxieties of powerlessness and marginalisation – villagers working through an entire dry season to build a road through the bush, or a bridge across a river, in the expectation that their collective fortunes would improve, only to find that nothing changed; young men, like Abdulai, back from the diamond fields, with little to show for their efforts; others back from the cities where they had hoped for a windfall, but found none; students unable to find the money to finish their schooling, or thrown out of college for protesting

against the government; men frustrated in their attempts to ally themselves with a powerful mentor and patron. At the same time, I was witness to the fantastic avenues to self-esteem and empowerment that
had begun to fill this existential vacuum, particularly among young
men. An alliance forged with a powerful bush spirit. The acquisition of
powerful medicines, or the ability to transform oneself at will into a
powerful animal. Or the hope that Islam and the spiritual authority of
the alhajis – those who had made the pilgrimage to Mecca – would
usher in a new age. And then, as corrupt governments and coups
destroyed the civil state in Sierra Leone, and the economy collapsed,
these thwarted dreams had assumed increasingly violent and vengeful
shape, mixing indigenous fantasies of magico-phallic power with
images from kung fu movies, fixations on invincible trickster heroes
like Rambo, and the possession of lethal weaponry.

Conclusions

In this chapter I have eschewed explanatory models that trace out
lines or trajectories of determination, explaining social crises in terms
of cause and effect. Whether one considers the play of emotions, the
snatches of thought, and the strategic shifts that Sewa experienced
during the rebel invasion of Kabala, or the 'grotesque realism' that
characterised the comportment and attire of some of the rebels, or, for
that matter, the complex constellations of the illusio that have figured
in the consciousness of Sierra Leonean youth in the modern era, one
is struck by the kaleidoscopic combinations and recombinations of a
finite set of social factors (gender, estate and age-status distinctions)
and key symbols (education, wealth, power), as well by the metaphor-
like transfers of behaviours, images and ideas from one field of social
life to another. This field of stochastic chaos or turbulence, though neither consciously created, culturally scripted, geographically closed or
historically determined, may be compared to the field of myth, in
which, as Lévi-Strauss has shown (1963), a finite set of elements are
endlessly combined and permuted, as well as transferred from one
region to another, or undergo sudden disappearance and reappear-
ance at different moments in time. Though neither intention nor purpose govern this play of forces, and determinate beginnings and
narrative-like closure simply do not exist, this chaos is not devoid of
order, for our own human interests – our needs, our grievances, our
expectations, our mindsets – are constantly playing upon and entering
into this flux, giving it a semblance of meaning. Thus, human beings,
'in degrees beyond all other creatures ... consciously participate –
albeit meagerly – in the selective mutations and accelerations' of their

own cultural history (Fuller 1970: 297), much as one wakes to one's dreams and bestows order upon them. War is simply one transitory crystallisation of processes that are at once phylogenetic, cultural and biographical – one expression, as it were, of a play of forces that, at other times, crystallises in the form we call 'peace'. But though war and peace are both products of the same forcefield, and may be construed as variations on the theme of renewal, war rapidly becomes entropic – transforming social distinction into radical otherness, taking life rather than creating it, and losing the ludic vitality that gives myth and ritual their regenerative power. To invoke the Bambara metaphor, fire gives birth not to fire, but to ashes – which is to say that the social ceases to reproduce itself, and produces the antisocial (Kassim Kone, personal communication[16]). Yet, say the Bambara, just as ash often conceals fire, so someone who has become lost to his or her society may be returned to it, and ashes then give birth to fire.

Notes

1. The Tamaboros were a civil defence militia made up of mainly Kuranko and Yalunka recruits. Kuranko informants gave me two versions of the etymology. Tamaboro may mean 'walk-about bag', because hunters never announce directly that they are going to the bush; they use the circumlocution 'I am going walkabout'. Alternatively, Tamaboro may be loosely translated, *ta ma bo aro*, which means 'go and free us', i.e., from this war, this mess, this plight. Under the leadership of Komba Kambo, the Tamaboros enlisted the support of hunters (*donsenu*) and others with special powers of witchcraft, shapeshifting, and traditional hunting skills (cf. Leach 2000, Ferme 2001a: 223, 2001b).

2. An American consortium had been mining gold in Diang for several years, though the war had forced a momentary suspension of operations.

3. Sewa later told me that he had sought to appease his captors and make his escape, because as the son of a chief he dreaded the shame that being with the RUF would visit upon his family.

4. In his monograph on formations of violence in northern Ireland, Allen Feldman has explored how the dialectical tension between 'doing and being done' (vernacular markers of the difference between being an active subject and being violently subject to the actions of others) is nowhere more powerfully expressed than in the subjective meaning of being armed. 'To wield a weapon is literally *to take one's life in one's hand*. In violent praxis the fate of embodiment ('life') is detached from the self and transferred to the instrument of violence. In turn the weapon as a

political and forensic artifact of both the self and the Other is encoded with the reversibility of doing/being done' (1991: 102).

5. Elsewhere, in remarks that speak directly to the rebellion in Sierra Leone, Hannah Arendt writes: 'If tyranny can be described as the always abortive attempt to substitute violence for power, ochlocracy, or mob rule, which is its exact counterpart, can be characterized by the much more promising attempt to substitute power with strength' (1958: 203). She adds presciently: '*The vehement yearning for violence ... is a natural reaction of those whom society has tried to cheat out of their strength*' (ibid: 203–204, emphasis added).

6. This was vividly brought home to me when Sierra Leonean friends described, not without self-deprecating humour, their unstable behaviour during the war years, when one was susceptible to every rumour of impending danger. The sounds of gunshots, or even a car backfiring, would send one into a paroxysm of fear, so that one found oneself trying to hide or flee to Lumley beach, waiting until things seemed to have returned to normal.

7. Carl von Clausewitz observed that warfare, as 'an act of violence intended to compel our opponent to fulfil our will' is 'nothing but a duel on an extensive scale' (1982: 101).

8. Veena Das makes brilliant use of Nietzsche's comments in her account of the Partition riots of 1949 (1995: 182–185). Writing of 'invisible' forms of symbolic violence in Sierra Leone, Marianne Ferme observes that getting 'satisfaction' through the actual physical punishment of a political opponent is rarer than public ridicule and shaming – 'singing in public songs that revealed embarrassing, concealed physical deformities, the infidelity of a spouse, or quirky personal habits' (1998: 570).

9. This radical subversion is what defines rebellion, and it is this same phenomenon that Frantz Fanon famously invoked when he wrote that decolonisation is the 'putting into practice' of the well-known phrase *the last shall be the first and the first last* (1968: 28).

10. Max Gluckman argued that life crises 'disturb' the 'intricate set of relationships' that comprise 'the moral order' of a society, and that life crisis rituals are means of righting this disorder (1956: 134. In my 1983 analysis of the imagery involved in rituals of rebellion, and of the ways in which such rituals crucially enable actors to reassert individual and collective agency in the face of unpredictable and disturbing events, I showed how Kuranko initiation involved the borrowing or transferral of iconic behaviours from everyday contexts, as well as from mortuary rituals, and concluded that though this radical reconfiguring of behaviours, roles and images may occur 'spontaneously', it is ritually contrived at critical moments of disruption or disjuncture in a social environment, and it is precisely this 'magical manipulation' of objective symbols that stand for a subjectively confused situation that enables people to grasp and recreate their social world (Jackson 1989: 327–345).

11. Slavery is frequently invoked in Sierra Leone as a metaphor for social degradation, and Rosalind Shaw has perceptively traced out the ways in which the trauma of slave-trading continues to be inscribed in the 'ances-

tral' practices, images, rumours and beliefs associated with witchcraft among the Temne of Sierra Leone (1997, 2002).

12. Paul Richard's has also noted the parallels between initiation and rebellion in his account of the RUF, who sought to 'manipulate to its advantage the cultural 'infrastructure' of rural life in Sierra Leone' (1996: 30, 81). My argument, however, is that cultural precedents for armed rebellion are not so much invented as exploited, since these cultural thought-models for comprehending disorder and managing misrule already exist *in potentia*, and do not necessarily have to be orchestrated to appear *in presentia*. Several trenchant insights on the gendered symbolism of the rebellions in Liberia and Sierra Leone are to be found in Marianne Ferme's essay on the violence of numbers (1998: 560–561).

13. Krijn Peters and Paul Richards argue that 'confusing war and play, child combatants are heedless of danger' (1998: 183). Though young men often go to war as if it is an adventure or game, combat quickly destroys this illusion. Fear is endemic to all warfare (which is why the rebels devoted so much effort to combatting or masking it), and I agree with Johan Huizinga, that combat can only be called play when 'it is waged within a sphere whose members regard each other as equals or antagonists with equal rights.' This condition changes, Huizinga observes, 'as soon as war is waged outside the sphere of equals, against groups not recognized as human beings and thus deprived of human rights – barbarians, devils, heathens, heretics, and "lesser breeds within the law"' (1970: 110–111).

14. Bourdieu's notion of 'symbolic capital' covers this same field of rare, incalculable and 'priceless things' – of '"fair words" or smiles, handshakes, shrugs, compliments or attention, challenges or insults, honour or honours, powers or pleasures, gossip or scientific information, distinction or distinctions, etc.' (1977: 178).

15. In a study of the culture of education in Sierra Leone (1992), Caroline Bledisloe observes that formal education is never enough to guarantee one's future; blessings must be earned as well. While knowledge may be learned from books, blessings are earned from obedience and respect toward one's teachers, work performed for elders, as well as the endurance of hardship and the cultivation of benefactors. But while Bledisloe spells out the means whereby one deserves such favours, she does not explore the vexed reasoning that follows from the split between what a person feels he or she is owed and he or she actually receives.

16. Bambara images of life's capacity for natality and self-perpetuation ('fire producing fire') include allusions to the *zaban* vine, which sprouts anew whenever cut, and the following proverbs: *Foronto boro koro mana koro cogo o cogo* (No matter how old the bag of hot pepper gets, you will find something capable of causing a sneeze in it), *Ni kononin kili cera, ni a boda ma kala, a na kili were da* (When the little bird's eggs are taken away, unless it's anus is sewn up it will lay more eggs), *Kelenkelensa te du ci fo den wolobaliya, do be sa, do be wolola* (Dying one after another does not destroy a family; unless the family is barren some die and others are born).

Chapter 5

WHAT'S IN A NAME?

AN ESSAY ON THE
POWER OF WORDS

... mastery over reality, both technical and social, grows side by side with
the knowledge of how to use words ... The right word for an action, for a
trick of trade, for an ability, acquires *meaning* in the measure in which the
individual becomes capable to carry out this action. The belief that to
know the name of a thing is to get a hold on it is thus empirically true.

Bronislaw Malinowski (1965b: 233)

About the time that the controversial BBC interview with Michael
Jackson aired on national TV I received an e-mail from a woman in
Copenhagen who was writing an article for the Jyske Bank's youth
magazine on 'people who share their names with famous people'.
Since I was the only Michael Jackson she could find in Denmark, she
wanted to know if I would answer a few questions, such as 'What did
I think of the singer Michael Jackson?' and 'Did I have any experience
in the same fields as my name brother?' and 'Did I have any funny stories to tell that involved my name?' After responding to these questions in a fairly cavalier way, I found myself pondering more deeply the
mystique of names, and recalling incidents over many years in which
the other Michael Jackson had encroached upon my life, and wondering, finally, whether names are as arbitrary as we like to think, and
whether in fact 'that which we call a rose by any other name *would*
smell as sweet'. In the scene in Romeo and Juliet when this famous
question is asked, Juliet is wrestling with the fact that while Romeo's
family name denotes his *social* identity and destiny, it fails to do justice

---

Notes for this section can be found on page 91.

to the *person* with whom she has fallen in love. She then declares that neither of their inherited names should determine their fate:

> Tis but thy name that is my enemy;
> Thou art thyself, though not a Montague.
> What's Montague? it is nor hand, nor foot,
> Nor arm, nor face, nor any other part
> Belonging to a man. O, be some other name!
> What's in a name? that which we call a rose
> By any other name would smell as sweet;
> So Romeo would, were he not Romeo call'd,
> Retain that dear perfection which he owes
> Without that title. Romeo. Doff thy name;
> And for thy name, which is no part of thee,
> Take all myself. (11,2)

The famous Michael Jackson, who lives in Neverland, north of Los Angeles, California, and has proclaimed 'I *am* Peter Pan' and 'I never want to grow up', was not the first 'other' Michael Jackson I encountered. The first was a minor character in Charles Dickens' *Bleak House* (2003: ch. 57).

> 'And who told you as there was anybody here?' inquired Jenny's husband, who had made a surly stop in his eating, to listen, and now measured him with his eye.
> 'A person of the name of Michael Jackson, with a blue velveteen waistcoat with a double row of mother of pearl buttons,' Mr Bucket immediately answered.
> 'He had as good mind his own business, whoever he is,' growled the man.
> 'He's out of employment, I believe,' said Mr. Bucket, apologetically for Michael Jackson, 'and so gets talking.'

The second Michael Jackson who crossed my path was a previous tenant of a converted garage, known as the 'tree house', at 29 North Terrace, Wellington, New Zealand, where I lived for a year when writing my M.A. thesis on the impact of literacy on the New Zealand Maori in the early nineteenth century – a topic which touched on the potency of names in oral cultures, and on the way print culture saps and destroys this potency, and with it the lifeworld that is so intimately bound up by the spoken word. Among the mail addressed to this other Michael Jackson that I opened inadvertently and then returned to the GPO 'Not known at this address' were several invoices from Wellington's largest bookshop. It was around this time that the accountant at the bookshop refused me credit on the grounds that the probability of two persons having an identical name *and* identical address was 'in the order of a million to one'. I think he was under-estimating. But this mysterious other Michael Jackson may well have been the same one who had a brief affair in London with a girl from Johannesburg. In any event, after returning home to South Africa, the girl wrote a letter to Michael Jackson, c/o New Zealand House, London, and the letter was eventually forwarded to me in Kabala, northern Sierra Leone, where I was doing anthropological fieldwork among the Kuranko. I steamed open the letter to find an address to which I could return it. Inside was a money order for fifty Rand and a request that my namesake buy and send her several records that were currently banned in South Africa. One was, I remember, *More Sex on Black Velvet* by Engelbert Humperdinck, whose 'real' name, incidentally, was Jerry Dorsey. But what's in a name?

Much to my wife's disapproval I used the 50 Rand to purchase a set of African TAT (Thematic Apperception Test) protocols from the University of Durban. As for the letter, I sealed it in a new envelope, stuck Sierra Leone stamps on it, and sent it back to Johannesburg. I cannot remember whether the TAT tests I subsequently did with kids in the Kabala secondary school covered the subject of names, but I was already aware, from my fieldwork, that a person could be prosecuted for calling a person's name into disrepute, and that sharing a name betokened a shared identity.

Almost twenty years after this particular Michael Jackson disappeared from my life, I went to live in the United States, where I heard of a certain Mike Jackson whose name had appeared in a judgement entered in the Small Claims Court of Monroe County, Indiana, where I had found work after several years of being 'out of employment', as Mr Bucket puts it in *Bleak House*, speaking of *that* Michael Jackson. Not long afterward, when I took out a bank loan to buy a house, I was asked to sign an affadavit declaring I was 'not one and the same person' as this other Michael Jackson, and therefore not liable for his debts. Why, I asked myself, was I always picking up after these other Michael Jacksons?

Then there are the famous Michael Jacksons – the first, whose life's work has been travelling the world in search of 'characterful beers, whiskies and spirits' and who has written seventeen books on the subject. The second has made his life's work himself. That Michael Jackson, the expert on beer culture, has had a hard time raising his profile above his namesake is clear from his website (www. beerhunter.com) which says, 'Hello, my name is Michael Jackson, no, not that Michael Jackson'.

Over the years, I have often wondered whether, instead of trying to distinguish myself from my namesakes, there might be something to be learned from the shared identity that is implied in the endless, if embarrassed, allusions people persist in making to the fact that I have the same name as the King of Pop. Is there, indeed, something in a name? And is this comparable to being a look-alike – to sharing the physical features of another person, a kind of accidental and unrelated twin? I would like to ask Valentino Johnson this question, and know whether the $US40,000 he had spent up to 1990 on having his features cosmetically altered to look like the star actually made him feel like Michael Jackson. Though there is also the question of whether Valentino's cosmetic surgery could ever keep pace with his role model's ceaseless shapeshifting.

That shared features may, like a shared name, entail, even in modern times, a shared fate was suggested by the strange story of Kay Kent, a 25-year-old English photographic model and Marilyn Monroe look-alike who killed herself in August 1989. Kay's suicide would have been unremarkable, noted the obituary writer in *Paris Match*, 'had she not chosen to impersonate in dying the person who she imitated in life' (Golberine 1989).

I am older than the 'other' Michael Jackson, and no one teased me about my name until the 1970s. I minded the teasing less than the banality and unoriginality of it. 'Do you sing and dance?', 'You're not black!' This sort of thing. And even though people would preface their comments by saying, 'I suppose everyone teases you about your name?' they would not wait for my reply (which would, of course, have been a weary or irritated 'Yes they do'), but proceed immediately with their predictable observations. Sometimes this play on my name was more endearing than annoying, as when kids in Sierra Leone asked me for Michael Jackson posters, or when my daughter was in High School and brought some classmates home who wanted to see Michael Jackson, as if I would afford them some magical connection with the pop star.

In trying to work out an anthropological answer to Shakespeare's question, 'What's in a name?' the playfulness of the situations I have described offers an obvious starting point. Indeed, in many societies, the sharing of a name invites a teasing relationship. For the Tallensi of Ghana, for example, 'this feeling about the individuality of a name is shown in the delight with which Tallensi meet someone bearing the same name as themselves. Two persons with the same name call each other "*n-wu-uri*" (my namesake) and exchange friendly banter' (Fortes 1955: 339). Among the Kuranko, a similar familiarity is assumed between namesakes, as when a grandmother jokingly calls her grandson 'my husband', not only because of the structural 'identity of non-adjacent generations' but because the grandson will often bear the same name as his grandmother's husband. Significantly, this joking involves sexual banter. By contrast, certain Australian Aboriginal societies impose an avoidance relationship on namesakes, and 'two persons found to have an identical name [have] to be freed by ritual in order to speak to each other' (Coombs 1978: 43). Since joking and avoidance are both strategies for dealing with ambiguity and ambivalence, one may reasonably ask what is ambiguous about sharing a name? In the case of the joking relationship between grandparent and grandchild, the two categories are simultaneously the same and different. In so far as they are dependents, possessing no *real* authority or wealth, and lacking procreative power, their situations are comparable. Yet in so far as the old are nearing the end of their adult lives, and the young are about to begin theirs, there is all the difference in the world between them. Joking is a way of laughing off these contradictory ways of experiencing and framing the relationship. A similar anachronism determines the joking relationship between a married woman and her husband's younger brothers. From one point of view, she should keep a respectful distance between herself and her husband's younger brothers, yet from another she is mindful of the fact that should her husband die she will become, through leviritic inheritance, the wife of one of these men. Again, the contradiction between distance and intimacy finds expression in the sexual banter that is licensed between them.

Sharing a name involves comparable contradictions. The common name suggests a common identity, while the manifest differences between the individuals who share the name confounds this assumption. But joking and teasing are not simply social markers that a relationship cannot be taken seriously; it offers people a means of acting out, playing with, and even exorcising the awkwardness, embarrassment and absurdity involved, just as avoidance offers a means of exorcising the shame that is felt between mother-in-law and son-in-law. Joking and avoidance are thus coping strategies that both mark and help us manage confusing social situations. The words and images we use in giving objective, public expression to our ambivalent feelings and contradictory thoughts enable us to bracket or frame the situation as absurd, while at the same time enabling us to structure those thoughts and feelings, thereby giving us a sense that the world can be manipulated through the ways in which we speak about it.

Can we then say that what is in a name is a potentiality, not only to re-present reality to ourselves in a form that makes it less anxiety-provoking, less refractory to control, but to act more confidently in situations that are unpredictable, dangerous and subject to a high degree of uncertainty?

Let me explore this hypothesis by going back to one of the pioneering ethnographic works on the magical power of words, Bronislaw Malinowski's *Coral Gardens and Their Magic* (1965a, 1965b).

Spells

Central to Malinowski's 'ethnographic theory of language' was a prioritising of the instrumental over the expressive. For Malinowski, the most compelling thing about language (and he emphasised that he was 'not speaking here only of the Trobriand language, still less of native speech in agriculture' [but] 'the character of human speech in general') was not its capacity for articulating thoughts, ideas and feelings, but its pragmatic capacity for making things happen (1965b: 8). 'Speech is ... equivalent to gesture and motion', he wrote. 'It does not function as an expression of thought or communication of ideas but as a part of concerted activity ... Speech ... is primarily used for the achievement of a practical result' (ibid: 8). Volume 1 of *Coral Gardens* provides numerous examples of what Malinowski had in mind, and the Trobriand spells that accompany every phase of gardening, as well as the building and decoration of canoes, and the enhancement of health, wellbeing and beauty, help us understand how the magic of words actually works. Consider, for instance, the 'most important formula in the whole system of Omarakana garden magic' – the *vatuvi* spell – uttered over the axes after ground has been cleared and soil prepared for planting. Before any spelling takes place, the axes are dressed with magical substances – including aromatic herbs, leaves, clumps of soil taken from the nest of a bush-hen, chunks of hornets' nests, and bits scraped off coral boulders – and participants anoint their bodies and put on armulets. The spell typically consists of a string of references to critical aspects of the work to be done – in this case striking the soil – followed by repeated verbs, which impart to the spell an incantatory and imperative power.

> Show the way, show the way
> Show the way, show the way,
> Show the way groundwards, into the deep ground,
> Show the way, show the way,
> Show the way, show the way,
> Show the way firmly, show the way to the firm moorings.

The names of the gardener's ancestors, and his grandfather and father are now invoked, before the magician continues:

> The belly of my garden leavens,
> The belly of my garden rises,
> The belly of my garden reclines,
> The belly of my garden grows to the size of a bush-hen's nest,
> The belly of my garden grows like an ant-hill;

The belly of my garden rises and is bowed down,
The belly of my garden rises like the iron-wood palm,
The belly of my garden swells,
The belly of my garden swells as with a child.
I sweep away.

There follows a lengthy recitation of all the things that are to be swept away – including various pests and blights:

I sweep, I sweep, I sweep away. The grubs I sweep, I sweep away; the blight I sweep, I sweep away; insects I sweep, I sweep away; the beetle with the sharp tooth, I sweep, I sweep away, and so on. (1965a: 96–97)

Studying such spells, and the contexts in which they are uttered, brings home the fact that most ritual action depends on core metaphors that link and liken a mode of human being to an extra-human thing. Relationships are likened to paths, nets and bonds, understanding is thought of as a coming into the light, ignorance is equated with darkness, freedom with the flight of a bird, dilemmas with knots, persons with places, and the human body with the body of the land. In ritual these links provide a means of acting, for by manip-ulating the accessible and sayable element in the symbolic equation one can change the way one experiences the more elusive, unman-ageable and ineffable element. It is therefore difficult to accept Mali-nowski's separation of the expressive and the instrumental, for it is obvious that the practical outcome of these recitations is intimately connected to the expressive power of the metaphors used, as well as the intentions, desires and wishes they convey. These forms of willing or wishful-thinking are deeply embodied, for the spell conveys subjec-tive intentions from the belly (which is also the seat of memory), via the voice and breath, into the object (Malinowski 1922: 408–409).

As Malinowski notes, the 'magic words are, so to speak, rubbed in by constant repetition to the substance' (ibid: 408). But that the object must be within reach of the voice, within 'hearing', suggests that it is spoken to as though it were another person (ibid: 404–405), capable of responding to, or reciprocating, the words that are addressed to it. This focus on *external* inductive effects gives the impression that Tro-brianders lack any rational understanding of the relationship between words and the world. Put bluntly, no Westerner in his or her right mind would try to influence the growth of crops by talking to the soil in which they are to be planted. If, however, we place more emphasis on *internal* inductive effects, the gap between premodern irrationality and modern rationality is significantly narrowed, for *all* human beings seek to augment and increase *by all means possible* their capacity for effectively working on the world. Thus, as Malinowski himself observed, the spell is also addressed to the speaker himself. Although the spells for a yam house are seemingly directed at anchoring and filling the yam house, the Trobrianders themselves are under no misapprehension that it is the belly of people that is the real object of the spell, for, logically, if bellies remain empty the yam house will be full (Malinowski 1965a: 226–227). As Malinowski puts it, 'In the majority of cases indeed, magic refers to human activities or to the response of nature to human activities, rather than to natural forces alone. Thus in gardening and in fishing, it is the behaviour of plants and animals tended or pursued by man; in the canoe magic, it is the carver's magic, the object is a human-made thing; in the Kula, in love magic, in many forms of food magic, *it is human nature on to which the force is directed*' (Malinowski 1922: 401, emphasis added).[1] In other words, spells work simultaneously on *intersubjective relations* between persons and the soil, crops, yam houses, canoes etc., *and* on *intrapsychic* experience – encouraging self-restraint in consumption.

This is the meaning of the metaphorical connections between growing yams or taro, and pregnancy or phallic vigour in the *vatuvi* spell. Relationships between people, and an individual's relationship with his or her own emotions of hunger or desire, are identified metonymically with relationships between people and the physical environment, such that actions in and on any one of these spheres will have repercussions in the others. Though Malinowski did not explore the subjective implications of these metaphorical correspondances, he did speak of the way in which magic inspired hope, bolstered confidence and concentrated the mind (1965b: 246), though considered this an 'indirect' function of spells, and insisted that social integration was the principal need being met. But rather than sideline the psychological effects of naming, spelling and cursing, I share Tambiah's view that 'all ritual, whatever the idiom, is addressed to the human participants and uses a technique which attempts to re-structure and integrate the minds and emotions of the actors' (1968: 202).

This is reminiscent of Sartre's view of magic as a way of transforming our *experience* of our relation to the world (including objects and others), especially under circumstances in which we find ourselves frustrated in, or unsure of, our ability to act effectively upon it. As I have argued elsewhere (Jackson 1982: 149–151), it is characteristic of ritual praxis that when action proves difficult or unpredictable in one domain, people will exploit correspondences supposed to exist between that domain and others in order to regain the power to act. (Synecdochic correspondences between the social body, the human body and the body of the earth are the most common of these). This is surely why the words of Trobriand spells are 'primeval' and often 'meaningless', and why they 'are not words of ordinary speech' and 'are pronounced according to a special phonology, in a sing-song, with their own rhythm and with numerically grouped repetitions' (Malinowski 1965b: 219). All magic requires a sense that the words and actions being used are distant and disengaged from mundane life – something Malinowski called 'the coefficient of weirdness' (ibid: 218).

In his famous essay on the effectiveness of symbols (1963), Lévi-Strauss examines a Cuna Indian spell[2] for facilitating difficult childbirth. The spell takes the form of a shamanic quest, in which various obstacles have to be surmounted, wild beasts fought, and the demiurge Muu, who is responsible for the formation of the foetus, is defeated and forced to release the 'spirit-double' of the mother-to-be. For the Cuna, however, Muu connotes not only a foreign power, but the vagina and uterus of the pregnant woman, and the recitation of the spell thus involves a metaphysical journey into the visceral depths of the pregnant woman's body.

> The (sick) woman lies in the hammock in front of you.
> Her white tissue lies in her lap, her white tissues move softly.
> The (sick) woman's body lies weak.
> When they light up (along) Muu's way, it runs over with
> Exudations and like blood.
> Her exudations drip down below the hammock all like blood, all red.
> The inner white tissue extends to the bosom of the earth.
> Into the middle of the woman's white tissue a human being
> Descends. (Lévi-Strauss 1963: 190 ; cf. the same text translated by Holmer
> and Wassen, and published in Severi 1993: 175)

The shaman also recounts in great detail, and as if in slow motion, the events that preceded his intervention.

> The midwife turns about in the hut.
> The midwife looks for some beads.
> The midwife turns about (in order to leave).
> The midwife puts one foot in front of the other.
> The midwife touches the ground with her foot.
> The midwife puts her other foot forward.
> The midwife pushes open the door of the hut; the door of her hut creaks.
> The midwife goes out ... (Lévi-Strauss 1963: 192)

As Lévi-Strauss observes, it is 'as though the shaman were trying to induce the sick woman ... to relive the initial situation through pain, in a very precise and intense way, and to become psychologically aware of its smallest details' (ibid: 193). But this replay of events is also a re-cre-

ation of them in which the woman is induced to experience her own
physiology in cosmological terms. The cure depends on this objectification, through myth, of the subjective experience of being in pain. As
Lévi-Strauss puts it, 'The shaman provides the sick woman with a *language*, by means of which unexpressed, and otherwise inexpessible,
psychic states can be immediately expressed' (ibid: 198). But the
expressive value of the spell, which translates lived subjectivity into
the objective language of myth, is linked to its instrumental purpose.
For in so far as her *experience* of her situation is changed, the woman is
better able to overcome the pain, distress and exhaustion that may be
contributing to the difficult birth. It is in this 'inductive' property of
symbols, says Lévi-Strauss – their power to induce or persuade us to
think differently about our relationship to a task at hand, or a situation
in which we are experiencing great difficulty – that their effectiveness
lies, and this process is, moreover, common to both shamanism and
psychoanalysis (ibid: 198–205). Expressing one's inner intentions,
hopes and desires – whether ill-will in the form of a curse, or goodwill
in the form of prayer or blessings – has effect, not simply because one
has said what one thinks or feels, but because one has said it in the
accepted, formulaic manner, *thereby merging one's own ill with the social
will*. Thus, in the Trobriand Islands, the power of magic is inextricably
linked to the warrant of tradition (Malinowski 1922: 400), and any
spell derives its force from the knowledge that the words uttered are
not one's own but are ancestral words, carrying the voice and presence of those in whose footsteps one walks. The same is true of the
Cuna, where both tradition and the spells themselves 'minutely
describe' the appropriate ritual setting (a semi-darkened corner of a
hut, at night, in front of two rows of statuettes, with cacao grains or
red-pepper pods burning in a small hearth), as well as the way a
shaman should comport himself, and the sexual and alimentary
embargos upon him (Severi 1993: 177). All this makes the spell more
than esoteric speech, implying cosmological meanings; it is, as the
Cuna themselves observe, a form of *action* upon the world (ibid).

The Language of Kinship and the Naming of Children

It is intriguing that though Malinowski emphasises speech (parole)
over syntactical structure (langue), and Lévi-Strauss does the very
opposite, and though Malinowski finds meaning in the pragmatic,
social functions of language, while Lévi-Strauss locates it in the
unconscious structures of the mind, both anthropologists are occasionally drawn, despite themselves, to an existential theory of meaning. Thus, when Malinowski observes that speech is a way of

achieving 'mastery of reality', and that 'to know the name of a thing is to get a hold on it' (1965b: 233), or Lévi-Strauss writes that ritual and play typically re-present an intransigent aspect of the lifeworld on a reduced scale, thereby enabling a person to manipulate and master it (1963: 198, 1966: 23), they are identifying, albeit inadvertently, our capacity to use language to create a simulacrum of a lived event which can then be invoked and consciously deployed in ways that reality could not be. Malinowski writes: 'From the very use of speech men develop the conviction that the knowledge of a name, the correct use of a verb, the right application of a particle, have a mystical power which transcends the mere utilitarian convenience of such words in communication from man to man' (1965b: 233).[3] But there is nothing mystical about this process, for by affording us opportunities to replay or anticipate real events through objects, words and images that stand for those events, we achieve what play achieves for a child – a sense of being able to vicariously act on a world that is, in reality, refractory to our will and outside our control. Thus, to bestow a nickname is to alter our perception of a person. Or to name a place is to possess it, to think of it as a part of oneself. But we do not simply internalise a language; we learn how to use it intentionally, to create a world that is within our grasp and answers our demand for meaning. This *existential* value that a belief or an action has for an individual is intimately connected to the value it has for the group. For no one invests for long in a society that provides no sense of worth or wellbeing, and no society survives for long unless it provides some modicum of satisfaction to its individual members.

Naming and Unnaming People

In many Australian Aboriginal societies, a person's name is not widely used or generally known, and it is customary to place a complete embargo on speaking a person's name when he or she dies. Among the Warlpiri, for example, a deceased person's name is put out of circulation for a generation, and his or her footprints are ritually erased from the earth. The person is now known as *kumanjayi* – 'no name'. To refrain from speaking the personal name, or using any homonym that might call it to mind, effectively transforms one's experience of that person, and hence of one's relationship with him or her. Tabooing the name is not simply a technique for forgetting the person who had borne the name; it is a way of manipulating social reality and transforming the intersubjective field that connects the living to the dead.[4]

To remember a name has the opposite effect. By putting a 'forgotten' name back into circulation, the essence of all those who carried the name in generations gone by is now brought back into existence. This is why Warlpiri say that the presence of a name, after a generation in which it was absent and out of mind, signifies a rebirth – a re-embodiment of a now ancestral essence, and a proof of the continuity of kinship over time.

Consider the way this works among the Kuranko.

To label Kuranko a 'patrilineal' society is to endorse a classical anthropological bias toward the 'politico-jural domain' – a bias that itself reflects the ideology and interests of a male standpoint (cf. Piot 1999: 122). The Kuranko lifeworld, however, reflects a dynamic and indeterminate interplay between what Kuranko call *na ware* (mother's side or place) and *fa ware* (father's side or place). One must know 'both sides', and be able to recall and call the names of both one's paternal and maternal ancestors at a family rice-flour sacrifice. Not to know one's patriline and matriline means, as one informant (Duwa Marah) once put it, 'that you do not know where you are from'. Kuranko naming conventions exemplify this general principle of complementarity. The first-born child is customarily named after a predecessor on the father's side. The second born 'goes to the mother's side', and successive children are named alternately for the father's side and the mother's side. Of course, variations exist – as when Muslims name a child for a Koranic saint, or naming commemorates the unusual circumstances of a child's birth, as in the following, possibly apocryphal, story. A house caught fire while the woman of the house was away fetching water from a stream. While her neighbours struggled to rescue the woman's belongings from the burning house, unaware that her woman's infant was asleep inside, her dog dragged the infant from the house and saved its life. The child was named Nyawule, meaning 'life-giving dog'.

Here is a genealogy of the family I was closest to during my fieldwork:

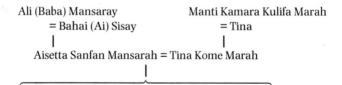

```
Ali (Baba) Mansaray              Manti Kamara Kulifa Marah
   = Bahai (Ai) Sisay                    = Tina
        |                                   |
   Aisetta Sanfan Mansarah = Tina Kome Marah
                        |
```

1 Kulifa Bockarie (named for paternal grandfather)
2 Ai (named for maternal grandfather)
3 Sewa Bockarie (named for paternal grandfather's younger brother)
4 Ali (named for maternal grandfather)
5 Tina and Dondon (twin daughters, named for paternal grandmother and paternal grandmother's sister)
6 Abdul (Islamic name)
7 Noah (born on a Friday, and named for the Islamic 'star name' of that day)

This customary way of identifying the living with the dead, and of recognising a complementarity between male and female lines, does not, however, determine how such identifications and complementary relationships will be actualised or experienced in the course of a person's life. Thus, while Abdul is a Muslim, as the name would suggest, Noah is staunchly pagan. And though Sewa is nominally identified with his grandfather, he feels no special affinity for him, but identifies strongly with his own father. In other words, naming defines a potentiality that may or may not be activated, or taken up. This is also the case with clan names. Even though all Marah may, in theory, claim hospitality and help from one another (as well as from people from other clans that are historically cognate with Marah, such as the Temne Bangura, the Maninka Konde, the Mende Mala, and the Yalunka Samura), this cannot be presumed, and must depend on a person's finer judgement of the situation in which he finds himself. This is also true of joking relationships between namesakes, for though the shared name suggests a deeper identification, invoking it requires subtle judgement.

How Words become Realities

For structural linguistics, the arbitrariness of the sign is axiomatic. For phenomenology, however, what is most compelling about signs – including names, images and figures of speech – are the conditions under which they are deployed and experienced *as if they were* 'motivated' and non-arbitrary. This fetishisation of signs, that effectively fuses words with the things they represent, may, at one extreme, define madness. Yet it also defines one of the most ubiquitous and powerful means by which human beings, in all cultures, manipulate reality and cope with life. For example, among the Umeda of the West Sepik District of New Guinea, the organic metaphors that coalesce botanical and social dimensions of reality – likening the structure of coconut, Areca, sago and other palms to the structure of social relations – involve systematic semantic, phonological and morphological correspondences between the relevant terms (Gell 1975: 121–123, 1979: 44–62). Thus, the Umeda word *pul* refers to the Areca palm, a garden fence and a mythological hero, the logic being that all imply the transgression of boundaries. Chewed with lime and betel, Areca induces 'a 'marginal' state of consciousness, putting the user slightly 'outside' himself' (Gell 1975: 124); it is also chewed at transitional moments during the day and at night, or before undertaking a journey or task. Fences, of course, define social boundaries, and the Oedipal hero Pultod (Areca-nut man) is a 'marginal' figure.

Similar homonymic correspondences are implicit in the word *naimo* ('wild sago' palm). *Naimo* combines words which concern 'femininity and matrilateral relations' (ibid: 129). Hence *nai* (skirt), *na* (sago, mother's brother), *naina* (matrikin), and *mo* (gullet), *mol* (vulva), *mov* (fruit), *mol* (daughter, girl). Gell concludes that a 'complex word like *naimo* is not simply a lexical counter, an 'arbitrary' sign, but is, in itself, a complex statement about relationships' and in a Heideggerarian vein he asserts that 'through looking at vocabulary [one is] able to reconstruct the Umeda 'world-view' – or at any rate certain aspects of it' (ibid: 133). But the point of such structural homologies, as Gell himself suggests, is not to create an intellectual system for its own sake but to produce a template for ritual action – in the Umeda case, the Ida fertility ritual – and it is this praxeological aspect of naming that interests me here.

As Dwight Bolinger and David Sears observe, though it is practically impossible to invent a new suffix or a new syntactic pattern, 'one of the few truly inventive privileges that our language affords us' is the privilege of inventing new nouns and names. 'The act of naming, with all it implies in the way of solidifying and objectifying experience, becomes one of our most powerful suasive tools, enabling us to create entities out of nothing' (1981: 145). Consider, for example, a child, taunted in a school playground, and called names, who retaliates by chanting 'Sticks and stones may break my bones, but names will never hurt me'. The chant is a way of coping with the hurtful name-calling by a kind of magical inversion of the situation. Sticks and stones would, in truth, be more bearable than the verbal slingshots. In March 2003, as the Bush administration prepared for war against Iraq, President Jacques Chirac of France promised to veto any UN security council resolution that would give the U.S. a green light for military action against Saddam Hussein. Angered by French intransigence, many U.S. food outlets rebranded french fries 'freedom fries' – which brought to mind the French rejection of foreign language borrowings as a way of preserving its cultural purity. As for the similarity between the magical power of words in Trobriand gardening magic and Western advertising, Malinowski himself was well aware of this, observing that the advertisements of modern beauty specialists like Helena Rubenstein and Elizabeth Arden would make interesting reading if collated with the formulae of Trobriand Beauty magic, reproduced in Chapter XIII of *Argonauts of the Western Pacific* (1922) and in Chapter XI of *Sexual Life of Savages* (1929).

I smooth out, I improve, I whiten.
Thy head I smooth out, I improve, I whiten.
Thy cheeks I smooth out, I improve, I whiten.

Thy nose I smooth out, I improve, I whiten.
Thy throat I smooth out, I improve, I whiten.
Thy throat I smooth out, I improve, I whiten.
Thy neck I smooth out, I improve, I whiten. (Malinowski 1965b: 237–238)

Which brings me back to Michael Jackson.

For is it not true that the ways in which we use words may be likened to the ways in which we work on ourselves, conjuring with whatever resources and materials we can command, an appearance that we find more bearable or more satisfying than the one that was visited upon us by circumstance or birth? And is it not also true, that what makes a situation abhorrent is determined less by any objective characteristic than by the extent to which we experience it as imposed upon us, as something we are forced to suffer in silence, and that deprives us of our will?

To conflate magicality and pathology, as media accounts of Michael Jackson so commonly do, asking for example 'Is Michael Jackson for Real?' (Goldberg and Handelman 1987), is the same error that underlies anthropological attempts to determine whether beliefs and practices are rational or not. Both are forms of sophistry[5] that deploy category words to play up a difference between self and other, or downplay the similarities between them. Whether the other is Michael Jackson – coping with a sense of being cut off from the rest of humanity and dealing with an unhappy childhood – or a Trobriand gardener, trying to increase his confidence that his earth will yeild an abundant harvest, our exoticising images and language conjure the illusion that such forms of thought are less typical of 'us' than of 'them'.

If I have taken an interest in Michael Jackson over the last twenty-five years it is not only because of the shared name, but because his biography is a window on the same hyper-reality that influences us all, and because the role of magic in his life illuminates the role of magic in our own. In 1982, Michael Jackson said, 'With acting, it's like becoming another person. I think that's neat, especially when you totally forget ... which I love to do ... That's when it's magic' (cited in Lippert 1988). But we are all actors. We would find life insupportable if we felt utterly at the mercy of our circumstances, and could not respond.

This, then, is my answer to the question, What's in a name? Language is perhaps the most 'natural' form of human intentionality, and naming the most rudimentary expression of our need to act in and on the world, at least to the same extent that it acts upon us, so that we live, not passively and blindly, in the face of events we neither comprehend nor control, but actively and intentionally, as if we had a hand in shaping those events, and deciding their meaning.

Is this to say that willing, wishing and desiring are existential imperatives? Following Brentano, Husserl (1962) made intentionality central to his notion of human being. We do not exist in a social vacuum. Our being-in-the-world is an unceasing interplay of wills or intentions, a struggle for what Foucault called 'governmentality' – 'a mode of action upon the actions of others' (1983: 221). Accordingly, the critical question is not whether we have or do not have wills, but the social and ethical contexts in which one's will is realised.

A Kuranko story that I recorded in 1970 (Jackson 1982: 164–167), begins with a dilemma. A young man, frustrated in his search for the bridewealth needed to marry a woman whose hand in marriage is also sought by several other men – all better off than he – happens to meet an old woman in the bush who gives him a fetish, and instructs him on how to use it. He has only to point this fetish at a person or animal while declaring 'I have *nyemakara* this at you' and the person or animal will die. However, the young man so abuses the power of the fetish that God finally takes it from him, which is why God alone now has the power of life and death over human beings.

The fetish and the word *nyemakara* constitute the material and verbal embodiments of the young man's will and desire. Indeed, in Mande, the prefix of the word *nyamakala* (which designates a group of inferior clans posessing superior powers of influence, through the command of words, fire and breath), is *nyama*, which may be translated as the 'energy of action' (Bird 1976: 98), 'life force' (Tamari 1995: 65), or 'the necessary power source behind every movement, every task' (McNaughton 1988: 15). Yet it is clear that *nyama*, though somewhat mystified in these translations and said, among the Mande, to be present to some degree in all life forms, including plants and animals, is essentially the power to do – the potentiality of human wills 'to be done', of projects to be realised, of efforts to 'pay off', and actions to take effect. As pragmatists, the Mande make no hard and fast distinction between real and magical effects; the proof of the pudding is in the eating. But a distinction *is* made between ethical and unethical expressions of human will-power, for uncontrolled individual will or desire is a danger to all, a source of misfortune, and of social death. This is the moral of the Kuranko story, in which the young man's reckless, heedless use of the fetish threatens the very existence of society. This same ethics and this same logic, governs all action, 'magical' as well as 'rational'. Will-power must be controlled and used for the social weal – for all, rather than for the advantage of one.

I think it is consonant with the conclusion of this Kuranko story to argue for bracketing out any consideration as to whether spoken words are rational or irrational, or true or false representations of 'reality', in order to focus on the ethical and existential implications of the words we speak and the names we use – the degree to which they enable us to create a viable social world in which the right to speak and act are the prerogatives of all.

Notes

1. In her ethnography of Bemba female initiation (*chisungu*), Malinowski's student Audrey Richards is led to a similar conclusion. Rites of passage do more than create or represent 'group ties', she notes; their 'pragmatic effects' include the inculcation of 'moral attitudes and obligation', and assure the neophytes that they are 'fit to assume' their new roles as women (1982: 161–163)

2. Lévi-Strauss refers to it as a 'song' or an 'incantation,' not a spell. Severi notes that it is an example of a 'therapeutic chant' (*ikala*) that applies to a variety of somatic and mental illnesses and generally involves 'the narration of a journey during which the auxiliary spirits of a shaman travel in the underworld, searching for the lost or kidnapped *purpa* of an ill person' (1993: 166).

3. Such observations anticipate Austin's speech act theory (1962) and Wittgenstein's notion that words are not pictures as much as ways in which we play with our relationship with the world (1953). Citing Goethe's phrase from Faust, *'Am Anfang war die Tat'* (In the beginning was the deed), Ray Monk captures the drift of Wittgenstein's later thought on language by noting that 'The deed, the activity, is primary, and does not receive its rationale or justification from any theory we may have of it' (1990: 306).

4. 'Social forgetting' is ascribed the same therapeutic value in postwar Sierra Leone; not to speak of the traumatic past is seen as a way of bringing it *socially* under control and making it vanish, which is why many Sierra Leoneans criticise the Truth and Reconciliation Commission, with its emphasis on public confession and endless talk, raking over the coals, bringing up painful memories.

5. The Sophists took the view that certainty was impossible, and that an ability with words counted more than knowledge of the truth.

Chapter 6

MUNDANE RITUAL

> ... magical or religious actions are fundamentally 'this-worldly'
> (*diesseitig*), as Weber puts it; being entirely dominated by the concern to
> ensure the success of production and reproduction, in a word, survival,
> they are oriented towards the most dramatically practical, vital and
> urgent ends.
> Pierre Bourdieu (1990a: 95)

In his seminal study of transitional objects and transitional phenomena, the psychoanalyst D.W. Winnicott describes the actions of a troubled seven year-old boy whose parents had sought his professional help. The boy's mother suffered from depression, and during her times in hospital, he had stayed with his maternal aunt. Increasingly, however, his parents had become concerned by his behaviour – a compulsion to lick things and people, a habit of making compulsive throat noises, threats to cut his little sister into pieces, overcontrolling or losing control of his bowel movements. In his first personal interview with Winnicott the boy revealed an intense preoccupation with string, and subsequently his parents told Winnicott that this 'obsession' worried them, for their son had gotten into the habit of tying up tables and chairs, and had recently tied a piece of string around his elder sister's throat. Winnicott suggested to the mother that her son was dealing with his fear of separation, and using the string in an attempt to deny it, much 'as one would deny separation from a friend by using the telephone' (Winnicott 1974: 17).[1] With this insight, the mother talked to her son about the times she had gone away from him, and about his fear of losing touch with her. Six months after the first interview, the mother told Winnicott that her son had stopped playing obsessively with string, joining objects in the way he had – though the string play

---

subsequently and temporarily reappeared, once when the mother had to return to hospital, and another time when she again suffered a bout of depression.

Winnicott's analysis provides invaluable insights into ritualisation – the subject of this chapter – for it succinctly demonstrates that the manipulation of objects, abstract ideas and personae in our *external, social environment* is analogous to, but possibly more significant than, the *intrapsychic* manipulation of *images* of these things (symbolic disguise, displacement, repression, projection, reversal, rationalisation, scotomatisation) in enabling human beings to come to terms with distressing situations. Both fantasising and ritualising are predicated on the logic of intersubjectivity. By this I mean that all human beings tend to equate, or draw analogies between, their relationships with other persons, their relationships with their own thoughts and emotions, and their relationships with things, ideas and words. As a corollary, human beings tend to act in critical situations *as if* one of these modalities of relationship could be effectively substituted for the other. In Winnicott's view, these are all 'object-relations'. 'Transitional objects', such as pieces of string, teddy bears, or toys enable children to manage their difficult but inevitable separation from parents or caregivers, as well as laying the foundations for adult responses to traumatic change, separation and loss (*passim* 1974).

The question I explore in this chapter is just how far object-relations theory can take us in understanding ritualisation cross-culturally. That I broach this question reflects my view that the anthropology of ritual has been vitiated by a preoccupation with complex cultural forms, and that we have all too often dismissed the mundane forms of ritual life as 'trivia', 'superstitions', 'obsessional habits', or neurotic idiosyncracies.[2] I also think that anthropology has focused so much on the sociocultural functions or conceptual values that ritualisation 'takes on' that we have overlooked the ways in which ritual procedures are perennially reinvented as human beings struggle to restore a sense of understanding and control in the face of perturbing and overwhelming *everyday* events. It is my view, first, that ritualisation is synonymous with the mindfulness and meticulous care that people in precarious or critical conditions tend to display, like not walking on the cracks in the sidewalk, obsessively cleaning a house, or a golfer, after making a critical shot, bending his or her body to induce the ball to follow the intended line across the green, as onlookers shout 'Get in the hole!' Such magical devices and practices are to acting as aide-memoires are to remembering – props and supplements to the will.

Second, as I pointed out in the previous chapter, ritual *knowledge* simply provides a pretext for ritual action, and has little value in and of itself. Like others, I share a dissatisfaction with the ways in which ethol-

ogists and evolutionary psychologists tend to exaggerate the phylogenetic basis of ritual behaviour, reducing the *meaning* of all ritualisa-
tions – grieving, courting, initiating, birthing – to their alleged adaptive
value for our species two million years ago (Gould 1997). Structural-
functional models are no less flawed, for to assert that the meaning of
ritual lies in the way it conserves or reintegrates social and psychological order, is to trap oneself in a form of circular reasoning, conflating
cause and effect (cf. Bateson 1958: 3–4, and Houseman and Severi
1998: 166), as well as to ignore the patently antinomian character of
much ritual. By this I mean that many rituals, like creation myths, systematically invert or confound the order of things as a prelude to
reconstituting it – as in carnival, saturnalian rites, role reversal and
initiations (Leach 1966). Finally, intellectualist accounts of ritual,
which emphasise the search for a personal or cosmological logos, are
flawed to the extent that rituals are not always motivated by ideas, or
conceptually or verbally 'scripted' and 'orchestrated' (Bourdieu 1990a:
80–97; Jackson 1989: 119–136). When anthropologists try to understand rituals by asking informants what is going on, what it all means,
they often get few answers. One reason is that ritual practice, in its very
nature, lies on the periphery of what can be thought and said (Jackson
1989: 133). But while sympathetic to recent approaches to ritual that
refuse to explain ritual processes in terms of adaptive advantage, social
function, conceptual meaning or the transcendence of nature (see
Houseman and Severi, 1998: 165–202 for a superb review), I think it
is a mistake to conclude that ritual can be studied 'in itself and for
itself' (Lévi-Strauss 1990: 669)[3] or construed as 'pure activity, without
meaning or goal' (Staal 1989: 131), 'the activity' being 'all that
counts' (ibid: 133, see also Staal 1979). My view is that 'the relational
field' of which Houseman and Severi speak cannot be analysed as pure
form, but has to be explored as a field of *lived* relationships, and ritualisation understood existentially, as a strategy for transforming our
experience of the world. Fantasy and ritual are *supplements* to real
action, not substitutes for it – vital means of making life more think-
able, and hence more manageable, under trying conditions.[4] When a
Dinka knots a tuft of grass in order to constrict, delay or 'tie up' an
enemy, or binds a stone with grass to restrict the movement of a prowl-
ing lion, he does not desist from practical action, for these devices are
but 'models' of his 'desires and hopes, upon which to base renewed
practical endeavour' (Lienhardt 1961: 283). 'Symbolic actions,' Lienhardt goes on to say, 'recreate, and even dramatize, situations which
they aim to control, and the experience of which they effectively mod-
ulate. If they do not change actual historical or physical events – as the
Dinka in some cases believe them to do – *they do change and regulate the
Dinka's experience of those events*' (ibid: 291, emphasis added).

Separation and Loss

Merleau-Ponty once observed, accurately I think, that a small 'child lives in a world which he unhesitatingly believes [is] accessible to all around him. He has no awareness of himself or of others as private subjectivities, nor does he suspect that all of us, himself included, are limited to one certain point of view of the world. That is why he subjects neither his thoughts, in which he believes as they present themselves, without attempting to link them to each other, nor our words, to any sort of criticism. He has no knowledge of points of view' (1962: 355). What then happens to a child when someone who is familiar, beloved, and integral to his world suddenly disappears? If he has no way of taking up a point of view on this, how does he objectify it, express it, and think it through? Above all, how does he deal with it? And what part do nature and culture play in this? Do phylogenetic and cultural elements entirely shape his experience, or do these elements simply provide a repertoire of possibilities that he strategically selects and deploys in dealing with his loss, through trial and error, in dream and in deed, *and with whatever lies to hand?*

My son, just turned four, has a soft heart. At the pool today, despite the ninety degree heat, he said he did not want to swim or play on the water-slide. Instead, he spent the morning rescuing June bugs from the pool. Later, we walked home in the heat. I was steadying his brand-new bicycle as we went along. His talk was all about how he was going to put the half-drowned June bugs in the bughouse that his friend Harry had given him as a birthday gift.

Josh also likes to collect action figures. They have scary names, these figures his parents buy him from K-Mart, Target or Service Merchandise. Tremor, Venom, Violator and Overkill. Josh has explained to me, however, that some are 'naughty ones', others 'good ones.' Hence his innocent query at K-Mart yesterday. 'Is this a good one or a naughty one?' We bought Spawn – a 'naughty one', Made in China.

I could not exactly understand the link between his compassion for June bugs and his liking for these gothic and mutant superheroes until Josh got his bughouse. He filled the bughouse with wood lice, spiders, ants and various insects from the garden, then watched in fascination as they fought and killed each other, vying for space.

Josh has got a pretty amazing collection of action figures now. In fact, he is a part of it. He calls himself Creepy One. Adopting a karate stance, he frowns at me and throws up his blade-like hands.

'Looking good,' I say.

The other day at Josh's school, one of his friends pointed me out to his father. 'That's Creepy One's father,' the little boy said.

'Big butt head!' Josh says, and explains: 'That's what Roger said to Doug.' Doug is a TV programme on *Nickelodean* that Josh and I sometimes watch together.

'We should have a doug house as well as a bug house,' I say.

'Doug's not in this land,' Josh rejoins, seriously. 'That's on TV.'

'What are some other things that are not in this land?' I ask, curious to know what he considers imaginary, by contrast with what is real.

'Rug Rats. Nickelodean. Beetlejuice. It not in this land. Beetlejuice doesn't keep me awake.'

That night, writing this dialogue in my diary, I note: the imagined is that which cannot hurt us.

Yesterday evening, Josh and I were fooling around on the sitting-room floor when the phone rang. 'Can you get it?' I called to my wife. As I tried to shush Josh, yet still respond to his desire to continue our rough-housing, I noticed that Francine was not saying much. But her face was grave, as though the caller was unburdening himself or herself of a matter of life and death. Every now and then Francine said, 'Oh my God,' and I tried to guess what was wrong. Had someone been hurt in an accident? Someone in her family? 'Yes,' she said, 'yes I will,' and then 'yes' again.

When she hung up she did not say anything.

'Has something happened?' I asked. 'Is someone hurt?'

'Baba is dead,' she said. 'She must have had a stroke or heart attack while she was splitting firewood. Lois found her this morning.'

I thought it odd that she should refer to her mother as 'Baba' – the word Joshua used. I got up and went to comfort her, but she said she was all right. So calm. So detached.

We went for a walk in Bryan Park, and under the big chestnut tree by the tennis courts we sat Josh down and told him that his beloved grandmother, his Baba, was dead.

After taking this in for a while, he said very simply, very emphatically, 'I'm angry. I'm not sad, I'm angry.'

The following day we flew to New Zealand. Baba had lived on the coast. Her living-room windows overlooked an estuary and dark green hills. It was unnerving to enter her house and find, on the dining table, a list she had written of things to do before she travelled to the U.S. in ten days' time to visit us – air tickets to be collected at Campus Travel, potatoes to plant – and then, beside the list, a sweater she had knitted for Francine, ready to have the buttons sewn on, and two knitted teddy bears she had made for her grandchildren.

One of the first things Francine did was telephone the mortuary in Hamilton. She wanted her mother back home. And so for two days and nights Baba lay in a casket in her bedroom. Josh went in to see her from time to time, to touch her face, to hug her. We cautioned him from trying to prise her eyes open, from kissing the dead body. It was not healthy.

I gazed out the window at the mudflats along the estuary where Baba and Josh used to gather periwinkles, the two of them out there for hours in their Wellies, even when rain swept in from the ghostly hills. A fishing boat chugged down the estuary as I watched, its wake spreading from one side of the estuary to the other. I called Josh to come to the window. 'Come here,' I said, 'it's the fishing boat you used to watch out for with Baba.' He did not respond.

After the funeral there was a lot of legal business to take care of, and Francine had to organise the sale of Baba's car and house. The work of cleaning the house and sorting through Baba's possessions was interrupted by numerous visits. Members of the family, their faces grave, their voices lowered, commiserating.

Ten days later, we returned home, still in the shadow of Baba's death. We all, in our different ways, felt abandoned and lost. Francine had lost her mother, her confidante, her mainstay in troubled times. I had lost, with Baba, my last niche, my last place of anchorage in my homeland. As for Joshua, it seemed at times that he had lost his reason.

Late one autumn afternoon I guided him down to Bryan Park on his bicycle, negotiating the broken sidewalk, looking out for traffic at the intersections.

'You know my *old* Baba,' Josh said, out of the blue. 'Not Emily or Baba,' he explained, mentioning his other grandmother, who died two years ago and who he did not remember, 'well, she was eaten by a crocodile.'

I tried to take this in, the past split off from the present, and death as a predator. But Josh went on:

'My old father,' he said, 'not you. You're not my real father.[5] My old father was eaten by a crocodile too. And my old mother.'

That night, as I tucked Josh into bed after reading to him from his *Book of Fabulous Beasts*, he said: 'I want you to die. I want to be ayone (alone). I don't want to be with you. I want to be naughty. I want to stay up all night yong (long).'

Indeed, at 9.15 p.m., as I recorded his comments in my journal, he was still awake, reading his Book of Fabulous Beasts, entranced by the Phoenix that is consumed by fire, yet every morning is reborn from its own ashes.

'He feels that the rug has been pulled out from under him,' I wrote. Through no rhyme or reason known to him, by dint of things beyond his comprehension and control, a vital element in his world has been cruelly and unjustly snatched away. Desperate not to be a victim, not to suffer this outrage in silence, and to feel that the world recognises and responds to his needs, he inverts his relationship to everything and everyone around him. He speaks of Creepy One, his alter ego, who has no mother or father, who exists alone, a law unto himself. His anger at Baba, or the forces that conspired to take her from him, is turned against us. At preschool, he is incontinent. In a place where routines and rules provide no room for emotional outbursts, he has recourse to his own body, his own inwardness. Relinquishing sphincter control gives him a perverse sense that he is in fact in control of his own situation. Maybe this is why he fears passivity. He dislikes recess at school. He wants to stay up all night long. He does not want to go to sleep. If he slept death would come. We would disappear. The world would ring terrible changes in his absence, and the morning would be unlike the morning he last woke to.

'He keeps telling me how much he would like to fly.

'The truths we live by are not always the same as the truths we swear by.'

A friend and I took Josh with us to Dunn Wood in search of edible fungi. We found a box turtle, which Josh grasped, kissed, and said he would care for. He was convinced it was the same turtle we had found in the woods behind Mary-Helen's house, miles away, not long before we heard of Baba's death. It had returned from nothingness, and now he could take charge of it, and make it his own.

Back home I made a cage for Josh's turtle. Josh packed the cage with sphagnum moss, placed a dish of water under the turtle's nose, and tried to feed it some leaves. He said he wanted to take it to school for show-and-tell.

The box turtle seemed to make a difference. Josh seemed calmer, more in control, more his old affectionate, trusting self.

Josh's feelings are easily hurt. When I ask him not to hammer his bicycle with the spanner, he dissolves immediately in tears.

On the way to Bryan Park, Josh tells me, 'I don't want you to die'. For a split second I felt the beginning of a rush of great relief. Then he added, 'I want tyrannosaurus to eat you.'

First thing in the morning, Josh climbs into bed with us and hugs Francine. 'I really love you, Storm,' he says. Storm is one of his mutants.

That evening, I am late home on account of a student exam. Josh is elated to see me, and eager to show me the hairy caterpillar bugs he has found. 'I really love you, Wolverine,' he says.

The X-men are safe, I tell myself. He feels he can control them, these miniature figures he keeps in a box in his room. These guys he can trust. But not his parents. Not yet.

As if to hammer this home, he once more asks me: 'You know my old Baba? Not Emily. Not Baba. My parents who lived before, in Africa?'

The parents who were real and reliable, and did not let him down, I think.

That night, after Josh has gone to sleep, Francine and I talk things over. Francine recounts how she took Josh to Bryan Park, and he poked her with a metal rod of some sort. When she asked him not to, because it was hurting her, he retorted, 'I want to do it. I want you to die.'

'But it won't make me die,' Francine said.

'What if I make you bleed?'

'It won't make me die, it'll just hurt me.'

'What if I cut off your arm?'

'I still won't die. It's pretty hard to make someone die, you know, if you're healthy.'

'What if I cut off your head?'

'I still won't die.'

'I want you to be dead. Pretend to be dead.'

Francine pretended, but without lying down.

'Lie down on the ground!'

'No, I'm holding Freya, I'll just have to be a ghost.'

Josh's shoe came off. He wouldn't let Francine tie it back on. He ran off.

Francine said to me: 'He's so sweet with living things, so sad if he hurts a butterfly. And she described how he had found one bruised and battered by the creek. 'Look,' he told her, 'it's still alive, I want it to fly away.'

Josh took Francine outside. 'I want to show you something,' he said. 'It's *very* interesting. Come with me, I'll show you.'

Out on the lawn all his action figures were 'dead' in a bucket. 'They are dead now,' he explained. 'We are burying them up. Don't touch them.'

He transferred the action figures to an old barrel, then tore up tufts of grass, and emptied ash and dirt on top of them. He then up-ended the bucket over the buried figures in the barrel. 'They got to stay warm. If they stay here they going to die.'

As he performed the funeral, he asked Francine to say something good about each of the buried figures. 'Creepy One Supersaver,' he prompted her. 'Wonder Woman. Boo-in-Bub.'

'Staging this funeral, replaying the tragic events over which he had no say, is how he begins to bring his feelings until control.' At least this is how I reasoned in my journal. 'In creating a miniaturised simulacrum of the world – exchanging real figures for superheroes – he is able to play out as theatrical events what befell him as reality, re-empowering himself, regaining a sense that he too can make things happen in this world, rather than be at the mercy of things happening to him. But whatever truth there is in this theorising, the fact is that both Francine and I are at our wits' end, coping with his accident-proneness, his throwing things at us, his declarations of his need to be alone, to be elsewhere, for us to die, his anger, his vulnerability when reprimanded (breaking into tears and protesting that we should not be angry at him).'

In the late evening we stroll along our street. 'I'm going to Africa,' Joshua announces, a propos of nothing. 'That is my land. I have to go there or I will die.'

Is it the autumn? The colder air? Or is it human warmth he wants? I remember how drawn he is to Salamander and Phoenix in his *Book of Fabulous Beasts*. But how can I guess at his need, except to compare it to my own, when I was his age, feeling the same abandonment, desperate to be elsewhere?

He rambles on about the father and mother and grandmother he had 'before', and how they all lived in Africa.

Before Baba's death? When the world was warm, and safe and secure?

I drove to Barnes and Noble and asked the assistant if she could help me locate anything on children's bereavement. She fetched the two titles they had in stock. One promised the reader that his or her loved one was in heaven, safe with God. The other was a secular equivalent, giving assurances that trees and flowers spring up anew from the ashes of the dead, brightening the world over which darkness has momentarily fallen. Life goes on. Loss is an illusion.

What feeble imaginings, what corny scenarios! When I compared these glib consolations, these saccharine evasions, with Josh's complex and heart-rending fantasies, I felt outraged. How easily adults insult the intelligence of a child. I told myself that Josh did not need explanations. He did not want assurances. He did not want to be distracted, to be bought off. He wanted an arm around him. He wanted his parents to be close. He wanted them to listen to his nightmares. Just listen. So that, in his own way, in his own good time, he could see this thing through.

Another day verging on chaos. Josh brought home a cheap box that belonged to one of his friends. He says he found it in his locker at school, and supposed it was his. He will not be persuaded to take it back, to return it to Harry. He clings to things now with the same ferocity that he clung to Baba, to his parents, to this world of human subjects that has let him down.

Luckily Francine finds an identical box at K-Mart. Chaos is averted.

At bedtime I speak to Josh about his sadness and anger.

'Where do your feelings come from?' I ask.

Again he tells me about his 'other grandmother' – not Emily, not Baba, 'who was eaten by a crocodile.'

'Did this happen in New Zealand?'

'Yes.'

I tell him we are not going to be eaten. No crocodile is going to get us. He has nothing to fear.

'I want to be ayone (alone),' he says. 'I want to grow up and be an adult.'

I tell him that he does not have to grow up for a long long time yet. He should let himself be four, be himself. He does not have to be alone. We will be here with him, loving him, looking after him, making meals for him, always. I will be here, Mummy will be here, Heidi will be here. And Freya.

He tells me we are all going to die. He has to get another Mummy and Daddy.

I try to explain that Baba had been old. Old people die. We are young and healthy. We are not going to die. 'You don't have to think of dying,' I tell him. 'Old people sometimes worry about that. But not children, not young healthy people like us. Tell me that you will not worry about that any more.'

'I won't,' he says. 'I understand.'

It is now almost three weeks since we arrived home. Things are becoming resolved now. At breakfast this morning Josh said, 'I had a dream about Baba alive.'

'That's good,' I said. 'I'm happy you had a dream about Baba alive and happy.'

Josh said that Baba had been taking him to the ice cream shop.

That night, after I had read him his bedtime story, he said he loved me, and he hugged me spontaneously for the first time in four weeks.

Jerry and Betty Mintz live three doors from us along University Avenue. Jerry is a colleague and a friend, the first person in the anthropology department to go out of his way to make me feel at home in Bloomington when I first arrived. He walked me around the campus, showing me how to find my way to the library, to the Kinsey Institute, and the gym. Then he invited me to a screening of some of his ethnographic films.

These days I do not see a lot of Jerry. He has leukemia. He is off work, and if he goes out, it is always with Betty, and a respirator. One turn around Bryan Park, then home.

Today I saw him standing on the sidewalk in his bathrobe, watching Betty weed the garden. I walked along the street and we talked about the fall. Then he asked me how Josh was getting on, and I told him how Josh had used his action figures to get a hold on his confused and painful feelings after his grandmother died.

Jerry told me a story about a friend of his in Brooklyn. His friend is an obsessive collector. 'Street signs, stamps, coins, you name it, he collects them all. Even insulators.'

'Like the insulators on telegraph poles?'

'Yeah,' Jerry says. 'He steals them. Only he hasn't got a red one yet. The only colour insulators don't come in is red. And this bothers him.'

'Why would anyone want to collect insulators?'

'He got started collecting things when his father killed his mother when he was a kid.'

A year passed. I showed Josh a photo of himself painted as Creepy One, a photo that went back to just before Baba died.

'I hate Creepy One now,' Josh said, 'because he's not a real superhero.'

There is always an arbitrariness about the strategies or objects we use in our attempts to grasp the world. Many children, dealing with traumatic events, draw or paint pictures – graphic images of dreadful experiences. Inside a concentration camp. People jumping to their deaths from the World Trade Centre towers on 11 September 2001. Homes destroyed by bombing, or an earthquake, or buried under a mudslide. Others turn to objects, and small rituals to re-enact the catastrophe that has befallen them. Children after the Skopje earthquake in 1964 played games that involved burying things. Something has to be seen through, and the child goes over and over the ground again until it is done. Like Joshua's gradual reconciliation to the fact that no one, himself included, was invincible. Superheroes did not exist in the real world. When our subjectivity is swamped, inundated, overwhelmed by events over which we have no comprehension or control, we need to get some distance, to stand back, to objectify. So we turn to paint, or doodling, or playing with toys, or objects, or scribbling poetry – whatever comes to hand, whatever is already there – and from these vantage points that are removed from the immediate subjective world in which we are floundering, we recover a sense of our ability to grasp, to manage, to act in the world. Even though 'grand rituals' deploy extramundane objects and images, close study often reveals that this ritual paraphernalia, though manifestly more exotic and avowedly more 'sacred' than superheroes, scraps of cloth and tufts of grass, has its source in the everyday lifeworld. That ordinary actions of washing, dusting, tidying, burning, eating, killing or cooking, and social relations between men and women, the old and young – the stuff of quotidian life – are typically taken up and elaborated in ritual is a reminder that ritual has its perennial origins in our unremarked habitual use of whatever comes to hand to 'get a handle' on our thoughts and feeling, to implement our will. Culture is the word we give to this potential world of images, stories, objects and ways of acting to which we may have recourse in our struggle to exist. But culture is not what determines the acting, or the need to act. These are existential imperatives.

And we can discern them in others because we have experienced them in ourselves. And seeing them in others can be our way of objectifying experiences in ourselves that are too close, too confused, to admit of direct comprehension.

Ritualisation

I hope I have made clear that ritualisation is often mundane and unspectacular, and that it cannot be understood without reference to the critical existential situations that precipitate it – such as a perturbing and radical change in a person's situation, or traumatic separation and loss.[6] This is not, however, to reduce ritual to private, idiosyncratic or emotional behaviour, for human beings suffer the loss of loved ones, prized possessions, beliefs and convictions, self-esteem, homeland and employment, with similar intensity, the reason being that our subjectivity, will, consciousness and purpose become invested in all 'objects', to varying degrees, so making them, as it were, metonyms of ourselves. This is why I cannot accept Lévi-Strauss's argument that ritual 'is not a reaction to life; it is a reaction to what thought has made of life. It is not a direct response to the world, or even to experience of the world; it is a response to the way man thinks of the world' (1990: 681). Such an artificial polarisation of 'epistemological' and 'existential' anxieties (ibid: 680) is analytically unhelpful, since human beings find themselves just as troubled by emotional, environmental and social difficulties as they do by conceptual ones. Accordingly, the ways in which we organise the world into comprehensible categories – object/subject, verbal/non-verbal, male/female, elder/younger, human/animal, kin/non-kin – is not just something *against* which ritual works but often the raw material *with* which it works. But whether body or mind, thought or feeling, social or material reality is emphasised in a given ritual practice will depend entirely on how a person identifies the source of his or her distress.

Several years ago, I explored the ways in which metaphorical connections between the human body, the social body and the body of the land, are often made the basis for ritual action, arguing that it is 'because anthropomorphic metaphors unite these various domains in the one image that they facilitate movement from one domain to another' (Jackson 1989: 149). In ritual, appeal is made to a domain analogous to the domain in which anxiety is located, and this relatively, though only momentarily, neutral domain is then subject to manipulation and play in the hope that it will change one's immediate situation and alleviate one's distress. The grounds for the possibility of such symbolic transferences and substitutions are the deeply engrained metaphors that fuse *eigenwelt* and *mitwelt*, a fusion that reflects the mutually defining mirroring of primary intersubjectivity in which whatever changes occur in the self will have repercussions in the other and vice versa.[7]

Let me briefly consider some of these symbolic substitutions.

A Foi man from Papua New Guinea, about to plant *wasia* pitpit (sago) recites a spell in which he denies that he is planting the pitpit; he is 'planting the feathers of a hawk as it flaps its wings' (Weiner 1991: 17). The logic here is to 'effect a transfer of properties from one domain to another. In this case, the sudden enlargement of the hawk as it spreads its wings is used to represent the desired sudden and rapid growth of this cultivar' (ibid: 17).

A pubescent girl is oppressed by all kinds of external expectations as to how she should look, how she should behave, how she should feel, how she should think. These expectations as to how she should comport herself in relation to others might be visited upon her by an overbearing mother, by popular images of svelt fashion models or media celebrities, by the physiological changes taking place in her body, or by her peer group. Feeling she has no power to determine her own destiny, feeling she is a creature of forces outside her control, she falls back on her own inner emotions, her own body, *her relationship with herself*, as a domain that *is* within her control. She effectively makes her body a substitute for the external world, and by starving herself, or gorging and vomiting, she becomes an actor again, repudiating the social reifications that have reduced her to the status of a 'mere appendage', a mere thing (Selvini 1974: 88).[8]

In the mortuary rituals of many societies, the immediate bereaved – in whom distress and anxiety is most keenly focused – are often sidelined, and surrogate mourners perform, in a controlled way, the emotions of grief and loss. Often, these 'reversed emotions' (Goody 1962: 107), that affectively distance the living from the dead, involve badinage and mockery, thus symbolically dismissing the idiosyncratic personality from memory and preparing the way for the idealisation of the deceased as an ancestor. Among the Kuranko these surrogate mourners are logically 'joking partners' of the deceased – at once structurally identified with the bereaved, yet seen as 'other' – for they belong either to another generation, or to the matriline (Jackson 1989: 70,79–80).

In eastern traditions of yoga and meditation, attention is moved from one's relationship with the external world – which is a source of illusion, vexation and frustration – to the inner world of one's consciousness and emotions. Bringing stillness and steadiness to thought, stability to the body and smoothness to one's emotions induces an experiential transformation in one's relationship to the external world. But yoga practice is not an escape from this world into a substitute reality, but a supplementary modality of acting that makes one's social and practical action more effective. By contrast with these techniques focused on interiority, Mary Douglas in *Purity and Danger* (1966: 12) suggests that inner turmoil or disorder may be managed by 'ritually' reorganising one's mundane environment – cleaning or redecorating a house, rearranging furniture, weeding a garden, buying new clothes. In both these cases, changes in one's experience are 'induced' by working on an aspect of one's lifeworld that is amenable to manipulation. But in both cases, the action is supplemental. It offers respite, assists focus and induces a sense of being in control of one's circumstances. If the ritual action becomes an end in itself, consuming all the time and energy of a person, then, and only then, can we speak of madness. For what defines an action as 'obsessional' rather than sane, magical rather than realistic, is not the form of action per se, but the extent to which one has lost oneself in it, leaving, as Freud puts it, one's 'whole world ... under an embargo of "impossibility"' (1950: 27).

Let me explore this further, with an example from my fieldwork in Aboriginal Australia.

Among the Kuku Yalanji of southeast Cape York, thunderstorms are a constant menace during the wet season, and people are often fearful of their approach. This is partly because thunderstorms are thought to be agents of retributive justice (if you break food or sex taboos, you will be struck down by lightning), partly because thunderstorms are the means whereby sorcerers and enemies attack their victims.

How does one act when storms approach? How does one avoid being wholly at their mercy, a victim of their destructive power?

Among Kuku Yalanji, two analogous domains of relationship are posited: relations between social categories, and relations between environmental elements.

The key terms, and the relations posited between them, are: mother-in-law is to son-in-law as thunderstorm is to grasstree.

Now, when thunderstorms approach, it is supposed that social categories that should be kept apart are coming dangerously close together: you and your enemies; outsiders and insiders. This situation is compared to the infringement of the avoidance relation between mother-in-law and son-in-law.

The problem: how to drive the thunderstorm away?

The solution: activate the analogies alluded to above.

The practical action: grass-tree logs are burned. The grass-tree is son-in-law to the thunderstorm. The thunderstorm smells the grass-tree smoke. And just as mother-in-law will avoid her son-in-law if she smells him (social categories are identified with different odours among the Kuku Yalanji), so the storm smells its son-in-law and moves away.

A comparable situation is described in Ghassan Hage's essay on reading a newspaper (Hage 2002). Here, the migrant's relationship to an Australian Lebanese newspaper substitutes for the migrant's relationship with Lebanon – a relationship which has become attenuated, compromised or blocked by distance. News items in the Australian Lebanese paper 'operate metonymically as a fragment of an imaginary Lebanon' – as a way of bridging 'the distance between Lebanon as an imagined totality and the migrant' (ibid: 195). But what is compelling about Hage's account is not the metonymical relationship posited between the migrant and the newspaper, but the way this relationship is embodied, and performed, in the mutterings, slaps and exclamations of the reader. Reading the paper gives the reader a means of performing his Lebaneseness, despite the distance that actually exists between him and his homeland. These gestures may be understood, Hage notes, as 'strategies of intensification' (ibid: 197) – strategies for narrowing the physical and symbolic gap between the news event and the reader. It is a magical action, in Sartre's terms (1948), since it produces an experience of intense closeness to events in Lebanon without actually altering the real distance between the migrant and the homeland.

But do we want to sustain this distinction between real and imaginary? Is magical action necessarily a form of false consciousness? And under what conditions does it become pathological?

Magical Reason

Ritualisation, in the sense I have been using the word, is an aspect of everyday human action and speech in all societies, and springs from the ways in which human beings learn to play with transitional objects, words and images in managing the contrary and contradictory impulses, imperatives and imaginings that make up the field of primary intersubjectivity. Purely sociological analyses of ritual are of limited value unless they are grounded in an understanding of the dynamics of primary intersubjectivity. This is why I have argued that ritualisation has to be approached not simply as a social phenomenon that reorders and reintegrates *social* relations, but existentially – as an ontologically 'primitive' mode of action that plays upon the emotions, manipulates the body and changes consciousness. One effect of such action is to transform subject-object relations, such that a person comes to experience himself or herself as an actor, and not just acted upon – as a 'who' and not merely a 'what'. In Sartre's discussion of such 'emotive behaviour' he gives the example of a bunch of grapes that is out of reach. 'I shrug my shoulders, I let my hand drop, I mumble, "They're too green," and I move on' (1948: 61). In this 'little comedy', played out beneath the bunch of grapes, my frustrated desire for the grapes is transfigured by the magical effect my gestures and words have upon me. In repudiating the grapes as 'too green' I 'magically confer upon the grapes the quality I desire' and so change my relationship with them (*passim* 62). But, Sartre notes, the grapes are not *really* changed by my actions, and this 'emotive behaviour' is, strictly speaking, ineffective (ibid: 60). Though we 'magically ... invest real objects with certain qualities,' Sartre concludes, 'these qualities are false' (ibid: 72).

It is this distinction between true and false 'belief' that I want to question.

W.G. Sebald's account of the bombing of German cities in the period 1942–1945 begins with a series of awful statistics. The RAF alone dropped 1 million tons of bombs on 131 towns and cities, killing 600,000 civilians, destroying 3.5 million homes and, by the end of the war, had made 7.5 million people homeless. Yet, Sebald writes, 'we do not grasp what it all actually meant' (2003: 3), and he marvels that this terrible devastation 'seems to have left scarcely a trace of pain behind in the collective consciousness' (ibid: 4). Some of those who survived this period have left memoirs, to be sure, but most are sanitised, fictionalised or mythologised, as if, by tacit agreement, the unvarnished truth of this experience could never be made public, never be described. Throughout his book, Sebald makes it very clear that, in his view, people *should* have addressed the reality of what had happened, and left some record of what they witnessed and what they experienced. Speaking of such reminiscences as do exist, he acknowledges that these 'contain genuine insights, attempts at self-criticism, and moments when the dreadful truth makes its way to the surface', but then laments the way these writings 'quickly revert to the harmless, conversational tone that is so strikingly disproportionate to the reality of the time' (ibid: 85). While acknowledging 'the quasi-natural reflex, engendered by feelings of shame and a wish to defy the victors ... to keep quiet and look the other way', Sebald is mystified when he reads a report by the Swedish journalist Stig Dagerman, who travelled through Germany by train in the fall of 1946, that though the train 'was crammed full, like all trains in Germany ... no one looked out the windows' (Sebald 2003: 31). But why should people look at the ruins around them? Why should they dwell on the devastation? And why is Sebald so unable to empathise with the 'passive sadness' that had seized so many, and by the 'harmless, conversational tone' with which these people hoped to restore some semblance of a life?

In his essay on the emotions (1948), Sartre speaks of the way a novice boxer will sometimes shut his eyes and throw himself at his opponent as a way of 'symbolically eliminating' or neutralising a situation he cannot bear to think about, and cannot control. 'These are the limits of my magical action upon the world,' Sartre writes. 'I can eliminate it as an object of consciousness, but I can do so only by eliminating consciousness itself' (1948: 62–63). This is precisely what one sees in the behaviour of those who survived the fire-bombing of the German cities – haggard figures poking about in the rubble and detritus, burdened with parcels and sacks, crates and cartons, cooking meals in the ruins from dirty, wrinkled vegetables and dubious scraps of meat, or drifting about in such lethargy that they seemed to have lost the will to live (Sebald 2003 *passim* 36–38). But in one poignant account of Hamburg, a few days after the air raid that destroyed the city, the writer Nossack describes seeing a woman cleaning the windows of a building 'that stood alone and undamaged in the middle of a desert of ruins.' Nossack writes, 'We thought we were looking at a madwoman. We felt the same when we saw children tidying and raking a front garden. It was so far beyond all comprehension that we told other people about it, as if it were some sort of marvel. One day we came to a suburb that had not suffered at all. People were sitting out on their balconies drinking coffee. It was like watching a film; it was downright impossible' (Nossack 1972: 35, cited in Sebald 2003: 41–42). To me, these are glimpses into the human capacity for what Arendt called 'natality' – the capacity to initiate the new, even in the face of unspeakable calamity. But to Sebald, this is simply evidence of 'people's ability to forget what they do not want to know, to overlook what is before their eyes' and he takes the Hamburg citizens to task for continuing to drink their coffee as if nothing had happened – criticising their lack of empathy (ibid: 42).

Yet if Sebald had suffered this calamity would he, any more than they, have had the presence of mind, the energy, the incentive, to record the devastation around him, or would he have succumbed to the same appalling lethargy, struggling to get through the day, to find food, to keep warm, to survive the nights – a condition in which questions of theodicy would undoubtedly be the last things on one's mind?

If I am less inclined than Sartre to speak of magical activity as 'ineffective' or 'false', and reluctant to share Sebald's view of the Germans as alienated from the experiences that befell them in the closing years of the war, it is because I see nothing necessarily pathological or futile in the denial of reality. It is as much a coping mechanism as 'facing' or 'accepting' reality. The difference between pathological and normal reactions to crisis (if one is to use these words) lies not in the activity per se, but in the degree to which a person becomes stuck in that activity, so that what is a supplemental means of coming to terms with a difficult situation becomes an end in itself, a substitute for acting, and thus an escape, a refuge, a dissociated state of mind that prevents further growth or development.

Notes

1. One is reminded of Freud's famous example of 'mastery play' in *Beyond the Pleasure Principle*, in which a one-and-a-half-year-old child manipulated objects that came to hand in order to exert 'mastery' over his mother's going away and returning – throwing a toy out of his cot and declaring it gone (*fort*) before reeling it back in with an exultant 'there' (*da*) (1957,18: 14–16).
2. I later discuss briefly the Dinka practice of *thuic*, for example – a ritual action that Lienhardt describes as 'in itself trivial, and among the Dinka themselves ... not regarded in any way as an important ceremony' (Lienhardt 1961: 283) – because of the light this practice sheds on more complex and 'sacred' ritual scenarios.
3. Though we owe to Lévi-Strauss extraordinary insights into the internal logic of myth and ritual, the reduction of this logic to the structures of the unconscious mind suggests a confusion of means and ends, for what compels myth or ritual is not logic but life. Our social and historical situations do not simply provide the raw material on which the unconscious mind works its wonders; rather, it is our social difficulties and confusions that lead us to have recourse to myth and ritual as ways of comprehending and managing our lives.
4. This thesis is not a reversion to Tylor, Marett and Frazer, for I contend that (a) 'magical' thought and action is as much a part of modernity as premodernity, and cannot be used as a rhetorical device for separating 'us' from 'them', (b) magic is, except in cases of madness, a supplement to practical activity, not a substitute for it, and hence it should not be dismissed as a stuttering form of pseudo-science but seen as an aspect of science, (c) magic is less a way of way of coping with unpredictable natural phenomena, than transforming human experience of the environment, both social and physical, and (d) magic is as closely tied to the exercise of human will as to the reduction of anxiety.
5. In trauma, one recognises the physical features of the people one knew and loved 'before', but one no longer recognises them emotionally. It is as if the part of the brain associated with emotional recognition 'cuts' off, and no longer supplies the affective aspect of recognition, giving rise to the familiar protest, 'you are an imposter; you are not my real parent' (i.e., that which was 'real' to me no longer exists, except as a memory, a chimera, a simulacrum, a look-alike). This helps explain why the corpse of a loved one is at once 'she' and 'not she', and why memories suddenly define the 'reality' of the person one has lost.
6. Van Gennep's tripartite model of rites of passage (1960), so creatively 'reinvented' by Victor Turner in his ground-breaking studies of Ndembu ritual (1970: 93–111), is at once too abstract and too general unless we refer this cultural sequence of separation – marginality – reincorporation to the primordial patterning of separation anxiety, defined as a passage from protest, through withdrawal, to acceptance (see Bowlby 1971, 1975).
7. In his study of Yaka healing ritual, René Devisch makes a similar observation. 'The therapist treats the patient's body as if it enclosed or embraced the world, as if it were both a micro- and macrocosm ... The healer works upon the patient's inner world of passion and affects, her sensory and bodily forms of contact, and her social and existential involvement with the group and the life-world by metaphorically regarding them as bodily-cum-cosmic processes of depletion versus empowerment, obstruction versus flow, closure versus exchange, rotting versus fermentation, killing (in the hunt) versus regeneration (through cooking), and so on' (1993: 265).
8. Karina Toftgård Lindrup has kindly drawn my attention to Tsisti Dangarembga's novel, *Nervous Conditions* (2001), which depicts an African woman seeking to escape the 'double-colonisation' of patriarchy and colonial power by symbolically asserting control over her own body through bulima and anorexia.

Chapter 7

BIOTECHNOLOGY AND THE CRITIQUE OF GLOBALISATION

It is infinitely easier to take up a position for or against an idea, a value, a person, an institution or a situation, than to analyse what it truly is, in all its complexity.
Pierre Bourdieu (1998: 22–23)

The world of human subjects is surrounded and permeated by a world that is *without* subjectivity – the world of things. The intrinsic otherness of this object-world, that makes it so refractory to human understanding and so resistant to human control, is nonetheless subject to such intensive physical and intellectual labour – reworked by human hands, reimagined in narratives and rituals, elaborated in belief and systematised by science – that it inevitably comes to resemble the human world that it essentially lies beyond. Thus does intersubjectivity – through the idioms of vitalistic and anthropomorphic thought – absorb the object world into the subject world, and establish the ground rules for magical, ritual, dialogical and social relations between them. But because the basis of this relationship is contrived and unstable, we periodically come up against forces of nature or of sheer materiality that render absurd the notion that human beings may reason with or enter into social relations with such forces, while the natural world is itself so dominated, colonised and transformed by the brute force of human will that the notion of its being *extra*-human is equally subject to radical doubt.

These observations about the way human beings work to make the unalike seem alike, and act as if the extra-human and human were continuous with each other, are nowhere more sharply brought into

---

Notes for this section can be found on page 126.

relief than in the innovations of biotechnology. Alternatively regarded as a natural extension of our human bodylife or of human will, *or* demonised as unnatural, alien and inimical to our human integrity, new genetic technologies constitute a fraught and ambivalent arena – where age-old questions about the relationship between the human and the extra-human, the subjective and the objective, the natural and the unnatural, the spiritual and the material are contested and decided.

The Ambiguity of Technology

News stories like the following break almost every day:

> Monsanto, the international company that pioneered the use of genetically-modified crops, has revealed that its most widely used GM product contains *unexpected* gene fragments, *raising fresh doubts* that the technology is properly understood. (Meikle 2000: 1, emphases added)

This story concludes with a comment from Andy Tait, GM campaigner for Greenpeace, U.K.: 'This shows exactly what we have been saying for years, that genetic modification is *inherently unpredictable* and will have all sorts of knock-on effects once released into the environment' (ibid, emphasis added).

I see nothing intrinsically new in this kind of story, or in the reactions to it, and it is my view that biotechnology simply updates and re-dramatises the human anxieties that have always come with new technologies – anxieties that express deep misgivings about our human ability to comprehend and control any new phenomenon. In the case of gene technologies, the manifest lack of consistent and confident institutional or governmental control only exacerbates this crisis of agency. One simply does not know enough about the new technology to be able to feel that one can manage or predict its repercussions. Confronted by this kind of uncertainty and ambiguity, human beings typically switch their focus from the world around them to the world within – to their own emotions, their own thoughts, their own bodies, their own immediate social field – where an illusory yet consoling sense of being-in-control may be conjured. In such magical thinking, complexity gives way to simplicity. This is because the world of fantasy is non-dialectical. It is governed by a principle of parsimony, and by a static logic of polarisation. Accordingly the language we use in critical and disconcerting situations tends to be the language of morality – a language of either/or, of black and white, of good and bad. By seeing the world in what Bourdieu calls 'the reassuring dichotomies of Manichean thought' (1998: 22), one has only to make a single choice, and this choice, rather than leading one into a deeper understanding of the enigmatic, ambiguous and contextual complexity of the phenomenon provides an escape route from the phenomenon's gravitational field, a way of simply putting it from one's mind. To deliver a judgement is to close a case, and license the building of a wall. This polarising essentialism is, of course, at work in fantasies of racism (Jews and blacks are evil, whites virtuous), cultural fundamentalism (native peoples are spiritual, Westerners are materialistic), and biotechnology. There is no grey zone, nothing to be explored or tested, nothing to be thought through by dint of intellectual labour. It is a black and white issue, a cut and dried case. The new is either offensive to human, natural or divine orders – which is to say, the world one is already familiar with – or it promises salvation – a way of magically replacing the old with the new. Such strategies create a *discursive* boundary line that magically substitutes for the 'real' boundary line between self and other, known and new, that has been transgressed, and over which one feels one can no longer exercise control.

That these polar responses to new technology have been with us for some time is nicely demonstrated by the story of Mary Shelley's Frankenstein (1985, originally published in 1818). Raised and educated by parents who were also radical intellectuals, Mary Shelley was especially sensitive to the ethical issue of how far the new scientific possibilities in the late eighteenth century – which she saw as symbolic of a masculinist desire to dominate and exploit nature – should be allowed to go. The idea for Frankenstein came to Mary Shelley in 1816 during a summer vacation with her husband and some friends in a villa near Lake Geneva. One evening Lord Byron announced that everyone should compose a ghost story, and that each should tell his or her story on successive nights. Inspiration did not come easy to Mary, until one night, after reading an account of Erasmus Darwin's experiments with 'galvanism', she conceived her story about the 'frightful' effects of 'any human endeavour to mock the stupendous mechanisms of the Creator of the world'. In this germ of what would become the story of Frankenstein is a dramatic encapsulation of our modern ethical ambivalence toward the scientist-hero as Promethean creator of life, and about technology itself. Indeed, this vexed question concerning the extent to which technologies are 'natural' extensions of ourselves, or entail dangerous and unnatural interference in a divinely appointed or naturally-evolved order is written into the word itself – the root, *tuche*, suggesting chance, fate and things beyond human control, but the derivative term *techne* connoting chance assimilated to human designs and subjugated to human will.

Which sense of the word one emphasises will, I think, depend far less on one's cultural background per se than on the extent to which one feels ontologically secure, and in command of one's own life.

In an interview with Larry King on CNN in early 2000, the Hollywood actor Nick Nolte confidently confessed to using all kinds of artificial substances and techniques in an endeavour to keep himself young and maintain his health. But that he could celebrate the miracles of modern biomedicine and bioscience seemed, however, more an expression of his privileged position and healthy bank account than an objective confirmation of the therapeutic properties of the things he was doing and allowing to be done to his body. Thirty years ago in Sierra Leone I encountered a very different situation. Here, it seemed to me, Kuranko villagers' anxious attitudes toward the new technologies of the West were symptomatic of their growing sense of disempowerment, poverty and bewilderment, not only in relation to the Nation State whose power could neither be tapped nor ignored, but in relation to an international sphere that was no less powerful, and no less insidious.

Let me elaborate.

When NASA succeeded in putting a man on the moon in 1969, the event was widely celebrated in the developed world as perhaps the greatest technological and spiritual achievement in human history. For millions in the developing world, however, news of this event reached them belatedly and through rumour, and was glossed in ways that reflected local realities, local sensibilities. Having watched the televised coverage of the Apollo mission in Cambridge a few months before going to Sierra Leone to begin fieldwork for my Ph.D., I was in a good position to observe this contrast.

At the time I arrived in Sierra Leone, the country was in the grip of a conjunctivitis epidemic. I soon learned that this eye disease was known as Apollo, though several months later, when another wave of the epidemic swept the country, a distinction was made between Apollo 12 and Apollo 13. 'What was the connection?' I asked people in the town where my wife and I had settled. The American moon landings had disturbed the dust on the surface of the moon, I was told, and just as the sand-laden Harmattan blew south from the Sahara in the dry season, filling the air and irritating one's eyes, so this cosmic dust had brought its own discomforts and disease.[1]

Given my curiosity, people were then eager to have me clarify some of the anomalies in the accounts they had heard of the Apollo missions. Many villagers suspected that these accounts were untrue; no one could travel to the moon. Others (ignorant as to how far away the moon was, and believing it to be just overhead – no bigger than it appeared in the night sky) asked me to explain how a rocket large enough to hold three men could come to a standstill alongside the moon, and allow the men to get out and walk around on its surface. Still others demanded to know why the Americans wanted to go to the moon in the first place; what sinister designs and global repercussions did this presage? I had observed this same suspicion of America in local peoples' refusal to allow Peace Corps volunteers to photograph them. Anxieties clustered around the rumour that photos showing village women with bare breasts would be used by whites in the U.S. as racist propaganda, a way of arguing for the oppression of African Americans on the grounds that their origins and essence were incorrigibly primitive. In many ways these anxieties anticipated the fears of a later generation: that just as Americans had once tried to steal peoples' vital essence by capturing their likenesses in photographs, so foreigners were now out to steal and traffic in human body parts and vital organs.

But back to Apollo.

The questions put to me by Kuranko villagers in Sierra Leone in 1969 should not be read too literally. Kuranko were less interested in grasping intellectually the truth of the Apollo programme than in how to resolve an old existential dilemma that rumours of this programme had simply refocused and made more urgent. This was the dilemma of how to control traffic across the borders of their own local world, such that it would be perpetually revitalised by imports from the outside world – and these included magical medicines, commodities like salt, cloth, kerosene, seeds and women – rather than weakened and undermined by foreign influences or forces that they were powerless to control. It was not that Kuranko had hitherto lived in isolation; rather that the post-independence period signalled increasing hardship in negotiating relations with the outside world that were to their advantage. At the same time that people were building roads to gain access to markets, that young men were going south in increasing numbers to work in the diamond districts, that Muslim converts were making the pilgrimage to Mecca, villagers were coming to see that this outside world was much larger, much more complex and probably much less manageable than it had been for their forefathers. The Apollo stories encapsulated this widespread suspicion that the might of a foreign power of which one knew very little could cause things to happen in one's own backyard without one's consent, without one's comprehension, and without one's control.

Underpinning and possibly increasing these anxieties were assumptions familiar to us from Renaissance thought. In postulating profound functional correspondences between microcosm and macrocosm, one is ever alert to the ways in which events located in the cosmic realm presage changes in the social body and within the bodies of individuals. Thus, in Renaissance dramas such as Shakespeare's *Coriolanus* and *Hamlet* ('Something is rotten in the State of Denmark'), disturbances in the social order have dire repercussions in both the cosmic order and in the minds and bodies of individuals: people fall ill, the stars fall out of their courses.

The lesson I take from the myths of Apollo in Sierra Leone is that we would do well to explore the ways in which people's ideas about new phenomena and new experiences are grounded, not purely and simply in their culture, nor in the 'nature' of the phenomena themselves, but most significantly in their *relationship* with the phenomenon in question – notably the degree of comprehension and control they feel they have in this relationship. In brief it is power, as well as culture and technology, that conditions belief. And power is always *lived* within the space of intersubjectivity – which is to say, as a *social* relationship.

In *From Anxiety to Method in the Behavioural Sciences*, George Devereux argues that we share with all living organisms a deep-seated need to be recognised and responded to. 'Denial of response' can be so traumatic that in most societies cultural strategies exist that alleviate peoples' panic reactions to the unresponsiveness of matter. Most notably, physical occurrences are interpreted animistically, and human meanings are projected onto the extrahuman world (1967: 33–34). Thus, a thunderstorm will be said to embody the malicious intentions of outsiders, and a 'natural' disaster such as a flood, mudslide or earthquake will be construed as a manifestation of ancestral displeasure.

Ironically, both Nick Nolte in 2000 and the Kuranko in 1969 have one thing in common – recourse to magical thought as a way of coming to terms with technologies that are not only new, but are clearly beyond their effective comprehension and control. One reimagines or conceives one's relationship to the technology in intersubjective terms, so that one may then manipulate, appease, or bargain with it in the same way that one seeks to manipulate, appease, or bargain with *people* who lie on the margins of one's immediate world. In other words, this magicality is governed by the intersubjective assumptions I have already alluded to – the notion, the necessary illusion, that THE universe as a whole is subject to the same rules of reciprocity that make life meaningful and viable in one's immediate SOCIAL universe – the everyday life world in which one is recognised, in which one's actions count and one's words make a difference. Thus, as I hammered away on my Olivetti portable, sitting on the porch of my house in Firawa, or drove my Land Rover over rubble tracks between remote villages, rumours spread in Kuranko that I had a djinn (*nyenne*) working for me. Such an alliance with a bush spirit would have come, for them, at a terrible cost – forfeiting the life of one's child or kinsman. Whether they thought I had made such a sacrifice in order to carry out my research I do not know (that my family did suffer on account of my work might be taken as evidence that this was so), but the reasoning was that everything in this world is governed by the rules of sociality – the unceasing give and take of intersubjective life. This magical reasoning is evident in Melanesian cargo cults. Indeed, the whole idea of kako (cargo) is based on the assumption that the relationship between blacks and whites is essentially and was originally a socio-moral relationship. Among the Tangu of the Madang district, northern New Guinea, this was compared to the reciprocal relation between elder brother (*ambwerk*) and younger brother (*tuman*) (Burridge 1969). Although Tangu people's pervasive *experience* of whites was of a people who did not act like social – that is to say moral – persons, who seemed self-centred, materialistic, and indifferent to family and community life (ibid: 150–151), in *practice* they sought to restore the socio-moral covenant that had allegedly existed with whites in the mythical past.

As with whites, so with rocks and hillsides – the unresponsiveness of the extrahuman world cannot be countenanced; there must be a way in which its likeness to one's own human world can be revealed, recovered and made the basis for social interaction. In cargo cults, redress is sought for the gross inequalities that have developed between blacks and whites: cargo cults are magical experiments in figuring out the right practical or ritual procedures to secure this return to economic reciprocity and social justice, to confirm the essentially social or intersubjective nature of the universe.

We see this same strategising whenever people encounter new technologies of communication. As in cargo cults, endless experimentation takes place as people struggle to strike a balance between incorporating the new and preserving the old (Lattas 1998: 267), though this is less a matter of conserving old practices than of sustaining a sense of being in control of the boundary between one's own world and the world of the other (Lattas 1998: 110). Consider for instance the advent of literacy among the New Zealand Maori in the early nineteenth century.

In the fifteen years after the establishment of the first European mission in the north of New Zealand in 1814, most Maori remained indifferent to literacy, and had to be bribed with trade goods like blankets and hatchets to remain in the missions. This pragmatic attitude to both Christianity and literacy existed, even after Maori began to see literacy as a possible answer to their growing ills. As Maori began to suffer the debilitating effects of European diseases, they were also demoralised by the manifest economic wealth and power of the newcomers. As they sought access to and control of the knowledge behind European power, Maori began to demand books, printed materials and writing equipment – a demand that far exceeded conversion to Christianity. In the words of one young chief in the Wanganui area, the 'pukapuka pakeha [European book] contains his thought' (Taylor 1868: 16). Other Maori compared books to muskets, or used fragments of print as charms, or fetishes capable of warding off bullets. One missionary noted that five bushels of potatoes were offered to the Weslayans for a single copy of a 117-page book of selections from the scriptures, the catechism, the liturgy and hymns, printed in 1830. Others observed that Maori sought anything in print – an old ship's almanac, a castaway novel, a few stitched leaves from a newspaper – and travelled great distances to get books. Long before missionaries penetrated the interior of the North Island, native catechists (many of whom were liberated slaves or commoners, seeking alternative avenues to *mana*) had gone ahead, establishing village schools. When the missionary Wade first visited the Waikato he encountered an exorbitant demand for printed matter and was told *E mate ana matou I te pukapuka kore* [We are sick from lack of books]. The price of four shillings per book proved no deterrent (Parr 1961). Indeed, by 1845 there was at least one Maori Testament for every two Maori people in New Zealand – a proportion which compared with any other country in the world (Wright 1959: 52–53). But at this time – which coincided with large-scale European settlement and the loss of Maori control over their lands, resources and autonomy – the interest in literacy dramatically waned, and Maori turned to new forms of political organisation and resistance as a way of controlling their increasingly dire and beleaguered situation (Jackson 1975).

The lesson to be drawn from the Maori 'conversion' to literacy in the decade between 1830 and 1840, and the wholesale repudiation of literacy from the beginning of the settlement period[2] is that people only embrace the new if it can be made to answer *their own needs* – not the needs others project onto them. For many Maori children today, the school is a place of demoralisation and defeat, a place where one learns that one is a failure. Under these circumstances, the only dignity lies in repudiating the institutions that are experienced as oppressive, even though one is told that education is the way of improving one's lot, and liberating oneself from a life without work, without a future. In other words, it is not technology per se – whether a technology of communication or a technology of medical care – that is in question, but a sense of the technology being inimical to one's need to feel that one is in command of one's own life. Thus, as colonisation led to the increasing alienation of Maori land, the undermining of Maori sovereignty, and the demoralisation of Maori people, many turned back to oral culture as a means of salvaging their *mauri* – their essence, their life. In this process, pakeha 'culture' came to be essentialised as 'materialistic' and 'imperialistic', hence inimical to *mauri Maori* (Maori spiritual vitality and cultural integrity). For many Maori today, extirpating or purging this alien and corrupting essence is not only a way of redressing *historical* wrongs but of reversing processes of *personal* degradation and loss – a theme that runs through the following *waiata haka* (dance poem) from the 1950s by Tuini Ngawai (cited in Dewes 1975: 58–59).

> Te matauranga o te Pakeha
> He mea whakato hei tinanatanga
> Mo wai ra?
> Mo Hatana?
> Kia tupato i nga whakawai
> Kia kaha ra, kia kaha ra.
> (Pakeha education
> is propagated
> for whose benefit?
> For Satan's
> Be wary of its temptations.
> Be strong and firm)

> Te matauranga o te Pakeha
> Patipati, a, ka muru whenua
> Kia kaha ra, e hoa ma
> Ka mutu ano
> Te tanga manawa
> Oranga, a oranga.
> (Pakeha education
> sucks you in then confiscates land.
> Be strong friends,
> Land is all we have
> To rest a throbbing heart
> And for our sustenance)

> Te matauranga o te Pakeha
> Ka tuari i te penihana oranga
> Hei aha ra?
> Hei patu tikanga
> Patu mahara
> Mauri e.
> (Pakeha education
> dispenses social security benefits.
> Why?
> To suppress customary ways,
> To confuse us,
> To kill our sacred and cultural spirits)

An Existentialist Critique of Globalisation

In volume one of his *History of Sexuality* (1978), Michel Foucalt speaks of a new modality of power that he calls 'bio-technico-power' –

the kind of power produced when the potentiality of the human body is augmented and expanded by technologies and techniques that improve or prolong life, create reproductive viability, enhance pleasure and otherwise make good the deficiencies and finitude of one's 'natural' endowment. Speaking of these new forms of 'biopower' and 'biosociality', Paul Rabinow not only endorses Foucault's vision of 'the practices of life as the most potent present site of new knowledges and powers' (1996: 92); he confidently asserts 'that the new genetics will prove to be a greater force for reshaping society and life than was the revolution in physics' (ibid: 98). But Rabinow fails to recognise that neologisms such as biopower and biosociality tend to disguise the ways in which the 'new genetics' is imbricated with the 'new' global capitalism – in which corporate and state interests in the north compete for control over this new form of power – in roughly the same way that the term eugenics – the 'old genetics' – once disguised insidious state programmes for the manipulation of individual fates and national destinies. This is why I think that any discussion of the new technologies of life must begin, not with an attempt to evaluate their ethical, economic and political implications for our future, but with a critique of the ways in which these technologies are *already* implicated in global patterns of inequality and injustice. As an anthropologist, my focus is understandably the ever-widening politico-economic gulf between north and south. This is why I feel it is imperative to counter the intellectual confidence of Paul Rabinow (1996) and Donna Haraway (1991), who see in biopower the dawning of a brave new world, with the cautionary, even cynical tone of several First Nation's calls for the urgent protection of indigenous cultural and intellectual property rights in the face of corporate bioprospecting, biopiracy and genetically engineered foods and crops. The caution and suspicion of the south stems, of course, from the fact that the south knows all too well, from its historical experience of colonisation, that the corporate, political, economic and even intellectual interests of the north are not only far removed from, but deeply inimical to, its own.

But though this power inequality between north and south seldom figures in contemporary critiques of biotechnology, it is another sense of the word 'power' that interests me. This is power defined not through its outward manifestations and instrumentalities, but inwardly, in the ways in which interpersonal life is mediated and experienced. Here, our analytical task is to understand 'what is at stake' for any individual, and how he or she feels that the balance between life and death, being and nothingness is changed by biotechnology.

But before elaborating further on this assertion I want to say a little more about the ways in which current discourse on biotechnology and biopower often shows the same objectivist bias that pervades discourse on globalisation. In both cases, so many untested assumptions are made about the ontological reality of the phenomena, that scant attention is paid to how these phenomena are actually apprehended, experienced, imagined and symbolically articulated by real human beings in the context of their actual social lives. This widespread avoidance of detailed and in-depth empirical, emic, or cross-cultural, explorations of biotechnology leads all too easily to the assumption that what the north thinks and feels, and how the north anguishes over the ethical issues, defines the agenda for all thought about biotechnology; the voice and views of the south may be different, but they are clouded by superstition and ignorance, and therefore only marginally relevant. It is my view, however, that it is precisely these marginalised and disempowered voices that should *determine* the agenda, because the central issue we face is the relationship of biotechnology to globalisation, and the relationship of both to power.

There is so much literature these days on globalisation that it is easy to be seduced by it – to believe that the over-production of academic writing on the subject and the mantra-like repetition of the term constitute evidence for its phenomenal reality and discursive salience. For me the most pressing questions are: who produces this discourse, for whom is it important, and is globalisation of truly global significance – in the sense that it matters deeply and in a similar way to every individual on earth – or is it rather, as Bourdieu puts it 'a myth in the strong sense of the word, a powerful discourse, an idée force, an idea which has social force, which obtains belief' (1998: 34)? By buying into the very idea of globalisation are we risking buying into yet another fetishised byproduct of the self-extolling discourse of capitalism, which has always sought to justify its particularistic interests with a universalistic rhetoric – what is best for the corporate giant being, by extension, what is good for the world. But one size fits all is the catchcry of the powerful, not of the powerless.

Consider Ulrich Beck's *World Risk Society* (1999) – a book that is powerful and persuasive. But though the book appeals to the academic Westerners' desire to be up with the play, to be ahead of the game, what exactly is the empirical, experiential and cross-cultural basis of Beck's arguments? Apart from quantitative data and personal impressions informed by independent thinking, astute reading and conferencing with colleagues – activities all confined to a relatively homogenous social class – there are no in-depth data offered and no insights given into how people outside the social circles in which Beck and his colleagues move actually LIVE the condition that the latter so confidently describe as 'the second modernity'. When such empirical research is carried out and published, as for example by Bourdieu and his colleagues in *La Misère du Monde* (1993) – the conclusions reached are very different. Where Beck, from a situation of personal security can predict and describe neutrally a society of 'endemic' or 'manufactured' uncertainty, a society without expert knowledge, only irreconcilable 'expert opinions', a society where 'intelligent technologies' make human work redundant, a democracy of shared risk rather than shared welfare, Bourdieu describes – in stories of pathological insecurity, illness, pain, distress, madness and poverty – the lived reality of such a society already existing on the margins of Europe, and concludes that from this point of view, globalisation is a euphemism with which global capitalism masks the misery it creates. And when Beck joins forces with Donna Haraway and Bruno LaTour, arguing that we should drop the nature-society dualism in favour of a *sociology of artefacts* or – as they put it – of *hybrids*, what value are we to put on indigenous people's insistence on a holistic approach to nature and society that, rather than abolish the distinction, seeks adjustment and balance between the two poles? Such differences are not primarily a matter for epistemological deliberation; they demand that we consider how knowledge may contribute to social justice.

Such is the case in recent dialogues between pakeha scientists and Maori in New Zealand over biogenetic technologies. Debates have centred on Maori resistance to the Human Genome Project ('an insidious expression of genetic capitalism'), on proposed amendments to euthanasia laws ('yet another technology of genocide'), on GE (genetic engineering) techniques for the biocontrol of noxious weeds and possums, on GE techniques of livestock breeding, and on bioprospecting of native flora and fauna. Mindful of New Zealand's bi-cultural constitution, the Labour government that came to power in 1999 saw that any radical division between Maori and non-Maori over the uses of gene technology would have serious consequences for the economic and cultural future of the nation. A Royal Commission on Genetic Modification was therefore established in May-June 2000 to receive submissions, convene meetings and organise workshops that would explore the issues. A considerable body of material now exists on the Royal Commission website (reports at: www.gmcommission.govt.nz) and elsewhere (e.g., www.ermanz.govt.nz on Maori objections to the Ruakura Research Centre's experiments in genetic modification [GM], a Nga Kaihautu video on GE issues, a report from the University of Auckland on 'Maori and Genetic Engineering' [Cram 2001], claims before the Waitangi Tribunal for intellectual property rights over native species) that provides insights into the cultural and political dimensions of the ongoing debate. While many pakeha see biocontrol as a practical solution to an environmental problem, Maori argue that transferring genetic material across species boundaries constitutes a dangerous, unprecedented and irreversible intervention in the natural order of things for, like mixing waters from different catchments or sources, moving genetic material from one species (a virus or parasite) to another (the possum) outrages *tikanga Maori* (the Maori way of doing things), disrupts the *whakapapa* (genealogy) and *mauri* (life essence) of those species, destroys a primordial balance between Ranginui (sky/father) and Papatuanuku (earth/mother), and by infringing these *tapus*, threatens the world with illness and degradation (Parliamentary Commissioner for the Environment 2000: 25–27).

However, when the Royal Commission completed its work, lip service was paid to respecting the Maori point of view, but politically it was ignored, the unspoken assumption being that European 'science' and Maori 'values' could not be placed on the same epistemological footing. Maori lawyer, Moana Jackson concludes a trenchant critique of this double standard, and the way it deploys value-laden terms to suggest an opposition between allegedly superior and inferior ways of reasoning, by pointing out that epistemology is not the issue; the issue is a political one of recognising that the Maori viewpoint is not an intellectual conceit but a matter of existential survival. 'For the issue is not just about the potential and unknown risks of GE but also the nature of the constitutional relationship that the Treaty sought to establish between our people and the Crown. On a matter that holds so many risks for what Maori submitters called the "ira tangata," it is not enough that we be heard with "exquisite politeness" and then marginalised. Our mokopuna [grandchildren] demand more' (Jackson 2001).

The New Divide between North and South

I think that events in Seattle and Davos are significant, not only because they signal that the World Trade Organisation is clearly not working – at least not working as American interests would like – but because they suggest that we in the academy might do well to be more critical of the discourse of globalisation that currently dominates our field. Seattle has brought home to us that for those inside the conferences, and those outside on the streets demolishing McDonald's, globalisation has very different resonances. These differences are not erased by the ingenuity with which the local reinvents tradition or creates cultural hybrids, but imply questions of survival, matters of life and death. For a well-heeled executive in a booming high-tech centre in downtown San Francisco, globalisation is synonymous with success and security; for a refugee from the recent civil war in Sierra Leone, now the poorest country in the world, globalisation means despair and disorder. George Bush's 'new world order' in the north has become the 'new world disorder' in the south, for the simple reason that as capital, both real, symbolic and imaginary, comes increasingly under the control of first world elites it slips beyond the reach of those in the localised backwaters of the poor world (Baumann 1998: 58–59). Globalisation thus connotes, at one extreme, confident, utopian fantasies of omnipotence, and at the other, a sense of things falling apart, of centres that do not hold, and of a radically diminished sense that one's voice, one's actions, or even one's existence matters or makes a difference to the way things are. And perhaps nowhere is this more apparent than in contemporary responses to biotechnology.

I said at the beginning of this chapter that technology, and by extension biotechnology, is fearful and threatening to the extent that it confronts us as extrahuman and thing-like – as something alien to our comprehension and outside our control. But this fear of things that we feel are not exactly 'of us', that do not seem to share our natural essence, that appear to have a life of their own, like the computer Hal in Stanley Kubrick's *2001: A Space Odyssey*, this fear has its source not in some instinctual antipathy to the unresponsiveness and 'otherness' of matter, but in our being social and our social being. We fear the inert, unresponsive, silent and alien appearance of the extrahuman world because we see mirrored and magnified in it our deepest *social* anxieties – that we will not be recognised, that our voices will not be heard, that our actions are without significance, that we are mere means to genetic ends that far outreach the time-scale of our conscious lives, and that we possess no more meaning than grains of sand on a beach or flotsam along a tideline. Our ambivalence toward biotechnology is born of the ambivalence that pervades all interpersonal life – the interactions that fill us with a sense of being subjects for ourselves yet are inevitably countermanded by others that reduce us to nothingness, the exchanges that provide the wherewithal for life only to be eclipsed by those that spell death, the gestures that create empathy one moment and antipathy the next, the gifts that are also poisons. Our relationship with technology encapsulates, articulates, and has its genesis in the ways we relate to one another.

Most approaches to the ambiguity of new technologies speak of these innovations as transgressing or blurring *conceptual* distinctions between nature and culture, the familiar and the foreign, self and other. Thus Suzanne Lundin: 'When one's own bodily substances are inhabited by foreign matter, a special boundary is transgressed; in this movement, not only the frames of the body are exploded but also established cultural categories for what is truly human' (1999: 17). Or Marilyn Strathern in *After Nature*: '... what is in crisis here is the symbolic order, the conceptualisation of the relationship between nature and culture such that one can talk about the one through the other' (1992: 177). Or Donna Haraway on cyborgs: 'creatures simultaneously animal and machine, who populate worlds ambiguously natural and crafted' (1991: 149). My argument is that it may be more edifying to see this ambiguity, not as a conceptual problem, a logical anomaly, a cognitive confusion, but as an inherent condition of intersubjective transitivity – where we are one moment merging with another (or another thing), the next distancing or separating from it. This fluent experience of being self only in relationship to not-self, of subject only in relation to another that is 'object' sets the scene, in my view, for the ambivalence we experience when confronted by new technologies – for a technology is, intersubjectively speaking, no different from another person, a tool, a thing, a stranger, or the earth; it has the potential to become a part of us, a condition of the possibility of being ourselves, but it is also a perpetual reminder of what we stand to lose in any relationship with what we see as 'other'.

If biotechnology has become a potent contemporary symbol of risk, and of life in a risk-society, this sense of risk and peril has to be understood, therefore, as rooted not in the technological innovations themselves but in the power relationships of interpersonal life, and the analagous power relations between north and south that are the contexts in which biotech innovations consolidate their reality. There is, however, another compelling reason why we cannot approach technology without reference to social context, and this is because so few of the ethical, health, environmental and public policy questions raised by the advent of biotechnology in the developed world can be answered by having recourse to expertise. Is gene modification medically and environmentally 'safe?' Will biotechnology help the developing world or simply widen the global gap between rich and poor? Is it possible to regulate or control biotechnology in the face of competition between governmental and corporate interests? Only time will tell. Accordingly, we are obliged, by default as it were, to focus on the very kinds of emic questions that anthropology has made its own, exploring the ways in which people in different cultures perceive, discuss, imagine, interpret and respond to biotechnology as both a practical and symbolic reality, while seeking to give voice, as we have always done, to those whose voices are so seldom heard in the conversation of the West.

Notes

1. A compelling parallel is documented in Barbara Bode's account of the aftermath of the earthquake that devastated the Callejón de Huaylas valley in Peru on 31 May 1970. The earthquake was provoked, many locals argued, by the Americans' landing human beings on the moon, and the French carrying out atomic tests on Mururoa atoll. 'It is all because of the scientists. What can we do?' observed one survivor (Bode 1990: chapter 12).
2. Although title deeds to land were carefully filed, Maori newspapers and political broadsheets disseminated, and records kept of important *rununga* (meetings), many old chiefs and tohunga objected to the use of writing, referring to written texts as *putea whakairo* ('repositories of crabbed markings') (Best 1959: 23).

Chapter 8

FAMILIAR AND
FOREIGN BODIES

> Human-machine relations are existential relations in which our fate and
> destiny are implicated, but which are subject to the very ambiguity found
> in all existential relations.
> Don Ihde (1979: 4)

Most current debates about new technologies attempt to decide
whether the innovations are good or bad, or how they may be regulated. That is to say, the discourse is either ethical or governmental. But
in focusing on how the effects of new technologies may be evaluated
and managed, these debates often leave unexplored the more immediately empirical issue as to how we actually experience and interact
with technologies, and how our attitudes toward them are linked to
perennial human anxieties about the strange, the new and the other.
My thesis in this chapter is an existential one. I take it as axiomatic that
all human beings need to have a hand in choosing their lives, and to be
recognised as having an active part to play in the shaping of their
social worlds. As a corollary, I approach the meaning of what people
say and do in terms of the degree to which they accomplish a balance
between controlling their own fate, collective or otherwise, and accepting that which cannot be decided by human will or subject to human
designs. To define meanings without reference to this intersubjective
dynamic is, in my view, practically meaningless. Thus, an anthropology of 'human-machine interaction' is unedifying while it insists that
human intersubjectivity is reducible to cognitive schemata and com-
municative 'rationality' (e.g., Suchman 1987: 1).

Notes for this section can be found on page 141.

Over the last twenty years, several scholars have demonstrated that technology and society are intimately interconnected. Inspired by Heidegger's famous 1954 lecture on technology, Don Ihde's seminal *Technics and Praxis* argued that 'Human-machine relations are existential relations in which our fate and destiny are implicated, but which are subject to the very ambiguity found in all existential relations' (1979: 4). Although Ihde sees these existential relations as rooted in the lifeworld, he does not, however, explore the specifically social character of these relations. In anthropology, Tim Ingold echoes Ihde's repudiation of the split between technology and society, arguing that 'technical relations are embedded in social relations, and can only be understood within this relational matrix, as one aspect of human sociality' (1997: 107), though he says little about how this embeddedness is experienced, while Pierre Lemonnier's work on the 'social representation' of technologies tends to reduce the *experience* of technology to cognitive, formal and informational *models* (1992: 79–85). Bryan Pfaffenberger makes a powerful case against the 'standard view' of technology – as a body of techniques and material objects that answer human needs yet remain separate from ourselves – by describing the intimate and complex interactions that bind technology, human labour and social relationships into a 'sociotechnical system' (1988b, 1992). Recently, Gary Lee Downey has explored the blurred boundaries between technology and society by focusing on how such boundaries are variously 'drawn and lived in everyday experiences' (1998: 27). And anthropological studies of 'biographical objects' and 'the social life of things' – all of which trace their genealogy to Marx's insights into the experience of labour (Marx 1964: 89–91, Marx and Engels 1976:43) – have made us more acutely aware of the complex ways in which objects become personalised and persons become objectified in the course of social life (Appadurai 1986, Miller 1991, Hopkins 1998, Hornborg 2001).

In this chapter I pick up the existential-phenomenological threads in this body of work, and seek to demonstrate how this perspective may be more systematically explored. Methodologically, this entails bracketing out, or setting aside, questions concerning the large-scale social impact of new technologies in order to explore the intersubjective dynamics of the human encounter with technology.

Technology and Intersubjectivity

In his 1954 lecture on technology, Heidegger noted that technology (*tekhnê*) should not to be confused with techniques, and so reduced to mere instrumentality. Technology is an aspect of our human existence, 'a mode of knowing', that brings forth and makes apparent the very essence of our being (Heidegger 1977: 294–295).

For anthropologists, being is quintessentially social. We are social before we are anything else. Observes Merleau-Ponty: 'The social is already there when we come to know or judge it ... it exists obscurely and as a summons' (1962: 362).

What is it, then, that technology reveals to us about this field of social being?

I begin by noting that the social is *lived* as a network of reciprocal relationships among subjects, that is to say intersubjectively. This implies, first, that human beings everywhere tend to conceive of subjectivity not only as encompassing others *but* as extending into the extrahuman world, with the result that objects, words and ideas tend to become imbued with consciousness and will (Jackson 1998: 9). Although human worldviews tend to enshrine hard and fast distinctions between humans and animals, or living and non-living things, these distinctions tend to be transgressed in practice and in the imagination, so that in explaining events retrospectively people will have recourse to sophistry as well as technical aids in deciding whether impersonal and transpersonal *forces* were at work (ancestors, gods, or natural, cultural, historical and biogenetic preconditions, for instance) or personal *intentions* (love, witchcraft, ill-will, goodwill for instance), as well as how these may have combined to produce certain effects (see Gluckman 1956: 84–85). This is what Zande refer to as deciding between the 'first spear' and the 'second spear' (Evans-Pritchard 1934: 59), and suggests that in all societies people wrestle with the question of deciding the relationship between those things for which persons may be held accountable, and those things for which they cannot.

While the tendency to act as if the object world were obedient to the ground rules of interpersonal life helps us cope with what George Devereux calls 'the trauma of the unresponsiveness of matter'(1967: 32–34), it remains largely illusory and variable.[1] As with alien others, the world of the extra-human contradicts our anthromorphic assumptions and proves refractory to our intersubjective strategies of constructive engagement and control. It may be comforting to believe that we can negotiate reciprocal agreements with enemies, appease the unruly elements with sacrificial gifts, or strike bargains with the gods, but in reality the extrahuman world impacts upon us in unpredictable and ungovernable ways.

This brings me to a second point about intersubjective relations. They are characterised by struggle. To some extent we may see this as a struggle against alienation, though alienation understood as more than just the estrangement of a worker from his or her production. Thus, although Marx's main focus was on how a person loses himself in the object on which he labours, an object which then 'confronts him as something hostile and alien' (Marx 1961: 70), he also noted that a person may lose himself in alienating relationships with others – including the gods. 'The estrangement of man, and in fact every relationship in which man stands to himself, is first realised and expressed in the relationship in which a man stands to other men' (Marx 1961: 78). Intersubjective struggle also bears some resemblance to Darwin's struggle for survival, but the will-to-be cannot be reduced to the satisfaction of physical needs, the perpetuation of one's own species-being, or even the continuity of one's own society, for the scarce goods we compete for, lay claim to or exchange, on the grounds that they are essential to our existence, are frequently elusive, indeterminate and unstable qualities such as health, wealth, power, position, recognition, knowledge, dignity, happiness and love. Though our very existence is felt to depend on the possession of such 'symbolic goods', accessing and controlling them is difficult to achieve and almost impossible to fix. We are thus susceptible to feeling that being itself – in the form of everything from a sense of hope, a sense of purpose, a fulfilling job, a compliment, an improvement in our lot or time to ourselves – is something that must be constantly striven for. But to emphasise that this struggle for being occurs between people and not just vaguely, in relation to the world, is also to emphasise that in all human relationships the other is potentially a source of fulfillment *and* frustration, of being *and* nonbeing. And this ambiguity inheres in our relationships with both human and extra-human 'others', since in various contexts persons, animals, gods, spirits, material objects and technologies all hold the potential to sustain our lives or end them

Psychoanalysis traces this ambiguity back to the period of primary intersubjectivity when an infant's dependence on the mother entails both affirmation and negation. As Devereux puts it, 'The prototype of all panic caused by a lack of response is the reaction of the infant to the absence, or temporary unresponsiveness, of its mother' (1967: 32). Although we should be careful not to reduce all forms of sociality to the mother-infant bond, it is generally the case that human beings have great difficulty in coming to terms with the fact that others are seldom straightforward extensions of themselves, and that distant others are not governed by the same ground rules that govern interaction with those we like to call our own. It is in this unstable relationship between self and other – and by extension, between human and extrahuman worlds – that our ambivalent attitudes to technology arise. Rather like the body in Cartesian thought, technologies are sometimes seen as extensions of ourselves – and as such, subject to our will. But at other times they are felt to be alien, invasive forms of non-being that subjugate us, undermining our very notion of who and what we are. Nowadays it is often argued that developments in cybertechnology and gene technology have all but abolished the boundary between nature and culture, automaton and autonomy, humans and things. And it is already a cliché that information technology has brought all humanity together in a single global village. Such views, however, do not reflect universal experience. Confidently objectivist in tone (e.g., Gray 1995), these arguments seldom take into account the numerous contexts in which doubt, anxiety or powerlessness tend to make people dread such erasures of the line between themselves and others, or themselves and machines. In this respect the discourse on technology and the discourse on migrants and marginalised others run together, for both raise critical questions concerning not only our capacity to conceptualise the supposedly extrahuman as human *but our ability to actually incorporate and control it.*

The hypotheses I want to explore in the following pages are, first, that our human ambivalence toward new technologies must be understood against the background of our ambivalence toward others, and second, that the ways in which we experience our relationships with both persons and machines will depend upon *the degree to which we feel in control of these relationships, as well as the degree to which these relationship are felt to augment rather than diminish our own sense of wellbeing.*

Encountering New Technologies

My 9-year-old son, Joshua, is playing a 'hard version' of a game on his Gameboy. The game is not going well for him. He flings down the machine, and walks away, tears of frustration in his eyes. 'It's not fair!' he exclaims. 'What's not fair?' I ask. 'It isn't fair. If you miss just one thing the game ends. It should give you another chance to get something. But it keeps on making me lose.' It is not uncommon to hear people speak of their relations with machines in much the same way as they speak of their relations with people. When the relationship 'works', differences between self and other are experienced as complementary rather than antagonistic: everything is under control, reciprocity is balanced, self and other seem to be as one. But when the machine does not conform to human expectations of reciprocity or fair play, we get distressed and angry, much as we would if a person behaved unfairly toward us or failed to acknowledge a gift.

Consider, for example, human relations with computers. In his ethnographic fieldwork in a computer lab (1998), Gary Lee Downey observed numerous instances of 'boundary blurring activities'. When he asked students directly if they 'ever felt themselves merged with the machine' (ibid: 147), most responded defensively; they did not want to appear as 'geeks' who were more comfortable with machines than persons, and did not want to seem irrational or animistic (though one student admitted 'I'd probably say that I'm one with the computer' (ibid: 148). However, despite the students' reluctance to admit to any kinship with a machine, Downey's empirical observations led him to conclude that their experience of the boundary between themselves and their machines was continually shifting along a continuum: at times the students experienced agency as if it were located within them, sometimes as if it were located within the machine, sometimes somewhere in-between (ibid: 238).[2]

Although from an objective point of view a person and a machine are manifestly different entities, an experiential point of view reveals the extent to which our sense of being either essentially different from or symbiotically merged with a machine is a function of how we interact with it – specifically, how much we feel we understand it and how much control we feel we have over it. When this knowledge/control is lost, as Downey observed, people often feel vulnerable, frustrated, and outraged, as if the machine had somehow invaded them or taken something from them (ibid: 185–192).

Let us consider in more detail the kinds of things that happen when our relationships with machines 'do not work', or 'break down'.[3]

Some of the most sophisticated innovations in contemporary medical technology have been in the field of radiology. But new imaging technologies such as CT scanners pose problems of adaptation and understanding for radiologists, and problems of organisation for the departments in which they work. In a study of four community hospitals in Massachusetts, Stephen Barley observed several strategies staff used to deal with the anxieties and difficulties they experienced with the new technology. Some of these were 'ritual' strategies that created the impression that there was no problem, such as rebooting or downloading the computer when problems arose, and so making the problem 'disappear'. Others involved attributing technical problems to mechanical failures, as if recourse to the language of the old technology could alleviate one's anxieties in dealing with the new. Still others were 'magical' in character, and involved addressing the computer as if it were a person. Barley's comments on this anthropomorphism are worth quoting at length:

> As used by the techs, 'THE COMPUTER' implied a mysterious force which, if not malevolent, was surely fickle.
> ... THE COMPUTER was said to be capricious; it had, in the techs' own words, 'a mind of its own.' THE COMPUTER was a sentient entity that 'liked' or 'did not like' commands, that acted 'crazy,' and that beeped when it wanted to say, 'I'm hot.' In the throes of a persistent problem, technologists beseeched THE COMPUTER to do as they desired, and the bold among them even insulted THE COMPUTER with word and gesture.

Most important, however, when events went irretrievably wrong, it was THE COMPUTER that was said to have caused the problem. Although THE COMPUTER always lurked in the background, the techs usually kept it at bay with their mechanical metaphors, their confirmatory strategy of problem solving, and the ritual solutions and superstitions that the confirmatory strategy engendered. It was only when these practical tools failed that techs resorted to anthropomorphic talk. To say THE COMPUTER was a cause was, in effect, to admit that one didn't know what was wrong. (Barley 1988: 520)

Two insights are provided here into what I shall call the intersubjective imaginary. First, the computer is addressed not as if it were an alien object, but as something with which a reciprocal, symbiotic relationship is possible. As a corollary of this, the technicians' failures to understand or control the computer led them to behave toward it as they would behave toward a perverse or obdurate person – either ignoring it, or trying to force it into a more responsive relationship with them. However, it is generally when relationships with a machine (or person) suffer 'irreparable damage' that people begin to construct the other in terms of radical otherness – as an enemy, an alien, a threat. In this sense, the 'breakdown' of relations with a machine, or within a marriage, or between two nations all tend to entail similar compensatory strategies and counter strategies, whereby individuals seek to recover their own lost or compromised being.

Sartre's phenomenology of the emotions (1948) offers useful insights into these compensatory strategies, though I share Pfaffenberger's view that we would do well to bracket out questions as to whether 'a given activity "works" (i.e., is "technical") or "doesn't work" (i.e., is "magico-religious")' (1992: 501).

Sartre's argument centres on the strong *emotions* that are stirred in us when we feel that machines have ceased to do our bidding, or start behaving in incomprehensible ways. This emotionality may be considered in two ways. First, strong emotions spontaneously arise when we are frustrated in our attempts to comprehend and control others or objects. But second, and most importantly, we work on and play up these emotions, making them the means whereby we 'magically' recover our sense of lost power over others or objects. Nursing ill-will toward an enemy, cursing an errant computer, kicking a flat tyre or pitying oneself for one's inability to stand up to a tyrant, will not necessarily effect any change in the behaviour of the object or other, but it may reverse one's experience *of one's relationship with it*. One becomes, imaginatively and retrospectively, the determining subject of the events that reduced one to the status of an object.

Clearly, when we are blocked from acting, emotionality is only one strategy for recovering our existential footing. We also focus on words, thoughts and on our own bodies. Thus, in cursing a machine we cannot understand or manipulate, or in recounting a story about some humiliating event, or in inflicting injuries upon our own bodyself, we displace the role of the other, and recapture a sense of our own subjectivity – of ourselves as actors rather than acted upon, as authors of meaning rather than victims of circumstance.

The problem is that this process involves splitting self from other – a split that may become entrenched and habitual, as in Luddite views of technology, chauvinist views of asylum seekers, and racist views of foreign bodies.

In turning now to the field of allotransplantion, I want to probe more deeply the existential conditions and the limits under which human beings can encompass radical otherness.

Between Self and Other: a Phenomenology of Allotransplantation

Though organ transplants (allotransplants) are often spoken of as 'gifts of life' these gifts are ambiguous. This is not simply because a death is the precondition for the bestowal of this gift. It is because the giving of the gift is not grounded in any immediate social relationship between recipient and donor. As such the gift is asocial, and resembles an alienated object, a commodity. This otherness of the donated organ creates feelings of deep ambivalence, disorientation and anxiety in recipients. 'Sometimes I feel born again,' noted one individual, 'Sometimes I am very depressed' (in Forsberg et al. 2000: 331). This emotional confusion often precipitates an identity crisis: 'Who am I? Where do I come from? I was completely dizzy. It was like the familiar me but the safety I had felt was no longer there. Instead there was a new person.' These crises reflect not simply the 'foreignness' of the organ, but the anomalous *relationship* of recipient and donor – the incorporation into the bodyself of a vital organ that belonged to a complete stranger, that is, so to speak, quintessentially not-self. This problem is undoubtedly exacerbated in cases of xenotransplantation (cross-species transplantation), when the organ is from an animal, and in xenophobic societies, where there may be strong resistance to receiving organs from foreign, 'soul-less' sources (Papagaroufali 1996:251). Yet in every case, the struggle to incorporate or assimilate that which is construed as 'other' is directly comparable to the struggle that, for example, characterises the incorporation of in-marrying wives in societies with patrilocal residence, or the accommodation of immigrants, refugees and outsiders in countries of asylum. What kind of reciprocity will exist between us and them?

Before detailing some of the intersubjective strategies that are typically used to imagine or negotiate some kind of identification with the 'other', let us look at a case of transplantation where this struggle between familiar and foreign was absent, for it helps us see the extent to which the trauma of transplantation is a function of the experiential distance that exists between recipient and donor.

Valerie and Andrew Milne first met in 1993 through a lonely-hearts column and married two years later. In March 1999, Andrew, 46, was diagnosed with an acute kidney infection. Valerie, 40, proved to be a perfect donor match, and the transplantation took place a year later.

Andrew comments:

> The transplant made us feel more at one that we were before. We were pretty close then, but we have an extra-special relationship now. I've got a part of her inside me now. It's strange, Valerie is a chocoholic. Before the operation, I never ate chocolate, but afterwards, I craved it. It seemed her kidney had transferred her addiction to me. (Price 2001: 18)

What is compelling here is the image of union – of one incorporated in another, as in a love-match or marriage. Valerie comments:

> When I found out that I had the same blood type as Andy, I had an overpowering feeling that I wanted to donate him one of my kidneys. It was the same type of feeling I had when I first met him and I knew we were meant to be together. (ibid: 18)

This sense of intersubjective mergence – variously expressed in images of entwined destinies, spiritual affinity, marriage, friendship or kinship – is not uncommon in cases of organ donation, *but in almost every case it has to be contrived and created.* Not surprisingly, it is the logic of balanced reciprocity that governs the creation of this intersubjective imaginary. Sometimes this takes the form of donors demanding reciprocity for the gift of life by seeking to establish 'long-term social relationships with recipients' (Sharp 1995: 365), or of transplant recipients trying to establish a social relationship with the donor's surviving kin. Sometimes an intersubjective relationship between self and donor will be cultivated symbolically. Consider, for example, the case of Sandy, who received a cadaveric kidney from a woman who was killed in an automobile accident. When her body began to reject the transplanted organ, Sandy focused her 'mind' on making her body accept the kidney. 'And the only words I can put on it are just, it was sort of like, you know, "Welcome" to this new kidney. You know, 'Welcome, kidney, this is your body. This is your home." I've never been so focused on anything, ever' (Bloom 1992: 323). In the case of Lena, for whom 'all living things are part of a flow, a system of constant give and take,' it was easy to be reconciled to receiving the organ of a 'stranger' (Lundin 1999: 22–24). Likewise for Sylvia, who argued that 'there are invisible links between people' that are reinforced by the ability of donor cells to remember their origins (ibid: 18).

For individuals who see the world as more deeply divided into mutually incompatible domains (animals/humans, humans/machines) the work of reconciliation is more arduous. Some individuals are fearful that they will incorporate unwanted traits of the donor's personality, while others anxiously seek assurances that the organ is clinically sterile – cleansed of its association with the symbolically 'dirty' world of not-self (ibid: 12). Often, as with Sandy, recipients personalise the organ they have received. In one case, the recipient baptised the liver she had received, and gave it a name. 'In the beginning it was something unfamiliar which was left to me to take care, I walked around holding it like when I was pregnant. I was surrounding the liver with my hands the way you hold your stomach during pregnancy. As time went on it was more like a gift which ought to be treasured' (in Forsberg et al. 2000: 332–333). Typically, too, recipients feel concern, regret, sorrow, and guilt that someone should die in order for them to live (Weems and Patterson 1989: 30; Sharp 1995: 380; Forsberg et al. 2000: 330), as if they had received a gift at another person's expense. To redress this imagined imbalance and reciprocate the gift of life, patients often conjure strong emotions of gratitude toward the donor, and the same compelling logic of reciprocity often gives rise to the kind of binding relationship, physical identification and indebtedness between recipient and donor that we associate with balanced reciprocity and direct exchange. But because the gift *cannot* be fully reciprocated, there is often an emotional contradiction between the assumption of affinity and the practical problem of reciprocating the gift. Fox and Swazey (1972) speak of this as 'the tyranny of the gift' (cited in Sharp 1995: 365). At the same time, because official medical discourse dismisses anthropomorphism as irrational, these stratagems of the imaginary are often at odds with the objectivist, commoditising, depersonalised language preferred by surgeons and other transplant professionals (Sharp 1995: 378–382).

In sum, it is difficult for human beings to entertain or tolerate an intimate, intercorporeal relationship with the world they think of as not-self. Yet when one's life depends on entering into such a relationship and receiving the gift of life from someone who is radically other, people have recourse to the strategies of reciprocity in order to make the relationship viable.

Anthropomorphism

The implicit argument of this chapter has been for seeing the classic antinomies of reason and emotion, body and mind, self and other, nature and culture, subject and object not as competing ontologies, but as terms we deploy, variously and often interchangeably, to capture different modalities or moments of intersubjective experience – the sense that we are at times actors, in control of our situations, and at other times at the mercy of circumstances, and acted upon. In exploring how identity terms such as self and other are largely determined by the ways we interact with one another, I have suggested that the ways we think, act and reason are grounded in the forms and experiences of sociality – specifically of reciprocity – and that these are universal.

Yet we still persist in seeing some societies as collectively governed by anthropomorphism, and others by scientific rationality – or some by the logic of gifts, and others by the commodified logic of the marketplace. It is the same kind of division that led to the classic anthropological division between hi-tech and low-tech societies.

In Kroeber's seminal 1917 essay on 'The Superorganic', culture is etherealised; it is not only 'extrasomatic' but excludes material culture and most of what we would classify as technology (Jackson 1989: 121; Pfaffenberger 1992). This idealist split between culture and technology is central to Plato, and implicates other discursive divisions between theory and practice, and mind and body (Ihde 1979: xix–xxiv). And this bias against technology, embodiment and practice in philosophy presages the same bias in anthropology. In both cases, the world is divided into a world of subjects and a world of objects (the body often being assimilated, along Cartesian lines, to the object world as mere instrumentality, as *res extensa*). Phenomenologically, however, subject and object are not stable entities but simply words we give to two extreme modalities of human interaction – being an actor and being acted upon, being a 'who' and being a 'what'. To speak of intersubjectivity is to recognise that objects appear sometimes to be animated by human consciousness and will, and human subjects appear sometimes to be like objects, treated as if they were mere things. It is also to abandon attempts to draw a hard and fast ontological distinction between subjective and objective domains, for experience is continually switching between quite various senses of self and other depending on the context and character of the interaction. As Downey's ethnography makes clear, even 'human' agency is not a fixed attribute of persons; it will be *experienced* as oscillating between self to machine depending on how well the person-machine relationship is working (1998: 238).

Historically, the subject-object split, like the body-mind dichotomy, may be understood as a discursive strategy for drawing a line between ourselves and animals, and ourselves and things. Once this split is made, it is all too easy to associate anthropomorphic or animistic thinking with primitives, children or the insane, and reason made definitive of one's own privileged preserve. Empirically, however, this distinction is neither substantial nor stable. It is not even that we project human consciousness and will onto machines, or try to imagine machines as persons, for intersubjectivity so shapes our experience from early infancy that it constitutes a 'natural attitude' toward the world into which we find ourselves thrown – a world that includes persons, machines, words, ideas and other creatures. It is thus no mystery that human beings should speculate over whether computers 'think', or ask whether machines will 'save' us or pose a 'threat' to our existence; the questions are grounded in the habits of sociality well before they find expression in ethical or governmental debates, and reflect the ambiguity of all intersubjective life – the question as to whether the other, with whom I have yet formed no primary bond, is with or against me, friend or foe.

But my principal concern is neither the history of ideas nor epistemology, but the pragmatics of coping in everyday life. In trauma, the splits alluded to above between body and mind, and person and machine, figure among the strategies people use when trying to make good an existential loss, or regain a sense of comprehension and control. As a general principle, people tend to turn from or flee the source of their distress and take refuge in some surrogate object that they feel more comfortable with, that they feel they 'know' and can 'deal with'. If body is imagined to be split from mind, then body is made an object on which subjectivity can go to work, but from a safe distance as it were. 'You feel betrayed,' said one individual after liver transplantation. 'You can't trust your own body. In spite of all it hasn't become part of me' (cited in Forsberg et al. 2000: 332). In her research among infertile couples, Tine Tjørnhøj-Thomsen also observed that infertility can make a person feel guilty about, or betrayed by, her body, though this loss of control over the 'object body' is made good by various imaginative strategies of displacement and blaming. Thus one woman reasoned, 'Maybe it is because I led a wild life in my young days; maybe my infertility is caused by some drugs my mother took during pregnancy.' Said another: 'It is good to know that it is not me, but something chemical in my body' (Tjørnhøj-Thomsen in press).

A similar process of splitting separates words from world, enabling one to make use of language – particularly in the form of storytelling – as a way of obliquely and surreptitiously regaining a sense of mastery over events one has suffered passively or in silence (Jackson

2002a). And in the face of anxieties provoked by new gene technologies, many people seek to reinscribe the blurred boundaries between nature and culture, or the human and the divine in the belief that if nature and the divine are separate domains they may become places of refuge. The same principle may apply to the splitting of machines and men. But as the poignant case of Joey – 'a mechanical boy', reported by Bruno Bettelheim (1959), shows, some people may find refuge in machines where others find refuge in the world of other human beings. Unloved and rejected by his parents and starved of all human contact, Joey repudiated the human world altogether and came to imagine himself as a machine – ruled by mechanical routines and needs, and bereft of feeling. Though Joey was stuck with his belief, such fantasies are typical of the ways human beings invest in things that give them security when other objects of their will, affection or desire, thwart and negate them.

Within the field of intersubjectivity, then, the object of our focus is continually shifting. What governs these shifts is the degree to which we feel existentially fulfilled. When a person experiences a radical diminution of his or her being in relation to another person or an object, he or she will seek to compensate for this loss by focusing on or identifying with a person or object where he or she feels recognised, complemented or affirmed. Thus, in his study of software hackers and phone phreakers, Bryan Pfaffenberger notes that many of these marginalised individuals were seeking recognition, approval, prestige and a greater sense of self-worth from a 'central authority', in much the same way as a neglected child might seek to capture the attention and love of a negligent parent by misbehaving in a clever and audacious way, regaining 'entry to a world that has denied them' (1988a: 44).

As I noted in chapters 6 and 7, the problem with these compensatory strategies is that they are Manichean. That is to say that by affirming one object, one other or one world, the antithetical pole becomes an essentialised and scapegoated symbol of absolute negativity. Thus men, anxious about their control of the social world, conjure the image of the witch as the embodiment of chaos. Or nationalists engage in xenophobic rhetoric and conjure images of the minatory other in order to bolster their own sense of being. Or Luddites destroy all technology in their desperation to restore their sense of being in step with history.

Can we avoid these Manichean excesses? To what extent can we *live* with boundary blurring?

Critique of the Nature-Culture Opposition

Several recent writers have observed that the new gene technologies
render the opposition between nature and culture obsolete. Because
we can now manipulate genetic processes, the boundary between natural selection and cultural selection is blurred, and 'the 'natural' and
the 'social' are no longer to be seen as ontologically different' (Haraway 1991; Rheinberger 2000: 19). Paul Rabinow calls this
hybridised condition 'biosociality', for nature becomes 'modelled on
culture understood as practice' with the consequences that 'culture
becomes natural' and nature becomes 'artificial' (1996: 99). There
are three problems with this sort of pronouncement. The first is ethnographic. Although technologies such as xenotransplantation (gene
transfers between humans and other species) and transgenesis
(humans receiving human organs) are new, there is abundant evidence that ritual and intellectual techniques for crossing the boundaries between animal and human domains (shapeshifting, totemism),
or between nature and culture (fetishism, anthropomorphism), occur
in all societies and at all times. Indeed, 'primitives' possibly have no
more or less investment in the separation of nature and culture than
'we' do. The second point is political. If indigenous people insist on the
strict separation of the human sphere on the one hand, and the sphere
of divine or natural life on the other, it is often not primarily a statement of belief (cognitive commitment) but a strategic defence of local
interests and rights against new technologies over which they feel they
have little control or comprehension. Thus, in a submission to the
Royal Commission on Genetic Modification, the Maori Congress
declared that 'the Maori genome is a cultural resource ...' and that
'Maori have the right to control their resources as their own ... according to specific cultural preferences'. But the political agenda behind
this assertion is revealed in the ensuing clause: 'Most of the previous
160 years has been characterized by Pakeha indifference to Maori cultural and spiritual values associated so intimately with their lands and
their natural biodiversity' (Royal Commission on Genetic Modification
2001, Form 1: 1).[4]

My third criticism is phenomenological, and brings me back to a
recurring theme of this book – that lived reality cannot be reliably
inferred from the way reality is discursively constructed and cogni-
tively represented. Although we may ontologise, essentialise, reify or
actively deny the symbolic contrast between culture and nature, or
self and other, it is important to see these contrasts as part of the
rhetorical strategies we deploy in struggling to strike a balance
between our familiar, local worlds, in which we feel we have the right
to command our own destinies, and a world of otherness, governed

variously by global forces, by the gods, by contingency or elemental powers, in which we feel far less in command, and of which we have much less understanding.

To seek absolute separation between these domains is but one way of managing relations between them – hence the Maori Council's decision to keep biotechnology out of the Maori lifeworld as a way of defending 'effective *rangatiratanga*' (Maori autonomy). Such declarations do not however, preclude the possibility of seeking rapprochement between opposing domains; indeed, Maori have done just this vigorously on economic, political, educational and cultural fronts from the first years of contact and colonisation. What decides the difference between building walls and building bridges is, as in any intersubjective encounter, the degree to which a person or group feels ontologically secure. The less one's sense of comprehension and control the more one is likely to split self from other and construct the other as alien, minatory, dirty or dangerous. To rephrase the famous Marxian formulation, we could say that when we do not feel existentially threatened by things, relations between things assume the form of relations between persons, but when we feel existentially threatened by other people, relations between people assume the form of relations between things.

Notes

1. Consider, for instance, the following lonely-hearts columnist's advice to a woman who 'could not bear being on her own in her single-bed flat': 'If Elaine can look around her flat and see that everything in it, from the cat to the washing-up liquid to the very air itself, is as dependent on her for its useful existence as she is dependent on it, she may get great comfort. It sounds crazy, but if she can imagine that, say, the electric blender is actually looking back at her, as she looks at it, she may find a huge sense of calm coming over her. Oh, stop laughing. Just try it' (Ironside 2001: 19).
2. Devereux's work on the moveable boundary between 'I' and 'not-I' and the experience of inside/outside anticipates this point (Devereux 1967: 321–328).
3. In the following discussion I bracket out questions concerning the content of what is communicated via electronic means.
4. Nancy Scheper-Hughes dramatically makes a similar point, referring to the stories that circulate in the poor world about organ stealing. 'The rumours express the subjectivity of subalterns living in a "negative zone" of existence where lives and bodies are experienced as a constant crisis of presence (hunger, sickness, injury) on the one hand, and as a crisis of absence and disappearance on the other. The stories are told, remembered, and circulated because they are *existentially* true' (1996: 9, emphasis in text).

Chapter 9

THE PROSE OF SUFFERING

... and I realised then the unmitigable chasm between all life and all print
– that those who can, do, those who cannot and suffer enough because
they can't, write about it.
William Faulkner (1967: 262)

The subject of this chapter had its beginnings in my conversations and encounters with refugees in Freetown, Sierra Leone, in the wake of that country's decade-long civil war. My theme is suffering – how it is borne and how it is explained – by people in very different circumstances. It is difficult to do justice to what people suffered in the Sierra Leone conflict, but one may perhaps venture to describe how people responded to their suffering. And here I want to emphasise something that struck me years ago, living and working in Kuranko villages – the way people are taught to accept adversity, and endure it. It is the overriding lesson of initiation, when pain is inflicted on neophytes so that they may acquire the virtues of fortitude and imperturbability. It is pertinent that the Kuranko word for pain (*dime*) admits no distinction between physical, mental and social distress. Moreover, pain is seen as an unavoidable part of life; it can neither be abolished nor explained away; what matters most is how one suffers and withstands it. This is nicely expressed in a Kuranko proverb that exploits the fact that the words *dununia* (load) and *dunia* (world) are near homonyms – *dunia toge ma dunia; a toge le a dununia* ('the name of the world is not world; it is load' i.e., the weight of the world is a matter of how one comports oneself. According to this view, life is a struggle between one's inner resources and external conditions. Expressed in a more existential vein, one might say that human existence is a struggle to strike some kind of balance between being an actor and being acted upon. In the

Notes for this section can be found on page 157.

stories that follow, this balance between being an actor and being acted upon has been catastrophically lost. I begin with scenes from a Freetown refugee camp, then turn to a consideration of what Luc Boltanski (1999) has called suffering at a distance – the kind of suffering that liberal Westerners are wont to experience when confronted by the pain, distress and misery of others, and find themselves at a loss to do anything about it. I conclude with a critique, based on my observations in Sierra Leone, of the way suffering is commonly construed in the affluent West.

The displaced people's camp in Cline Town had once been a foundry. Only a stone's throw from the warehouses and workshops of the waterfront, it was now a complex of semi-derelict buildings and laterite yards.

Abandoned lathes and metal presses lined the interior of a vast corrugated iron shed. Outside, in the shade of similar buildings, scores of women sat on wooden stools, selling tomato paste, onions, magi cubes, okra and cassava leaf – ingredients for sauces that few could afford. Meat and fish were non-existent.

I picked my way past a group of kids playing soccer with a half-deflated ball, and headed toward a row of makeshift huts – white plastic UN tarps over frames of lashed poles – hoping to continue the conversations I had begun the day before. My aim was to write down what people wanted to tell me. As it turned out, some people wanted to recount their stories of the war, while others simply wanted me to record their names in my notebook or leave them my name and address, as if this would create a tenuous connection with the world outside the camp, a glimmer of hope.

'I was in Kono,' Adama Sisay said, 'when the rebels entered there. I was a business woman. I lost everything. We left Kono and walked on foot to Makeni [about eighty miles], and then to Kabala [another seventy -five miles] where I started over. When the rebels attacked Kabala in 1994 we ran away to Freetown. During the intervention in 1997 [when President Tejan Kabbah's government was overthrown by a section of the armed forces, led by Major Johnny Paul Koroma], soldiers looted everything we had. I went back to Kabala. That same year we were attacked again. We fled to the bush. We had no food to eat for a week. We came back from the bush and were told to stay in town. I had two sons. One is here. The other is sick. We have no money, no ointment, no medicine. I lost everything. When we came back to Freetown I was staying in Kabba town. I tried to start another life there. On January 6, 1999, when the junta entered the city, they burned down our house. They wanted to kill me. But God stayed their hand. We ran into the bush. When we came back to the city, they brought me to this camp. That is my whole story.'

'Did you know any of the rebels, or did any of them know you?'
I asked.

'Some school friends of mine in Kabala, I had to hide from them.
They would have killed me.'

'Did they have anything against you?'

'Well, if you have seen them, you know who they are, and if you get
away you might tell others I saw such and such a person there'.

'So they kill to keep their identity secret?'

'Yes.'

'What is the hardest thing about your life here now?'

'The hardest thing is that I don't have money. I can't do any business. I used to do business. Now I am only living by God.'

'Let me tell you what happened to me,' Abu Kamara said. 'I was at
Lunsar, attending school there in 1994, when the rebels entered and
we had to flee. It was the end of my schooling. We had to leave Lunsar.
The place was not safe. I went to Kambia. In Kambia I spoke to some
missionaries, and asked them to help me continue my education. But
then we had to flee Kambia too. We went to the bush, to surrounding
villages. From there we made our way to Makeni. We were searching
for somewhere we could settle and start a different life. We were there
for a while, but on the road to Kono one day we were ambushed by the
RUF [Revolutionary United Front]. We were with some ECOMOG [Eco-
nomic Community of West Africa States Monitoring Group] soldiers.
Many ECOMOG and RUF were killed. We went back to Makeni. We
stayed there for three years. When Makeni was attacked we went back
to Lunsar. The RUF attacked Lunsar. We came down to Freetown here.
But we were in the east, and the rebels came and stopped us going to
the west. They said they did not trust us. Whenever people came from
the west they were killed.'

Even before Abu had finished, his friend Amadu was taking up the
refrain.

'We are suffering,' he said. 'We the youths do not have work. We
don't attend school. We have nothing to do. They give us food, but it is
not enough for us. After two or three days it is finished and we have
nothing. Our families are scattered. We have nowhere to live together.
Everyone is living on his own. We have no hope, no progress, no job,
that is our problem.'

So many people were now crowding around that it was impossible
to allow each individual the time and space he or she wanted. So we
talked together.

'The more we explain our stories,' Abubakar said, 'like that woman
there [Adama], the more we are puzzled.'

'What puzzles you?'

'That we have no work, no money, nothing to do. That we have to leave our wives. That we are useless. Before this time most of us were working, some of us doing business, some of us farming, but now they have brought us to this camp we are doing nothing. They cut off some people's hands, burned our houses, killed many people, but still, everyone in the country has said, let us come together and build another Sierra Leone. There is nothing we can say.'

I was intrigued by this conflation of the RUF and those who ran the camp. This sense that one's life was hostage to some force beyond one's comprehension or control. The ubiquitous 'They'. The degrading state of passivity, bewilderment and waiting into which one had been thrown.

'We sleep on the floor,' said one young man.

'Where you're sitting right now, we sleep there,' said another.

'Who runs the camp?' I asked.

'We know only one man, but he does not stay here.'

'Sometimes,' a woman interjected, 'they give us a card on which our names are written. It is to get food. We make a line. Sometimes we spend the whole day waiting in that line. Sometimes it is two or three days before we get anything. Twelve cups of bulgar. Half a pint of oil. Sometimes they tell us, "You are not registered". The very same people that gave us the card.'

'Who gives you the food?'

'One agent they call Share. The truck stops in the street. There is a forty foot container. They open the door. They take out the sacks one by one. Sometimes you get something, sometimes you don't. After twenty bags ...'

'What do they tell you, the people who run the camp?'

'They say we have to be patient before we go back to our homes. But we are suffering. We have been told we have to forgive and forget, that we have to look up to the government now, and see what the government can do for us. The government says the war is over, but for us it is still going on.'

'We would be only too happy to go home, another young man added, but what would we do? I am a mechanic. All my equipment was destroyed.'

'I am a driver, said another. The Big Man I worked for lost everything. I am trying to get another driver's license, but it costs money. So I am sitting down here, no work, no clothes to wear, no food to eat.'

As if in response to these piled-up images of confinement and deprivation, Eddy Shuma pressed forward. 'We have many stories,' he said. 'They wanted to burn me and some others in a kiosk on 6 January. They locked eight of us in the kiosk. I thought I was going to die. We could not tell you all the stories we have. They are too much. If we started telling our stories it would take a day. You wouldn't go anywhere. You would be doing nothing but listen to all our stories.'

I thought of Keti Ferenke Koroma, whose stories I had recorded in Kondembaia thirty years ago. Keti Ferenke had also liked to boast that I had neither the time nor staying power to hear all the stories he knew. Stories that were often about bloody conflicts, which inexplicably I did not think of as memories of actual events or as presaging the possibility of real violence.

Several of the young men wanted me to see inside their hut. They wanted to show me their cramped living conditions, the dirt floor, the bed made of lashed poles and a thin styrofoam mattress, the makeshift towel rail on which were draped a couple of shirts, a blanket and a towel. 'Look at this place,' they said, 'look at the dirt here. At night we cannot sleep for the mosquities. The bed bugs. The rats that gnaw the soles of our feet.'

Outside the hut, someone had written on a scrap of wood: *You only know the value of shade when the tree has been cut down.* As I copied the words into my notebook, Abu was saying, 'I want to go back to school.'

'I need tools,' Mohammed said.

'We need help to get our licenses,' Tony added. '150,000 leones. Where could we find that money now? Who would give me 150,000? How long will it take? We need help.'

I shelled out all I had.

What overwhelmed me was not the demands, nor the sense of impotence I felt, but the realisation that these people needed so little to resume their lives, and that rather than dwell on what had happened in the past, they desired only to move on, to start over. It was this that made their immobility so painful, for if there is one thing that reduces a person to nothingness it is waiting without hope. Outside, on the busy street, the petty traders sat for hours on end waiting for a customer, but experience had taught them that one or two sales were enough to put food on their table. But for the camp people, their waiting was as endless as it was empty. This was what they suffered. This was their pain.

Driving back to my hotel through the thronged, polluted streets of the east end, I kept thinking of how these people were no less imprisoned than my friend S.B. Marah had been in Pademba Road jail, when a smuggled message, a piece of meat, or a memory of his children's voices was enough to sustain him for several days (Jackson 2004). In such dire situations we do not hope for much. We scarcely dream. Words fail us, conveying little of what we really feel. In these circumstances, it takes all our will simply to endure. Explaining, judging, blaming are luxuries we cannot afford. And theodicy is not an issue, because, as Odo Marquard writes, a mouthful of bread, a breathing space, a slight alleviation, a moment of sleep are all more important than the accusation and defence of God (1991:11–12).

Around the time I was visiting refugees in the Freetown camps, I was reading W.G. Sebald's great novel, *Austerlitz* (2001). At one point in his novel, Sebald's main character recounts the history of the area around London's Liverpool Street Station, in particular of a priory which, until the seventeenth century, stood on the site of today's main station concourse, and was connected to the hospital for the insane and other destitute persons at Bishopsgate that we remember as Bedlam. Austerlitz recalls how, on his many visits to Liverpool Street station, he would obsessively try to imagine the location of the rooms where the asylum inmates were confined, wondering 'whether the pain and suffering accumulated on this site over the centuries had ever really ebbed away, or whether they might not still, as I sometimes thought when I felt a cold breath of air on my forehead, be sensed as we pass through them on our way through the station halls and up and down the flights of steps' (2001: 183). This image of suffering seeping into the earth, and still haunting the place where it occurred so long ago, is, of course, suggestive of the way that suffering seeps into us, whose historical or social distance from it gives us little immunity from its ghostly influence.

Arthur Kleinman observes that the spectacle of suffering has become such 'a master subject of our mediatized times' (1997: 1) that the suffering of humankind now impinges on our consciousness to a degree that we find difficult to manage. But though 'compassion fatigue' may diminish our concern, and the commoditisation of suffering dilute and distort our experience of human grief, demands for revolutionary change, relief and reform go hand in hand with stratagems to distance or insulate ourselves – socially, psychologically and politically – from this overwhelming exposure to otherness in the form of what Pierre Bourdieu (1993) calls *la misère du monde*.

In what follows I want to explore the ways in which we address the suffering around us – we who feel we can do so little about it yet cannot dismiss it from our minds. Inevitably, this involves an evaluation of the burgeoning anthropological literature on violence and suffering.

Suffering at a Distance

When Bertrand Russell speaks of his 'unbearable pity for the suffering of mankind' (1967) or Richard Rorty defines liberals as those for whom cruelty is the worst thing that people can do (1989), or the anthropologist Nancy Scheper-Hughes observes of suffering that 'not to look, not to touch, not to record can be a hostile act, an act of indifference, and of turning away' (1995: 418), we glimpse what has been at stake for conscientious intellectuals since the late eighteenth cen-

tury, when the modern engagement with human inequality and suffering was first scripted. Until this time, and despite lip service to Christian precepts of mercy and compassion, it was by no means natural or
inevitable that people would be moved to pity by the spectacle of
human misery. However, by the mid eighteenth century, Rousseau's
'innate repugnance at seeing a fellow creature suffer' (1992) had
became commonplace in certain strata of European society, and the
cry to end what John Adams called 'the passion for distinction' (1851)
was critical to both the French and American revolutions (Arendt
1963: 66–67 passim). But men like Jean-Jacques Rousseau, Tom
Paine, Thomas Jefferson, Robert Owen, and John Adams, though
exposed to the spectacle of mass suffering, did not themselves suffer
the hardships, pain and deprivations that moved them so deeply.

What was it, then, that drove these men to want to alleviate the
suffering of 'the people', en masse, and to create a world in which
equal rights included the right to wellbeing and happiness, as well as
the right to decide how one was governed? For the Americans, 'the
abject and degrading misery' of slavery and African-American labour
'was present everywhere' (ibid: 65). For European intellectuals, urban
poverty and misery was equally ubiquitous and unavoidable, and it is
possible that their revolutionary thinking was driven as much by the
sheer awfulness of coexisting with such large numbers of distressed
human beings as by enlightenment and compassion. This situation
reflected the changes that had taken place in Europe as a result of
industrialisation. By the eighteenth century, the dense concentrations
of people in cities, and the intensification of urban misery, meant that
the effects of poverty, disease, overcrowding and pollution could not be
ignored. This was not just a question of how one related to the poor,
but of how one related to others who were strangers – of radically
rethinking the grounds of civilitas and community in an urban setting. As Richard Sennett notes (1977), the tradition of theatre provided one strategy for reducing social ambiguity, and from the
Reformation on people had recourse to a rich variety of wigs, cosmet-
ics and costuming to mark status and rank. But marking oneself off
socially from others did not alter the fact that one was *physically* unable
to avoid them, and the poor became the subject of increasing concern
and debate.

In 1818, the English poet John Keats visited the city of Belfast in
Northern Ireland. The scenes that met his eye are pretty much the
same that a traveller encounters in many Third World cities today,
crowded with youngsters from rural areas seeking their fortune or
people displaced by war. Since the turn of the century, rural poverty
and the effects of the Industrial Revolution had 'sucked so many people into Belfast that its population had expanded by 50 per cent'

(Motion 1997: 279). Keats, travelling with a close friend, Charles Brown, was deeply troubled by the suffering he saw. 'What a tremendous difficulty,' he wrote his brother Tom, 'is the improvement of the condition of such people – I cannot conceive how a mind 'with child' of Philosophy could gra[s]p at possibility – with me it is absolute despair' (cited in Motion: 279). But Keats' despair at how this suffering might be alleviated gives way to an acceptance of life's unavoidable hardships, and a fascination with how one might 'convert the brutal facts of life into *perceptions* which might 'do the world some good'' (ibid: 301, emphasis added). Subtly, the desire to reform a barbarous social system is tempered by a more fervent desire to transmute the suffering around him into a form that improves his own soul. 'Do you not see how necessary a World of Pains and troubles is to school an Intelligence and make it a soul?' he wrote to his brother George in 1819, observing that this 'system of salvation' was very different from Christianity, and did not 'affront our reason and humanity' (cited in Motion: 377–378).

This turn to inwardness is, of course, characteristic of romanticism. But it is a turn that is born of a frustration to change the world *politically*. Faced with entrenched inequality, and the impossibility of social change, the romantic falls back on his own emotions, his own thoughts, his own suffering – what Coleridge called 'inner goings-on' and Luc Boltanski calls a 'metaphysics of interiority' (1999: 81), and Sartre calls 'magical action' (1948: 58–61). That is to say, when action on the world around us proves impossible, we have recourse to action on our own emotions and thoughts, thereby transforming the way we *experience* the world. Unable to flee an assailant, a person may faint. Unable to win an argument, a person may resort to verbally abusing his opponent. Unable to do anything about an impending crisis, a person may worry himself sick about it, as if this increase in anxiety will make some real difference. Unable to stop thinking about a traumatic event a person may refuse to speak of it, as if silence will make the event go away – a view contained in the English saying 'least said, soonest mended'. These are not 'games', Sartre insists, because we commit ourselves to magical activity as though our lives depended on it. Nor is it reflective; it is a mode of action that arises unselfconsciously, whenever our words fall on deaf ears, our actions prove inefficacious, our intentions are misconstrued, and our desires frustrated.

Let me quickly review some of the ways in which we create the illusion of acting to change the world by acting on ourselves – on the emotions and thoughts we conjure, and in the words we use.

One option is to magic the problem away by merging oneself with it – identifying so completely with the misery around you that the boundary between oneself and the object of one's concern is effectively dissolved. Van Gogh provides a poignant example of this empathic identification. Writing to his brother Theo in the winter of 1880, Vincent confesses that his 'only anxiety is: how can I be of use in the world?' (1963:117). At this time he is preparing himself to be an evangelist among the coal miners of the Borinage region, west of Mons. In order to commit himself body and soul to the poor, he feels he must cut himself off from his family, to 'cease to exist' for them. He neglects his appearance, goes hungry and cold, and gives the little he has to peasants and workers. But who is helped by this self-abasing sympathy? What good can come of this identification with the oppressed? Vincent feels imprisoned and melancholic. Frustrated in his efforts to alleviate the misery of humankind, he ends up seeking to annihilate his anguish by steeping himself in the suffering around him. But nothing is really changed. In his act of martyrdom, the martyr has simply made his own troubled conscience disappear by a sleight of hand, donning the sackcloth of those he had set out to save.[1]

Another option takes the form of what Foucault calls 'pastoral power' (1983: 213–215). By throwing oneself into the tasks and routines of administration, the suffering of others is no longer a spectacle to behold, but a technical or logistical problem to be solved. In this exercise of administrative rationality, the suffering are metonymically transformed into an abstraction, a statistic, a 'problem', a stereotype. Writing research reports, recommendations and proposals, or participating in endless meetings, in which the issue is discussed, has the effect of both distancing oneself from the sites of suffering, and sustaining a sense that one is engaged in a worthy task.

A third response to suffering is to intensify one's engagement with an individual sufferer, thereby reducing the overwhelming *general* problem to manageable proportions. John Berger's account of a country doctor in England provides an apt illustration. 'Sassall meets anguished patients on his rounds – the close relatives of the dying, those who are ill and want to die, the immobilized who are made desperate by a kind of claustrophobic fear of their own bodies, the insanely jealous, the lonely who try to kill themselves, the hysterics' (1976: 124). Sometimes Sassall is able to help these people, often he cannot, and becomes increasingly susceptible to their suffering. 'To deny this,' Berger writes, 'he tries to compete with the intensity of suffering' by working as hard as his patients suffer. 'His attitude to his work becomes obsessional' (ibid: 145).

A more self-centred version of this heightened concern for an individual sufferer is to focus less on what one might do to alleviate the suffering, than on one's own sympathetic reaction to it. By cultivating emotions of righteous indignation, anguish, outrage or sorrow, one may fall into believing that one's own passionate intensity will make some real difference to the sufferer. Slavoj Zizek calls this transmutation of pity into self-pity a function of a libidinal economy (1991: 35), in which the feverish activity of the obsessional is predicated on the magical assumption that if he were to stop his anguishing, the dire situation that is the object of his concern would become invisible or worse.

A fourth option consists in intellectualising violence. Here, the lived experience of the sufferer is translated into a purely discursive reality – a problem not so much for administration as for analysis. This use of intellectual techniques for prioritising signification over what Zizek calls 'the senseless actuality' (ibid: 35) of the world, suggests that theoretical meaning may be just one of many consoling illusions for making our relationship with suffering bearable and endurable – taming and domesticating it with words, in order to make it seem safe. But this has real dangers, for, as Veena Das reminds us, in reconstituting suffering as something verbal, we may deny the reality of suffering as effectively as censorship and repression, since discourse all too readily dissolves 'the concrete and existential reality of the suffering victim' (1995: 143). Though, in the words of Lawrence Langer, we may call for 'a new kind of discourse to disturb our collective consciousness and stir it into practical action that moves beyond mere pity' (1997: 47), it may be more realistic to admit that suffering brings us to limits of language.

A fifth option is to speak truth to power. Nancy Scheper-Hughes exemplifies this approach in her call for anthropology to become 'politically committed and morally engaged' rather than a project of passively and indifferently chronicling life as lived, and she envisions a 'new cadre of "barefoot anthropologists"' – 'alarmists and shock troopers' producing 'politically complicated and morally demanding texts and images capable of sinking through the layers of acceptance, complicity, and bad faith that allow the suffering and the deaths to continue without even the pained cry of recognition of Conrad's [1910] evil protagonist, Kurtz: "The horror! The horror!"' (1995: 417).[2] Though this stance echoes the views of critical thinkers like Foucault, Sartre, Said and Adorno (who wrote that 'The premier demand upon all education is that Auschwitz not happen again', 1998: 191), a commitment to witnessing as a tactic for preventing violence and suffering may actually be compromised by its militant demands. As Adorno argues in his essay on resignation, 'the uncompromisingly critical thinker, who neither signs over his consciousness nor lets himself be terrorized into action, is in truth the one who does not give in' (1998: 292).

What it means not to 'give in' is very much at the heart of ethnography. It means coexisting with the subject of one's concern, sustaining an engagement over time, in his or her place, on his or her terms, and trying not to escape into consoling intellectualisations, sympathetic identifications, or political actions that reduce the other to a means for advancing an academic career, or demonstrating what a compassionate person one is, or changing the world. It is a form of sustained communion. And though, as Michael Oakeshott famously put it (1991), its analogue is conversation, words are not essential to this dialectic. Moreover, its aim is not to take it upon ourselves to redress the injustices of the world but to do justice to the way others experience the world, and whatever is at stake for them. As I see it, this necessitates placing oneself in the situation of the other – a sustained intimate, and often silent, involvement in his or her everyday lifeworld that inevitably transforms one's own worldview, and may involve the other seeing his or her situation from a new perspective. In this sense, the ethnographic method seeks not some form of abstract knowledge, but through a mix of osmosis and dialogue understands the other as oneself *in other circumstances*, and sees both self and other from the unsettling and unsettled space of the 'subjective in-between' (Jackson 2002a: 255–256).

However, training 'one's imagination to go visiting', as Hannah Arendt called this method of intellectual displacement (1982b: 43) is by no means straightforward.

Consider Arthur Kleinman's view that we do violence to others, not only in the ways we act toward them but in the ways we speak and write about them. Kleinman argues that by subjecting the experience of human suffering to anthropological theorisation we violate that experience in much the same way as medicalisation delegitimates the existential reality of illness. These 'professional transformations' turn 'an 'experience-rich and – near human subject into a dehumanized object, a caricature of experience' (1995: 96–97). Kleinman goes on to urge that ethnographers of suffering resist categorisation and stereotyping. The suffering should not be seen as patients or victims, nor the violated 'romanticized or cynically deconstructed' (ibid: 187). Our task is to describe 'what is at stake for particular participants in particular situations' (ibid: 98). But the trouble with making 'lived experience' and 'what is at stake' into measures of interpretive adequacy or authenticity is that these terms are as abstract and general as any other. *Whose* experience is to be prioritised – the sufferers or ours? And do we privilege what is at stake for the liberal spectator or what is at stake for the sufferer – for the issues are seldom the same? With the best will in the world, it is as difficult to distance oneself from one's own assumptions as it is to embrace the experience of the other. Consider, for instance, the seven and a half hours of conversation in August 1970 between James Baldwin and Margaret Mead that were transcribed and published as *A Rap on Race* (1971). While Mead approached race academically, as a non-racist social scientist looking for answers, Baldwin was 'bent on revealing pain and a larger "truth" than facts can provide', and he privately rejected Mead's detached historical point of view because, as he put it later, 'history was all very well but me and mine are being murdered ... in time' (Leeming 1994: 310). 'History is the *present*, the *present*' (Baldwin and Mead 1971: 197, emphases in text). The communication difficulties here, between someone who suffers racism as a traumatic everyday reality, and someone who suffers racism at a distance, implies the perennial difficulty of translating pain into a 'shape fit for public appearance' for, as Hannah Arendt observes, 'pain is at the same time the most private and least communicable' of all experiences (1958: 50–51). But can the intellectual succeed in accomplishing what the sufferer cannot? Or are our attempts to communicate or publicise the pain of others little more than stratagems for helping us deal with the effects this pain has had upon us?

In a world in which human misery is increasing as the divide between haves and have-nots widens, and wars are waged for control over scarce resources, liberal-minded anthropologists may have no other options than those that have been invoked and deployed by European liberals for the past two hundred years. We all fall back on time-worn liberal assumptions that improved knowledge – in this case, ethnographic knowledge of people's lives in marginal environments – will somehow facilitate real, practical interventions, or that exposing the self-serving interests that lie behind the discourses of dominant states and corporations will somehow embarrass the rich and powerful into making life less burdensome and miserable for the powerless, or that describing the intolerable conditions under which the poor live and die will 'speak truth to power' and somehow alter the way power is wielded, or we show that suffering is somehow redeemed by the creativity with which people rebuild and reimagine their lives (Nordstrom 1997), the patience and stoicism with which they go on. But these arguments are often forms of wishful thinking – ways of salving our consciences rather than saving the world – and make anthropology, in Boltanski's terms, a 'politics of pity' rather than a 'politics of justice' (1999: 3).

Boltanski's distinction builds on Hannah Arendt's observation that whereas compassion involves sympathy and solidarity with individual sufferers, pity is a 'perversion of compassion' (Arendt 1963: 84) that creates a sentimental distance from those who suffer by lumping them together into aggregates – the refugees, the poor, the suffering masses. Compassion is thus like love, for it 'abolishes the distance, the in-between which always exists in human intercourse' (ibid: 81). There is thus an uncanny similarity between our anthropological strategies of suffering at a distance and the strategies of laughter and stereotyping.

As Henri Bergson showed, the difference between tragedy and comedy lies not in the essence or nature of the event itself but in the degree of distance we create between ourselves and the event. In comedy, the human condition is reviewed disinterestedly from a general rather than exclusively personal standpoint (1911: 4–6, 165). It thus involves *an absence of feeling*. But if laughing at people less fortunate than ourselves is the apotheosis of this transmutation of the singular into the categorical, as Bergson argues, so too is indifference, for as Michael Herzfeld points out bureaucratic and administrative control over the complex and unruly reality of human life is accomplished by the very same techniques of stereotyping and generalising that underlie the politics of pity (1992).

Hannah Arendt also notes that while pity is loquacious, compassion has difficulty with words. 'Closely connected with this inability to generalize is the curious muteness or, at least, awkwardness with words that, in contrast to the eloquence of virtue, is the sign of goodness, as it is the sign of compassion in contrast to the loquacity of pity' (Arendt 1963: 84). Though the anthropology of suffering does not always fall into this error of over-generalising, it rarely escapes the trap of excessive verbalising – something which is, as Steven Sampson points out, symptomatic of our Western preoccupation with talk and with talking things through, and achieving reconciliation through dialogue and conversation (2003: 180). This may reflect a belief that the intensity of our verbal response to suffering will somehow do justice to the intensity of the suffering itself. It may also be a misplaced attempt to compensate in words for the sheer banality of suffering – the fact that though it is so devastating to the sufferer, there is little that he or she can say about it, except recount the kind of matter-of-fact summaries of events that I heard from people in the refugee camps in Freetown. Violence is a form of excess, writes E. Valentine Daniel (1996: 208). But loquacity is a form of excess too, that risks doing violence to the very experiences it struggles to make sense of. This is why our language must be measured and tempered, rather than used to fill silences, or speak that which the sufferer cannot speak. And this is why we should learn the value of silence, seeing it not as a sign of indifference or resignation, but of respect. This is not shocked silence – as when one is struck dumb by events that beggar belief, or cannot be narrated – but silence as a deliberate choice. For there are certain events and experiences of which we choose not to speak. Not because they hold us in thrall, freezing the tongue. Nor because we fear they might reveal our flaws or frailty. Still less because we feel our words can never do them justice. Silence is sometimes the only way we can honour the ineffability and privacy of certain experiences. This, said Miriam Cendrars (1992), was why her father could never write his book on the life of Mary Magdalene. *La Carissima*

In *L'Homme Foudroyé*, the French writer Blaise Cendrars refers to this work as his 'secret book' on which he had been working for a year (1945: 265–266). Entitled *La Carissima*, it was a fictional life of Mary Magdalene, 'the lover of Jesus Christ, the only woman who made our saviour weep'. Though the book was never written, Cendrars described it as 'the most beautiful love story and the greatest love that have ever been lived on earth' (Cendrars n.d: 547 and 599). The same experiences that compelled Cendrars to write this book, also demanded silence. 'His silence was its truth,' writes Miriam Cendrars (1992). 'Had he written it, it would have been, for him, a negation of this truth. Its truth is preserved in his silence' (cited in Ferney 1993: 134). One thinks of Wittgenstein, who fought in the same war as Cendrars, though on the other side, 'Whereof one cannot speak thereof one must be silent' (1922).

Such silence may be, as in Africa, a way of healing and reconciliation, and not a way of evading or repressing an issue. Indeed, it may be a consummate form of coexistence. To sit with a neighbour or friend, saying nothing, may seem like a negation of intersubjectivity, but among the Kuranko it is a form of exchange, an expression of solidarity. And if one's friend has experienced loss, it is to acknowledge that loss, and what cannot be changed, at the same time as one affirms and demonstrates that the sufferer is not alone. Little is said, apart from the phrase *in toro* – you suffer – but in silence the social world is restored. Speech disperses the world, say the Bambara; silence reassembles it. Speech burns the mouth; silence heals it. The secret belongs to he who keeps quiet (Zahan 1979: 117–118).

I do not mean to make a prima facie case against acting to alleviate suffering, or against speaking out against injustice. My argument is against judging human actions, including responses to suffering, in categorical terms, and for understanding each situation on its own terms. Consider, for example, the Hypocratic Oath that we do no harm.[3] Sometimes it is very clear what is harmful and what is helpful; at other times, active intervention in saving a person's life may prove misguided and harmful. Similarly, while silence can often have harmful consequences, as when we assent, by our silence, to atrocious acts, silence is sometimes a way of healing, as in Cambodia, where many people have had recourse to spirit possession cults rather than storytelling in dealing with the traumas of the Pol Pot years (Trankell 2001). For these reasons, one cannot be formulaic – arguing on a priori grounds for a particular course of action, or claiming that anthropology should be concerned with either ethical truth (Scheper-Hughes 1995) or scientific objectivity (D'Andrade 1995). Every human situation must be thought through anew, in terms of what is at stake and what might follow from a particular course of action. There is, as the 'liberal ironist',

Richard Rorty, puts it, no 'final vocabulary' for doing justice to experience, changing the world or speaking truth to power (1989: 73–74).

Where, then, does our moral responsibility lie? My view is that must have recourse to the phenomenologist's epoché, and endeavour to examine each situation *as if* there were no universal measure against which to judge it, only various points of view that must be taken into account in exploring it. This means restoring to the notion of responsibility a sense of what it means to be responsive.

In the modern world, we have become so used to the idea that science can save us from an untimely death, and that the state can protect us from threats of invasion – chemical, military or viral – that we expect, almost as a constitutional right, a painless life that is free from the kinds of adversity that afflicts the Third World. But suffering is not only an inevitable and unavoidable part of life; it will always have to be endured with resources that science and the state cannot provide – resources we find in ourselves, and in our fellowship with others.

It is here that we may learn a little from the stoicism and powers of endurance I saw among the people I spoke to in the refugee camps in Sierra Leone. If we yield to *our* anguish over *their* anguish we may all too readily rush to judgement, imposing our solutions on their situations, and dismissing the ways in which they deal with their adversity as something that would become unnecessary if they could share a life like ours. But perhaps, in our preoccupation with controlling the forces of life and death and insulating ourselves against baleful influences, we have lost our capacity to be open to the world, and depleted our resources to cope with unpredictable hardship. In which case, the situation of the other may be seen, not simply as one we want to save them from, making them more like us, but as one we might learn from, even if this means greater acceptance of the suffering in this world, less bellicose or concerned talk about how we may set the world to rights, and a place for silence.

Notes

1. This strategy often goes with an aestheticisation of suffering, that sees pain as a path to transcendence. In braving intense pain, facing death and undergoing ordeals, the sufferer acquires illumination, virtue, salvation or a new life. Here suffering, as in the passion of Christ or the death of a martyr, is a form of the sublime.
2. This same moral tone is characteristic of her *Death Without Weeping* (1992), with its constant shifts of register between 'righteous indignation' (xviii), 'moral outrage' (16), exhortation to bear witness 'lest we forget' (xiii), and the need for active engagement and useful work (18).
3. 'I will follow that system or regimen which, according to my ability and judgement, I consider for the benefit of my patients, and abstain from whatever is deleterious and mischievous'.

Chapter 10

WHOSE HUMAN RIGHTS?

> In the aftermath of the Cold War – and a spate of 'new' African civil wars
> – human rights has been proffered as a global framework within which
> peace and justice might be sought. Northern governments and
> international non-governmental agencies have quickly embraced the idea.
> Steven Archibald and Paul Richards (2002: 339)

When I returned to Sierra Leone at the end of the war in January
2002, signs of the new dispensation were everywhere. At the airport,
a placard in the old hangar that served as an Arrivals Hall read 'Under
Rehabilitation', reassuring you that this noisy, dismal shed was only a
momentarily inconvenience. 'Welcome to Sierra Leone', said the
hoarding outside, 'If you cannot help us, please do not corrupt us'. At
every city roundabout there were banners announcing Di Wor Don
Don, Now Wi Di Pwel Di Gun Dem (The war is over, now we will
destroy the weapons), and downtown, in the crowded streets, there
were poda-podas called 'Better Days Are Coming', 'Human Right', and
'O Life at Last'. A fishing boat on Lumley beach had been named
'Democracy'. Young men were wearing T-shirts, saying 'Forgive and
Reconcile for National Development'. And everywhere there were
vehicles and offices belonging to NGOs and UN agencies, with 'Reconstruction', 'Rehabilitation', 'Reconciliation', and 'Resettlement' the
recurring words. One could not help but be affected by this ostensible
spirit of renewal. But how realistic was it? The foreign aid. The disarmament process one read about in the daily papers. The Truth and
Reconciliation Commission that was beginning its work. Was this language of reconciliation not unlike the language of human rights, at
once too abstract and too Eurocentric? A moral order imposed by the

---

Notes for this section can be found on page 178.

north upon the south, and as such, simply a new variation of the old self-extolling theme of the white man's burden?[1]

A couple of days after arriving back in Freetown I was stuck in traffic. Ahead of me, a large truck, attempting to pass between the lines of parked and gridlocked cars had scraped against the side of a poda-poda and come to a standstill. Verbal abuse was shouted. Passengers from the poda-poda joined the palaver. And the truck drivers pitched in for all they were worth. An unremarkable incident, except that the most vociferous participant in this slanging-match was, I observed, a young man standing on the tailgate of the truck and wearing the ubiquitous 'Forgive and Reconcile for National Development' T-shirt.

In the following pages I want to explore the lived reality behind the rhetoric of reconciliation and human rights, and examine the relation of notions of truth and justice to power. I am particularly interested in the contrast between what Veena Das calls 'cosmologies of the powerful' and 'cosmologies of the powerless' (1995: 139–140) – the ways in which explanations of violence, as well as strategies for enduring it, reflect people's differential command of social power. My point of departure is the war experience of a young Kuranko woman. Though I heard and recorded many stories in the course of my few weeks' sojourn in Sierra Leone, Fina Kamara's story is not untypical. And though I present it here as a single case, I think it illuminates something of what is at stake for many Sierra Leoneans in the postwar period, and sets the scene for discussing the relationship between the Western discourse on human rights and the situation in impoverished countries such as Sierra Leone.

Fina Kamara's Story

The day I went to see Fina Kamara in the amputee camp at Murray Town, the question uppermost in my mind had less to do with the trauma of war than how a person addresses the losses she has suffered, the injustices she has endured. How, when lives are shattered, can life be renewed?

Three years before I had read a story in the *Guardian Weekly* under the headline 'Machete Terror Stalks Sierra Leone' (Rupert 1999: 12). It concerned a rebel attack on the Kuranko village of Kondembaia in April 1998, and its focus was the ordeal of a young Kuranko woman and her 6-year-old daughter.

Fina Kamara's husband was my field assistant's maternal uncle, and so we had little difficulty in locating her. After parking the Toyota 4-Runner and asking some kids if they knew where the people from Kondembaia were living, Sewa led the way through a labyrinth of alleys to the centre of the camp. Though many of the refugees were living in makeshift dwellings, made of white- and blue-striped UN plastic tarps pulled over lashed poles, Fina occupied a room in a disused barracks.

I recognised her at once from the photo that had appeared in the *Guardian*, and after Sewa had introduced me, I told Fina of the field-work I used to do in Kondembaia, and the recordings I had made of Keti Ferenke's stories. I then showed her the clipping from the *Guardian* that I had bought with me. She looked at it without emotion or inter-est before passing it on to the other refugees who, out of curiosity, had now joined us. No one commented.

When I asked Fina if she would mind if I tape-recorded her story, she raised no objection, but wanted to know if she should speak in Krio or Kuranko. I suggested she speak in Kuranko.

'We were hiding in the bush for three months,' she began. 'We were afraid the RUF[2] might come at any time and attack the town. But then we received messages from Freetown and from ECOMOG[3] to come out of the bush and return to town. So we came out of the bush.

'One day we went to our farm to plant groundnuts. We returned to town that afternoon. Suddenly, we heard gunshots. Because there were ECOMOG soldiers in Kondembaia, we were used to hearing gun-fire, but this time we were confused.

'The RUF came suddenly. They shot many people. They stacked the bodies under the cotton tree. Then they grabbed us. Their leader said they were going to kill us too. But then they sent their boys to bring a knife. My daughter Damba was 6. They took her from me and cut off her hand. After that they cut off all our hands. One man died because of the bleeding. We ran. We fell to the ground. After some time we got up. Damba said, "Mummy, I am thirsty". By now all the houses were on fire. We went behind one of the houses. One of the RUF boys came and said, "What are you doing there?" I said, "I want to give water to my daughter." I gave Damba some water. Then I sat down and tied her on my back. We began running again, but they stopped us in the back-yard of one of the houses. One RUF girl said, "You move one step and I will shoot you." I had to go back. But there was a place behind the houses. We went down there. After a while I felt hungry. I found a mango but could not eat because my blood was all over it. A little while later I overheard the RUF saying it was time for them to leave. When they had gone, I found my son, and tied Damba on my back again and went to the bush. From there I came out on the road and sat down. I met my husband and uncle there. Everyone was crying. I told them to stop crying. We went to our farm, and in the morning we set off for Kabala. We did not reach Kabala that day because of the pain. It took us two days. People in Kabala said we were lucky; the Red Cross was there. After treating us they brought us by helicopter to Freetown here.

We were taken to Connaught Hospital. They treated us there. Then we were taken to Waterloo. When the RUF invaded Freetown, we had to flee from Waterloo. We fled to the Stadium. From there we were brought to this camp. If you ask me, this is all I know. We were ordinary people, we were farmers, we had nothing to do with the government. Whenever I think about this, and about the time they cut off my hand, and my daughter's hand, only 6 years of age, I feel so bad. Our children are here now. They are not going to school. Every morning we are given bulgar. Not enough for us. We are really suffering here. We only hope this war will come to an end and that we will be taken back to our own places. If we go back home, we have our own people there who will help us.'

Three and a half years had passed since Fina Kamara's world fell apart, and she was still struggling to grasp how this could have happened. The rebels came and went within an hour. In this short time they murdered fifty people and mutilated another ten or fifteen. They also set fire to every building in Kondembaia, save the mosque which they used as a kitchen, the school, the church, and a house where they stashed their belongings. Though Fina had spoken of the RUF, many of the rebels were in fact young junta soldiers, avenging their ouster from power a few weeks earlier when the Nigerian-led ECOMOG reinstated the elected government of Ahmad Tejan Kabbah. Unable to defeat the ECOMOG soldiers or the Civil Defence militias, they took their revenge on the defenceless people who had allegedly voted for the government, or sheltered and supported the CDF. Of all this, Fina Kamara knew nothing. 'We are ordinary people,' she had told me. 'All we do is go to our farms.'

When I had asked her, 'Do you think you will ever learn to live with what has happened?' she said, 'I will never forget.'

'Would it make any difference to you, if the people that did these dreadful things were punished?'

'I no longer waste my anger on them. But I will never forget what they did. When they burned my house, how can I forget that? When I look at my hand, how can I ever forget? I feel the pain constantly. Even now, talking to you, I feel it. At times, I can feel my fingers, even though they are not there.'

When I saw my old friend Noah the following day, I told him of my visit to the amputee camp, and of Fina Kamara's description of the phantom pain she felt in her hand. The embodied memory of all she had suffered. But I was perplexed, I told Noah, by the way that Fina had explained her feelings toward those who had visited this suffering upon her, and upon her village.

Noah was ready for this conversation. He had come to see me at the home of his brother, Sewa Bockarie Marah (S.B.) the day before, only to be turned away at the gate. The soldiers and security guards had refused him entry, though they knew he was S.B.'s younger brother. Even now, the humiliation and insult rankled. 'You see,' he said, 'how I am shut out. How I have no one inside who can help me. How I have to look outside for help.'

I told Noah that when I had asked Fina Kamara what she might do to redress the damage that had been done to her and her daughter she said, 'There is nothing I can do.' And when I asked her what she thought about reconciliation, she used the phrase *m'bara hake[1] to an ye*, which Sewa translated as 'I can forgive, but I cannot forget'. What exactly did she meant by this?

'It's what you might say' Noah said, 'when someone offends or hurts you, and you are powerless to retaliate. If, for instance, someone takes something from you without justification. Or insults and humiliates you for no good reason. Say a hawk came out of the blue and seized one of your chickens. What can you do? You can't get it back. The hawk has flown away. You have no means of hunting it down, or killing it. All you can do is accept, and go on with your life. But you don't really forgive, you don't really forget. You simply accept that there's nothing you can do to change what has happened. Look at me. I have no way of taking revenge on the rebels who took away my livelihood, but at least I can rid myself of them. I can shut them out of my mind. I can expel them from my life'.

Noah's words were reminiscent of a passage in Hannah Arendt's *The Human Condition* (1958: 237). Forgiveness implies neither loving those that hate you, nor absolving them from their crime, nor even understanding them ('they know not what they do'); rather, it is a form of redemption, in which one reclaims one's own life, tearing it free from the oppressor's grasp, and releasing oneself from those thoughts of revenge and those memories of one's loss that might otherwise keep one in thrall to one's persecutor forever.

'If I say *i hake a to nye'*, Noah continued, 'I am freeing myself of the effects of your hatred. I am refusing to hate back. But this doesn't mean that justice will not be done. Most of us here feel that God sees everything, and that God will mete out punishment in His own good time. That's why we say, *Alatala si n'hake bo a ro*, God will take out my anger on him. So I might say, *m'bara n'te to Al'ma*, I have left it up to God. Same as they say in Krio, *I don lef mi yon to God*. I think this is what Fina Kamara meant. She was not saying that she forgives the RUF, but that she is leaving it up to God to see that justice is done. Because how can you ever be reconciled to someone who has killed your father or cut off your hand? Reconciliation, forgiveness, forgetting … these are all relative terms. In Sierra Leone right now, we are letting sleeping dogs lie. You understand? We are fed up with the war. Fed up with atrocities. If we talk about the war, it is not because we are plotting revenge or want to prolong the suffering. We simply do not want it to happen again.'

Though Fina Kamara and Noah had found it expedient to give up all thought of payback, this did not mean they rejected the possibility of retaliation or the principle of _lex talionis_. Indeed payback is an open and vexed question in Sierra Leone. For who will see that justice is done? How can apologies atone for the material and social losses people have suffered. Who will pay for reparations? And will the trial of war criminals in Special Courts set up at both national and village levels simply rub salt into old wounds, arouse bitter memories, cause resentment and enmity, and set in train another cycle of violence (Jackson 2002a: 57, 62, 164–167).

The people I spoke to were realists, acutely aware of what they could and could not do. Consider, for instance, the comments of Noah's brother, S.B. Marah, who was a prominent Sierra Leonean politician, and Leader of the House in Ahmad Tejan Kabbah's government. If S.B. was less forgiving when he spoke of the RUF, it was not because his anger was stronger but because he was in a stronger position. Justice was thus conditional on one's power to see that justice is done. Or, as Noah's put it, 'If you are in a position of power you'll seek revenge, saying "May my hake fall on those who have destroyed the country"'. S.B. echoed this point of view. When I asked for his opinion of the truth and reconciliation process, he said, 'I come from a warrior family. My ancestors went to war. So with this war now, I wanted to fight to the finish. I wanted the fight to go on to the end, until the RUF were defeated. The President knows my views. He knows I was against the Loma Peace Accord. This was a useless war. The perpetrators must be brought to justice, and not forgiven. They destroyed us. In fact everything I worked for over thirty years they destroyed. So I do not forgive or forget.'

S.B.'s attitude to his thirteen-month long detention in 1974, was, however, very different. When, in the course of researching his life-story, I had asked him what he felt as he recounted his experiences in Pademba Road prison, and the judicial murder of his peers, he said, 'It is painful, but it has happened, it has happened. But that is the price one has to pay if you go into politics'. The RUF atrocities were something else. Something beyond the pale, something outside the bounds of what was human, and could not be forgiven.

Though S.B., Fina Kamara and Noah were as different as any human beings could be, I had been struck by their sober sense of what, in any given situation, was possible and what was impossible – of where the limits of their freedom lay. Westerners often speak of truth and freedom in abstract terms, and we are encouraged in the belief that there is nothing we cannot do if we put our minds to it. That there is no corner of the universe that is intrinsically beyond our understanding and control. No limit to our power to manipulate genes, to prolong life, to alleviate suffering, to mete out justice and to find personal fulfillment.

What also struck me forcibly about Fina Kamara's story was not only her awareness of her own powerlessness, but the absence of any dwelling on the self. There are, I think, two reasons why this was so. First, is the Kuranko habit of recounting one's experience, not as a singular, *personal* story, based on 'autobiographical memory' but as a series of shared events, involving crucial *social* relations (Jackson 1989: 20). Thus, Fina and others who suffered in the war were well aware that the violence was arbitrary. If they were victims, it was because the rebels classified everyone who was not for them as being against them, and because they simply happened to be in the wrong place at the wrong time. It was not that they were singled out on account of their specific identity. This is vividly conveyed in the way Fina relates her story. It is only at the moment when her arm is severed, or when she tries to eat the bloody mango, that her narrative consciousness is fully on herself. At other times she is a part of the village, one among many, and she recounts events as they happened to 'us'.[5]

As a corollory of this emphasis on 'we' rather than 'I', Kuranko tend to construct experience as intersubjective rather than intrapsychic, though from an empirical point of view each obviously entails the other.[6] Although people suffered humiliation, bereavement, mutilation and grievous loss in the war no one spoke of unhinged minds, of broken spirits or of troubled souls. And healing was sought, not through words, but deeds. Not through therapy but through things. Fees to send children to school. Cement and roofing iron to rebuild houses. Grain. Microcredit. Food. Medicines. It may well be that a diagnostic label like PTSD (Post Traumatic Stress Disorder) is empirically justified,[7] but it is imperative that we acknowledge that intrapsychic wounds are not the burning issue for Sierra Leoneans, but rather the material means that are needed to sustain life, and ensure a future for one's children.[8]

This was vividly brought to home to me when Noah spoke about his son and daughter who had been abducted by the RUF. His son managed to escape during a battle to dislodge the Sierra Leone army from the town of Makeni, and returned home to Freetown and his family. Noah told him that he did not want to hear anything of what had happened. It made him feel bad. As for the boy, apart from saying he hated the RUF, and would never forgive them for what they put him through, he craved only that his ignominy not become public knowledge. During the disarmament period, Noah urged him to go and find his weapon and hand it in to the authorities, but his son said 'No, I want no record of the fact that I carried arms; I will not do it, even if I am paid millions of leones.' As for the daughter, she was sexually-abused and traumatised (Noah's word). When she finally came home, she refused to return to school. Like her brother, she was deeply ashamed of what had befallen her. Noah had to 'talk and talk and talk to her' before she enrolled in a vocational school in Freetown, and did a dress-making course for a year. Noah told her, 'You are not the only one this happened to. It happened to thousands. So you should return to school.' 'Now,' he told me, 'she is doing well at school and going on with her life.'

Sierra Leone and the Discourse of Human Rights

Although the issue of human rights was raised in classical Greek and Roman literature, and promoted in the English Magna Carta of 1215, it is, generally speaking, a product of the European enlightenment, culminating in the American Declaration of Independence and Con-stitution (1776, 1787), the French Declaration of the Rights of Man and the Citizens (1789), and the UN Universal Declaration of Human Rights (1948). The increasingly complex legalistic, ethical and politi-cal human rights discourse of the nineteenth and twentieth centuries is characterised by a striving for an overarching, disinterested, global point of view that may be made binding for all people, in all cultures, at all times. In other words, the focus is on enshrining human rights in international law, and implementing this law on a global scale.

In seeking to understand the discourse of human rights in contem-porary Sierra Leone, I want to begin with the ways in which phenom-ena that 'we' discuss under the rubric of 'human rights', are *experienced* in different cultures and contexts. My assumption is that the more deeply one explores the lived particulars of any human situ-ation the more difficult it will be to create classifications, impose defin-itions, or sustain categorial notions of right and wrong (This is what Primo Levi, writing of his experiences in Auschwitz, calls 'the gray zone' [1989: 38]). At the same time, I will argue that the predominant Eurocentricity of human rights discourse has disconcerting echoes of the colonial period, and of the 'civilising mission' of missionaries and colonial administrators committed to stamping out barbarianism in every society but their own.

Let me begin with the observation that people without 'rights' are the least likely to have their voices heard in the human rights conver-sation. This is partly because thinking abstractly about their 'rights' is a luxury the oppressed can ill afford. But it is mainly a function of the long-standing tendency of Westerners to regard 'them' as victims, who possess neither the material nor intellectual agency to protest their situation, pursue justice, or improve their lot, while casting themselves in the role of saviours. Paradoxically, therefore, the discourse of human rights is rarely the discourse of those without rights; it is the discourse of those who enjoy such rights. It is a discourse, not of the powerless, but of the powerful *on behalf of the powerless,* who all too often assume some kind of 'moral ownership' of Third World suffering as a license to intervene in the administration of Third World societies (see de Waal 1997: 217).

Consider the Sierra Leonean point of view.

Like thousands of others who lost limbs, loved ones and livelihoods in the civil war, Fina Kamara did not speak of human rights abuses but of *satanay* ('evil'). Evil simply exists. It cannot be comprehended. And there is often little one can do to protect oneself from it, or secure justice if one falls foul of it. Although the violence done to her and her daughter by the RUF was an 'evil' event that had no parallel in her experience, Fina Kamara responded to it in much the same way as Kuranko women respond to the unavoidable, everyday hardships of life – with stoic or defiant acceptance. For 'us' to categorise the RUF atrocities as 'human rights abuses' is, no doubt, to recognise an important distinction between the kinds of woe that are visited on people by human agency and 'natural' disasters that cannot be blamed on anyone ('acts of God'). This is, in fact, precisely the distinction that Kuranko make between afflictions and illnesses that are caused by witches and sorcerers (*morgo kiraiye* – caused by persons) and afflictions and illnesses that occur, as it were, in the nature of things (*altala kiraiye* – caused by God). In practice, however, it is seldom a cut and dried matter of deciding whether misfortunes were caused by God *or* Man, but deciding the relative weight of these factors and forces – which one was the 'first spear' and which the 'second spear', as the Azande say (Evans-Pritchard 1934: 59). This decision is never an 'objective' appraisal, since it reflects the subjective capacity of a person to do something about her situation. Thus, Fina Kama, powerless to take avenge herself against the people who assaulted her, acknowledges that her tragedy was caused by human agents while invoking God as an agent of retribution.

Whether we invoke the Western or the Kuranko distinction, the critical factor for a sufferer is whether or not he or she can do anything about his or her situation – whether the affliction can be cured, whether justice can be done, whether punishment of the perpetrator will make any difference to the victim, and whether redress is possible for what has been lost. To isolate a particular class of affliction, and call it human rights abuses or PTSD may be mere casuistry.

Advocates of human rights respond to this critique by pointing out that though we cannot redress the injustices of the past, we can prevent such injustices happening in the future if we agree upon a universal charter, and create an apparatus for implementing it. The counter-argument is that a focus on defining what constitutes 'a human rights abuse' may distract us from exploring the complex conditions under which such abuses arise. It is sometimes necessary to remind ourselves that upholding human rights does not necessarily protect people from poverty and hunger – the conditions that frequently lead to human rights abuses. Despite its 'bad' record on human rights, China had made extraordinary progress in conquering poverty, while, for all its much-vaunted democratic ideals, U.S. domestic policies create a widening gap between haves and have-nots. Second, to speak of a breach of human rights is to imply a distinction between violences that are caused by identifiable human agents – and can, therefore, be unequivocally and legalistically defined and prosecuted – and those that are too diffuse to be attributed to any single human agent or perpetrator, or redressed by legal means. These are 'the violences of everyday life', as Arthur Kleinman (2000) calls them, that encompass the deeply engrained, disguised and habitual forms of 'structural' inequality that systematically negate the will and deny agency to vast numbers of people in contemporary societies simply because they are poor, 'coloured', young, infirm, elderly, vagrant or migrant. Our notion of what constitutes 'violation' or 'human rights abuses' cannot, therefore, be limited to situations in which physical harm is done, for a person's humanity is violated whenever his or her status as a subject is reduced against his or her will to mere objectivity, for this implies that he or she no longer exists in any active social relationship to others, but solely in a passive relationship to himself or herself on the margins of the public realm.

The mutilation Fina Kamara suffered at the hands of the RUF was nothing beside the nullifying effects of her prolonged sojourn in a refugee camp where she could neither act on or understand her situation, and where, through some tragic irony and in the name of humanitarianism, an aid agency (she did not know which one) took Damba to the U.S. for advanced medical treatment, leaving Fina with no way of communicating with her, and no idea when her daughter would return to Freetown. I was unable to find out how this unidentified agency had justified this prolonged separation of mother and daughter. Perhaps the overriding consideration had been rescuing Damba from the brutality of war, and giving her a prosthetic limb, rather than the bond between her and her mother. In her despair, Fina had no option but to look for God, while I asked myself whether we in the West, in our complacency, have arrogated the power of God to ourselves, and as a consequence placed people like Fina in the invidious position of having to look to us for what we may not, in reality, have the means to give.

It is often the case that when we create categories into which we compress a vast array of human experience, we not only do violence to the complexity of life as lived; we risk violating the very rights we wish to protect. By focusing on the atrocities caused by the rebels, and on the business of bringing the RUF leadership to justice, we all too readily overlook the myriad of small wrongs that make up the violences of everyday life; but we also overlook the ways in which informal modes of indemnification and apology enable wrong-doers to redeem themselves. On 11 March 2003 the *Guardian* newspaper announced that the Special Court, established in Sierra Leone under the auspices of the UN, had indicted seven Sierra Leoneans 'for war crimes, crimes against humanity and violations of international humanitarian law committed during the West African country's decade-long conflict' (Carroll 2003: 6). Shortly afterward, the EU welcomed the 'prompt and diligent action' of Sierra Leone's Special Court, calling it 'an important milestone on the path for peace, justice and reconciliation for the people of Sierra Leone.' In a declaration by the EU's Greek presidency, the European Union reiterated its strong support for the court 'in its crucial task to bring the main perpetrators of serious violations of international humanitarian law in Sierra Leone to justice' and expressed support for Sierra Leone's Truth and Reconciliation Commission in 'its endeavours to contribute to the healing of the Sierra Leone society'. What neither the *Guardian* nor the European Union statement mentioned was that of the seven former RUF and AFRC junta leaders indicted by Sierra Leone's war crimes tribunal, two of the former RUF commanders had been about to launch projects funded by the Government's National Committee for Disarmament, Demobilisation and Reintegration (NCDDR), and that other ex-rebel commanders were also reportedly working on community development initiatives. 'We actually had already approved four fisheries projects for Issa Sesay, Morris Kallon, Gibril Massaquoi and Eldred Collins,' said NCDDR Executive-Secretary Dr Francis Kai-Kai. Yet another ex-RUF commander, Augustine Gbao, was already at an 'advanced stage' in implementing an agricultural project in his home village in Kenema District. As for the arrest of Hinga-Norman, who had led the civilian militias in their campaigns against the RUF, many were outraged that someone who helped save the country from destruction should be placed on trial for human rights abuses.[9]

My argument is not only that 'our' preoccupation with human rights often blinds us to the ways in which injustices are experienced and dealt with in Africa. It is an argument against the ways in which the discourse of human rights disguises and perpetuates power inequalities between Africa and the West and, despite its humanitarian rhetoric, continues to construe Africa as 'a heart of darkness' that needs the enlightened West to rescue it from its own barbarism (cf. Shaw 2003). Moreover, by focusing on spectacles of physical violence (murder, mutilation, torture) and issues such as 'child soldiers', the mediatised discourse of the West not only sustains its image of Africa as the antithesis of the West, but deflects attention from the ways in which global capitalism and the disaster relief industry actually foster the social, economic and political conditions that doom vast numbers of Third World peoples to social death, and so create the preconditions for violence.

Let it be understood that I am not advocating indifference to the suffering of Africa, but for a deeper understanding of African situations, both in their positive and negative aspects. To accomplish this we need sustained conversations, centred on concrete events, that disclose what is a stake for particular individuals in *their* lifeworlds.

Consider the following conversation I had with my friend Noah Marah not long before he died.

At the time, Noah was in Freetown, where he had just completed the first week of a two week course to become a Justice of the Peace. An entire day of this course had been devoted to the subject of human rights, and so it was understandable, when Noah visited me that weekend, that we should get to talking about whether or not universal human rights were a European construct, imposed upon the rest of the world, and the extent to which human rights are relative to time, place and circumstance. These questions were, of course, much on the mind of many Sierra Leoneans at the time, for the UN Special Court, set up to try those responsible for atrocities during the country's ten-year civil war, was seen by many to be a response to Anglo-American demands and a capitulation to Eurocentric notions of justice. Most Sierra Leoneans preferred to 'let sleeping dogs lie', to 'forgive and forget', not because they were indifferent to the horrors of the war, but because they saw that there was less profit in prolonging the agony and raking over dead coals, than in focusing on reintegration and rebuilding. This tacit consensus not to dwell on or talk about the war seemed even more prevalent in early 2003 than the previous year.

One Sunday I strolled past the building site in Jomo Kenyatta Road where the Special Court was being constructed (a row of cells had already been built). I was with Noah's son, Kaima, and asked him what he thought of the war crimes tribunal. He saw little point in it, he said. People were not going to confess to crimes they committed during the war, lest they get marked for revenge, or arrested and prosecuted. Like others I had spoken to, Kaima said that the past was past. One cannot undo what has happened, but there is a lot one can do to ensure that it does not happen again. This was the way people reasoned. There were, of course, other arguments in support of this view, such as the argument that God or retributive justice would in the fullness of time punish those who had done wrong, and that, if one was patient enough, things would gradually change for the better. But you could not force this change to come about.

This had been the gist of what Noah's friend Fatu Marah had told me about female excision. As a child, she joyfully anticipated her initiation. The prospect of dressing in fine clothes, receiving jewellry and being fussed over, made her feel that she was about to cross some kind of threshold. But the experience of excision itself, even though it involved, as she put it, 'only a symbolic snip', changed her mind, so that now it is something she would never do to her own daughters. 'But this change of attitude must occur in its own good time,' she said. 'It can't be imposed by law.'

When I told Noah what Fatu had said, I recalled the female initiations we had witnessed together in Firawa thirty-two years ago, and how, at the time, it never crossed my mind that this involved any infringement of human rights. But there was one incident during my fieldwork that year, I said to Noah, that troubled me so deeply that even now I keep returning to it, wondering about the ethical issues that were involved.

I then reminded Noah of the event I had in mind. We had gone to the village of Kamadugu Sukurela at a time when many people were seriously ill with insect-borne encephalitis. In an attempt to divine the cause of this epidemic the local chief had summoned a witch-finder from Farandugu, four miles away. After several days in the village, Noah and I returned to Kabala. When we came back to Kamadugu Sukurela, two weeks later, we asked Noah's friend Morowa to tell us what had happened during our absence. This is how I came to hear of the event that had affected me so much, and about which I would subsequently write (Jackson 1989: 88–89).

Eight days after the death of a man whose illness the witch-hunter had diagnosed as being the result of witchcraft, the man's sister fell gravely ill. In her pain and distress she confessed to having killed her brother by witchcraft. 'I was hunting him for a year,' she said. 'The first time I tried to kill him was when he went to brush his farm, but I missed him. The branch only knocked out some of his teeth. But this year we [her coven] lay in wait for him on the path to his palmwine trees. We beat him up and injured him. Then he fell ill.' The woman also explained her motive for wanting to kill her brother: she had once asked him for some rice and he had refused her. But why she had used witchcraft against her brother rather than cursing him, as is a sister's right, was left unexplained. As the woman lay ill inside her house, the witch-hunter came and ordered that she be buried at once. Men bound her hands and feet and dragged her to the outskirts of the village. There they dug a shallow grave and buried her alive. Banana leaves and stones were thrown in on top of her.

When Morowa gave us this account I did not hide my outrage. But Morowa wanted to help me understand what was at stake. 'If it had been my choice,' he said grimly, 'I would have had her thrown into the bush without burial. But we buried her in the grassland beyond the Mabumbuli [stream] so that when the grass is dry we can set fire to it and turn her face into hell. A witch deserves no respect. A witch is not a person.'

'For me this was murder,' I told Noah.

'But she was a witch.'

'Witchcraft is simply the distressed fantasies of a sick person, not a reality.'

'Then why is there a word for it? There are words only for things that exist.'

'Do dragons exist, then, simply because we have a word for them?' And I tried to explain the problem of determining what it is precisely that words like witch and dragon denote – since witchcraft means different things to different people in different societies, and there are countless imagined forms of dragons, or of heaven and hell. We have to make distinctions between what people experience and what they infer from their experiences – the interpretations they put on them.

Noah allowed for what he called hyperbole – the way we exaggerate. But he insisted that the existence of witches and dragons, heaven and hell, was neither imagined nor exaggerated. In each case there was a core reality that could not be contested.

'But what of the Kuranko adage, The word fire won't burn down a house?' I asked.

'It's true that the word won't burn down a house, but fire will, and fire is very real.'

Noah then recounted an anecdote to make his point.

Between 1939 and 1942 Noah's father was Staff Sergeant-Major in the Court Messenger Force at Bonthe. It was during his time there, Noah said, that many confessed witches were brought before him. He was skeptical of witchcraft and once demanded that three self-confessed witches explain how they were able to consume the vital organs of their victims. They said they could not explain it (any more, said Noah, than shapeshifters can explain how they transform into animals), but they could demonstrate what they were able to do. They had a pawpaw brought and placed in a certain house, some distance from the house in which they were put under lock and key. A day or two later they asked to be let out, and for the pawpaw to be opened up. It had no seeds inside; it was an empty shell.

There are many ethical and epistemological questions here. To what extent does wishing a person harm constitute a crime? To what extent does a person who violates the human rights of another person forfeit his or her own rights, and may be incarcerated for life or executed? To what extent does punishment lie with the gods or with men? And how are we to decide the status of beliefs in witches and dragons, heaven and hell?

In addressing these issues, I want to emphasise that the epistemological question – whether a point of view is right or wrong, rational or irrational – is less important for people than the *pragmatic* issue of what they gain from a belief, and the *social* issue of whether their belief is recognised and shared.

Although Noah had, as I remarked in the Preface to this book, a yearning to be looked after by a mentor or benefactor, he possessed a remarkable independence of mind, proudly calling himself *sunike* – a Kuranko word that at once designates a ruler and a 'free thinker'. (This association of ideas probably reflects the fact that Kuranko rulers historically resisted the impact of Islam; being a *sunike* thus connotes both political and philosophical autonomy). Noah preserved in his own worldview this same 'Kuranko' obduracy – this stubborn refusal to submit to the directives of others. When I met him in January 2002, after more than ten years' separation, one of the first questions I asked him was whether he was still *sunike*. Noah told me 'I have never embraced any moral system, and I hope I never will.' This courage of his convictions was evident when rebels broke into his house in Lunsar during the war and took him captive. 'They taunted me,' Noah said. 'They said, "Pappy, here, drink" and thrust a bottle of beer at me. I said I didn't drink. They pushed a cannabis cigarette into my mouth. I told them I didn't smoke. I said, "Would I eat if I were not hungry?" From Lunsar we walked to Masimera where we stopped for two days. I asked if I could talk to their CO. They said "What! A civilian like you wanting to see our CO!" One of them lifted his weapon to show what would happen if I went on pushing my luck.'

For as long as I had known him, Noah had struggled to keep his dignity in a world where being poor, unemployed and without any public position was both as difficult as it was ignominious. His intellectual acumen, his birthright and his association with my ethnographic projects had brought him a measure of respect. But despite his conversancy with European law and literature, he was intellectually defensive, and skeptical of Western notions of development and modernity. Though we never discussed the negative effects of humanitarian aid, structural adjustment programmes, the arms trade and global capitalism in impoverished countries such as Sierra Leone, Noah was mindful of the West's ignorance of everyday life in Africa, and was fervently against the erosion of 'traditional' values. Yet it was not modernity per se that he abhorred, but the imposition of a Western will on Africa – the new face of colonialism as a paternalistic, humanitarian mode of domination – and the way many Africans assented to these new impositions without questioning what they entailed.

In November 2002, after conducting an opinion poll in which 1,280 Sierra Leoneans were asked if they supported the UN- and Government-sponsored Special Court for the trial of war criminals and the Truth and Reconciliation Commission, the Freetown-based civil society group Campaign for Good Governance (CGG) announced that 60 per cent of those polled supported these institutions, though 76 per cent admitted that they did not understand how these institutions worked, or what they would actually do.

Like many others I spoke to, Noah was deeply concerned with questions of human rights – with how entrenched structures of social inequality could be challenged, and how civil war could be prevented from happening again. But the same people had misgivings about Western processes for securing justice and effecting reconciliation in their war-torn country. Social reconstruction was, they argued, a Sierra Leonean matter, and would not be helped by dwelling on the past, bemoaning one's lot, or seeing a foreign power as the source of one's salvation.

Behind these arguments I discerned a fervent desire for autonomy. It was not primarily a matter of whether one believed in bringing war criminals to trial, or rehearsing the traumas of war before a Truth and Reconciliation Commission, any more than it was primarilyy a matter of whether or not one believed in witches. It was at heart an existential question of having a voice, of choosing one's own vocabulary for describing the world, and not being regarded as some primitive backwater that could only be saved from itself through the intervention and superior knowledge of the West.

As Noah's personal situation had worsened during the war years, so his sensitivity to this had increased. In years gone by, Noah had shared my skepticism about the existence of witches, and been far less preoccupied by the oppressive aspects of global modernity. That his views had changed was not because he had reached a new conclusion as a result of ratiocination, but that his marginalised situation had forced him to seek for new ways in which he could affirm himself in the face of powers he could not tap, worlds in which he could not participate, systems he could not comprehend.

Noah's situation was typical, as were his notions of witchcraft. In Sierra Leone I heard numerous anecdotes concerning people who had the power to fly to New York in invisible aeroplanes, move about there, and return home – stories that mingled 'traditional' fantasies of unfettered movement, ambition and greed with images of global modernity, and were identical to those Rosalind Shaw has recorded among the Temne.[10] Such 'beliefs' in witches are symptoms of estrangement and marginalisation – ways in which the imagination compensates for the growing gap between expectations and opportunities. But in Noah's case, I suspect that his assertion of the validity of traditional beliefs was also a way of reclaiming some sense of standing and identity in the face of a modernity that had given him nothing. This same kind of Nietzschean *amor fati* typically appears among marginalised peoples who, unable to be what the world order expects them to be, fall back on a perverse and vociferous celebration of *cultural* being as a way of asserting their *human* right to exist. (Jackson 2002a: 107–126). Behind the widely reported honour killings in Sweden (Kurkiala 2003: 6–7), there lies not some cultural conditioning that makes certain Kurdish men incorrigibly barbaric (for not all Kurdish men kill their sisters and daughters when they date or sleep with Swedish men, or defy their fathers' wills), but specific backgrounds and biographies and, overridingly, an existential need to assert their *own* humanity in a society that decides and imposes a Eurocentric notion of humanity on all, and finds migrants wanting. Existential factors are more crucial here than cultural ones or questions of 'human rights'.

The Wrongs of Rights

When we examine actual contexts in which human rights are invoked, it is often the case that the very process that purports to defend a people's rights actually compromises them. Thus, in numerous meetings to prosecute Aboriginal land claims in Australia, claimants are asked to demonstrate their claims to 'traditional' land in a complex legal process that is dominated by non-Aboriginal lawyers, anthropologists, and other experts, yet is largely incomprehensible to Aboriginal participants who sit in stony silence, marginalised and confused by the 'hard English', and often outraged that land that was taken in a day cannot be just as expeditiously reclaimed.

In my account of the destruction of an Aboriginal sacred site (Jackson 1995), a similar paradox was implied. Though white lawyers and advisers prosecuted a compensation case on the grounds that Aboriginal 'traditional rights' had been infringed, I found that in talking with the people most affected by the event that the real issue was an existential one – a question of being consulted by whites, of being taken seriously, and not being ignored (Jackson 1995: 137–155). In an illuminating study of European approaches to AIDS in Africa, Quentin Gausset (2001) argues that Western assumptions of what is best for the Third World may not only be beside the point, but plain wrong – particular the assumption that African cultural practices such as polygamy, adultery, wife-exchanges, circumcision, dry sex, levirate, sexual pollution, sexual cleansing, etc., are the principal barriers to fighting AIDS. Gausset not only demonstrates that this is false, but shows that this view reflects a long-standing Eurocentric assumption that African 'superstitions' are an obstacle to enlightenment and development – the implication being that Western science can save Africans from themselves. In fact, as Gausset observes, controlling AIDS in Africa demands *exactly the same resources and the same improvements in communication that are demanded in the West*. Eradicating cultural practices anywhere is unrealistic and unhelpful, but adapting the basic preventive message to local cultural conditions ensures that information reaches most people, and enables them to reach their own consensus on how the problem can be addressed (Gausset 2001: 517). Let me give one final example of the way that Westerns seek to impose their will on Africa in the name of human rights or humanitarian benefit, without reflecting upon the existential consequences of their actions.

One evening, early in 2003, my friend and host S.B. Marah received a visit from an African-American pastor. The pastor was accompanied by the Sierra Leone Ambassador-elect to Liberia, and some other supporters. The pastor wanted to enlist S.B.'s backing for a development project that had been originally intended for Côte d'Ivoire. But with the unstable situation in that country, it had been decided that Sierra Leone should benefit from the scheme the pastor wanted to share with the Honourable S.B. Marah. The plan was to 'make Sierra Leone a model state, a gateway to West Africa.' It would 'utilise the huge demographic represented by West Africa's eighteeen countries' to create an economic block that would rival the EU. The idea was to train hundreds of young people in the interior in some, as yet, unspecified way, whereupon the pastor's organisation would bring in the machinery and infrastructure that would enable these people to produce 'not raw materials for export but finished products.' An air service between Freetown and Atlanta would be part of the deal. After S.B. had listened patiently for about half an hour and politely asked the pastor to send a detailed written account of this project to his parliamentary office in the morning, the visitors left. I then asked S.B., whose face had betrayed nothing of what had been going in his mind, what he thought of this ambitious scheme. 'These people talk big, but they usually come to nothing,' he said. Then he added: 'Many of them are crooks.'

The pastor may not have been a crook. But for him West Africa was as much a place on which to project his own fantasies as it had been for the ill-fated Kurtz in Conrad's *Heart of Darkness*. A place that had no existence in itself, no life of its own, no capacity for creating its own future. To see a country in such terms may be harmless; to see people in such terms is wrong, *even when the vision is justified in terms of human rights.*

I want to emphasise that I am not saying that we should do nothing to secure social justice for marginalised people, or improve their lot. I am arguing for an understanding of the human condition that does not reduce the existence of others to abstractions, whether these be cultural, ethical or social. And though I often feel that questions of human rights or indigenous rights are less imperative than the question how we can politically and practically narrow the gap between rich and poor, my main concern is that the very mechanisms whereby the powerful – who also dominate the discourse of human rights – distribute foreign aid to and seek to influence the political choices of the underprivileged, paradoxically undermine these people's existential quest for greater autonomy.

This is the argument that Aboriginal lawyer and activist, Noel Pearson, makes against the Australia state, whose welfare-based approach to the plight of Aboriginals actually diminishes these people's capacity to determine their own destinies. It is the same argument Steven Archibald and Paul Richards make in reviewing some of the disastrous changes that the West has attempted to impose on Africa in the name of scientific rationality or European law. Arguing for a more particularistic, local-level approach to both agricultural innovation and the implementation of human rights, they criticise the way that 'intellectuals, development agencies and governments' have conceived solutions to problems 'at too high a level of abstraction and generalization', overlooked the fact that human rights *are* generally enshrined in indigenous law, and all too often ignored the ways in which 'indigenous science' and 'indigenous technology' hold the key to development (Archibald and Richards 2002: 340, cf. Richards 1985: 12).

Methodological Relativism

More imperative than defining universal human rights or implementing some universal moral law is the *practice* of putting oneself in the place of another. This is what Hannah Arendt (1982b: 43) called training one's imagination 'to go visiting' and what Kwasi Wiredu, translating an Akan concept, calls 'sympathetic impartiality' (1996: 29,170). It is this openness to submitting one's assumptions to the test of dialogue and debate, and of allowing one's own thoughts to be seen from the vantage point of another, that offers us the possibility of evolving forms of understanding and action that are conducive to the general good. Such sympathetic impartiality was utterly absent when the Akan killed innocent people so they could attend a dead ruler on his journey to the land of the dead, when the frightened men of Kamadugu Sukurela put an alleged 'witch' to death on the grounds that she was 'not a person', when rebels mutilated Fina Kamara and her daughter because she had supposedly voted for a government that sought their destruction, when migrants and refugees in Europe are persecuted because they are not like us, when the Nazis killed jews with impunity because they were mere 'wood', 'rags', 'merchandise', or 'dolls', and whenever another person's being-for-himself is reduced by language, or by actions or by thought to nothing but an object for us.

The century that has witnessed these atrocious acts also gave birth to anthropology. Perhaps it is true that every act of evil so unsettles the human soul that it ironically sows the seeds of its own redemption. Thus, ethnographers may be compared with those palaeolithic hunters who so painstakingly endeavoured to bring back to life in painted or sculptured representations the very lives they had contributed to destroying. Whatever the case may be, it seems to me that anthropology, and the methodology of participant-observation that still lies at its heart, is one of the ways in which such redemption can be sought – not by recompensing those who have suffered the terror of invasion and colonisation, nor by advocating some form of moral or cultural relativism, but by exercising anthropology's capacity as an empirical science and art of dialogue to subvert abstraction, encouraging us to become more deeply involved in the local and particular lifeworlds of others, fostering forms of understanding that are reached through engagement rather than detachment, and thereby creating the *social* conditions under which coexistence is possible.

Notes

1.   Unlike India, where the British established a state apparatus and infrastructure, Sierra Leone became independent in 1961 with an untried and unviable system of government. Though it would become cited as a 'failed state' it had, in truth, never become a state, and as a succession of idealists, opportunists and military rulers filled that power vacuum over the next thirty years, the country slipped into decay and anarchy. The army of international entrepreneurs, peacekeepers, NGOs, administrators and advisers that entered Sierra Leone as the war ended shared an ideology of development and human rights whose vocabulary belonged to the new

century yet whose assumptions were those of the colonial past. Africa was
being recolonised.

2. Revolutionary United Front, otherwise known as the rebels.

3. Economic Community of West African States Monitoring Group – a military force,
made up mainly of Nigerian troops, that was brought into Sierra Leone to quell
the rebellion.

4. Hake is sometimes translated as 'sin', though the word covers a multitude of
motives – hatred, ill-will, malice, envy – and distracts from the principle of retributive justice that lies behind it. In Kuranko thought, intersubjective relationships are
governed by reciprocity, so that if a person offends, wrongs or injures another person without justification, the offence calls for payback (*tasare*). This compensatory
action may be effected through several means. It may follow a court hearing, in
which case the offender must indemnify the person to whom injury has been
caused. It may follow a verbal apology, in which the offender begs forgiveness. It
may, if recourse to legal means or the workings of individual conscience are
unavailing, lead the injured party to take matters into his own hand and seek sorcery as a form of revenge. Alternatively, if the injured party feels that no worldy
agency can secure redress, he may be inclined to leave matters in the hands of God.
In a previous discussion of hake (Jackson 1982: 29–30) I speak of automatic
redress, in which an unprovoked and unjustified offence will boomerang back
against the offender, particularly if the victim is protected by magical medicines. In
conversations with Kuranko informants in January–February 2002, however, such
redress was thought to require divine agency. As Noah put it, 'People feel that God
is just and omnipotent. One way or another He'll avenge the crime or wrong-doing.'

5. That all villagers were equal in the eyes of the rebels, may ironically have helped
them endure the trauma they experienced, for though RUF violence destroyed the
lives of so many, it has reinforced a sense of solidarity among the survivors. This
solidarity was clearly evident when the Civilian Defence Force War Widows,
Orphans, and Ex-combatants Association was launched in Kabala, northern
Sierra Leone, on 11 January 2002 with the aim of rebuilding villages, clinics and
schools, of offering vocational training in gara-dying, carpentry and tailoring, and
providing medicines and microcredit to villagers.

6. We in the West dwell much on the self. We make a profession of our wounds. In our
stress on psychic inwardness, our own sympathetic suffering all too easily blinds us
to those who are really suffering, or making our own feelings, rather than our
relations with others, our primary concern. This view informed Desmond Tutu's
invocation of the African concept of *ubuntu* at the South African Truth and Reconciliation Commission – for reconciliation, he argued, required a movement from
'I' to 'we'. More forthrightly, the psychologist Nomfundo Walaza condemned those
who put the salving of their own consciences, the saving of their own souls, the
absolution of their own guilt, before the actions that would, in concert with others,
create a new *social* order that might redeem the order of the past.

7. In a meticulous account of the social history of PTSD, Allan Young argues that
this syndrome is 'not timeless, nor does it possess an intrinsic unity. Rather, it is
glued together by the practices, technologies, and narratives with which it is diagnosed, studied, treated, and represented, and by the various interests, institutions,
and moral arguments that mobilized these efforts and resources' (1995: 5).
Though historically and socially constructed, this does not mean, however, that
what we label trauma or PTSD does not signify profoundly real *experiences* of
human distress (ibid: 5–6), it simply means that we should acknowledge that it has
the same 'fictive' status as 'witchcraft' among the Azande.

8. These opposing view of reconciliation were ever-present in the Truth and Reconciliation Commission hearings in South Africa. Archbishop Desmond Tutu, for example, saw reconciliation idealistically, in Christian terms, as a matter of saving one's soul and forgiving one's enemies ('You can only be human in a humane society. If you live with hatred and revenge in your heart, you dehumanize not only yourself, but your community'), Vice-President Thabo Mbeki placed far less emphasis on individual redemption, stressing instead the creation of a new and viable society (Krog 1999: 110–111). The same difference in emphasis emerged from debates over the allegedly self-indulgent and 'self-centred' attitude of whites (concerned solely with personal amnesty and absolution) and the so-called 'we-centredness' of blacks (concerned more with healing a damaged nation through piacular rituals, and new forms of social solidarity and shared belief (ibid: 160–161).

9. Arguing against the widespread assumption that contemporary international humanitarianism 'works' to alleviate poverty and inequality in Africa, Alex de Waal concludes that 'conflicts in Africa can have local solutions, military or political' and suggests that it would be better if the West intervenes less, not more, in these processes (1997: 216).

10. Muslims or Christians, rural farmers or members of the urban middle class, all 'drew vivid and remarkably consistent images,' Shaw writes, describing prosperous cities 'where skycrapers adjoin houses of gold and diamonds; Mercedes-Benzes are driven down fine roads; street vendors roast 'beefsticks' (kebabs) of human meat; boutiques sell stylish 'witch-gowns' that transform their wearers into animal predators in the human world ... ; electronics stores sell tape recorders and televisions (and, more recently, VCRs and computers); and witch airports despatch witch planes – planes so fast, I was once told, that 'they can fly to London and back within an hour' – to destinations all around the globe' (2002: 202).

Chapter 11

EXISTENTIAL IMPERATIVES

Man muss diese vertseinerten Verhältnisse dadurch zum Tanzen zwingen, dass man ihnen ihre eigene Melodie vorsingt (One must force the frozen circumstances to dance by singing to them their own melody).
Karl Marx, *Die Frühschriften* (cited in Fromm 1973: 83)

It is my conviction that the struggle for existence finds its most dramatic and perhaps universal expression in the Oedipus complex. For purposes of cross-cultural analysis, it is, however, important to free the notion of oedipal desire from its Freudian emphasis on 'the narrowly sexual problem of lust and competitiveness' (Becker 1973: 35, cf. Fromm 1973: 59–60, 103–104), as well as its patriarchal bias toward 'blaming' incestuous and aggressive impulses on the child rather than the parent (Devereux 1953: 132; Fromm 1973: 61–62, 101). That the will to be finds expression in some cultures and individuals in images of incestuous or patricidal desire should not distract us from seeing that what is universal about the Oedipus complex is, as existential psychoanalysts have pointed out, the imperative need of every human being to be recognised as a person in his or her own right, and not be reduced to an object of other people's wills, a slave to their desires. Such existential raisons d'être are often incompatible with 'western' rationales for social progress and development. That which is imported and imposed – no matter how 'objectively' important for human life and livelihood – will tend to be resisted and rejected as long as it is felt to reduce the recipient to the passive status of an object. Man does not live by bread alone. And this is why, in the previous chapter, I spoke of the invasion of aid and development experts in West Africa as implying a reversion to the paternalism of late colo-

Notes for this section can be found on page 192.

nialism, a second colonisation, and why many contemporary Maori in
Aotearoa New Zealand repudiate the new genetic technologies.

'Bury me standing', the Rom adage goes, 'I've been on my knees all
my life.' This is also a recurring theme of existential thought – this
stubborn human refusal to take life lying down, to resist subjugation,
to struggle against being seen as a mere instantiation of transpersonal
forces, a plaything of fate, driven by circumstances that one can neither comprehend nor control. Even if it is an illusion that we can determine our own destinies, people in all societies seem to need to believe
that this is, at least to some extent, possible. As the Maori proverb has
it, *Mauri tu mauri ora, Mauri noho mauri mate* – an active spirit means
life, an inactive spirit leads to death. But rather than make self-asser-
tion or rebellion central to what it means to be human, I have argued
throughout this book that the struggle for being is better understood
as a continual, if frequently unreflective, quest for some sense of balance between being an actor and being acted upon – negotiating a
'fair' trade-off between the need to decide our own lives and the need
to come to terms with the forces against which we cannot prevail. To
this end, conformity, forbearance, resignation and self-effacement may
be just as effective in salvaging one's sense of being, in parlous or
oppressive situations, as active resistance and wilful self-definition. To
feel that one is part of a mass movement, to embrace a cause, or yield
to the will of others may increase one's sense of significance every bit
as much as striving to stand out from the crowd. Even in those 'religious' traditions that cultivate stoic acquiesence and practice detachment from material and social ties, the prioritising of 'being' over
'doing' is no less dependent on a decisive attitude and 'techniques' of
self-control than the 'materialistic' tradition of investing one's time
and energy in the accumulation of capital. But however one construes
being, it involves a *relationship* between what is given by circumstance,
and what one brings into being by virtue of one's own desire or will.
Even in extreme circumstances, human beings find or imagine ways of
conniving in their own fate, yielding their own will to the will of others, or to God, or assenting to fate so that the inevitable seems something done of their own free will, 'pitiable though this may seem'
(Kazantzakis 1961: 274). Moreover, except in pathological cases
human beings seldom respond to the loss of being (humiliation, degradation, violence and indifference) by doing absolutely nothing about it.
Though one may not be able to act directly against alienating conditions, one can always act indirectly, through the resources of the
imagination, thought and language, and thereby change one's *experience* of one's relationship to the external forces that bear so heavily
upon one.[1]

It is to Dostoyevsky that we owe perhaps the most compelling description of this perverse need to live one's life on one's own terms.

> Even if man was nothing but a piano key, even if this could be demonstrated mathematically – even then, he wouldn't come to his senses but would pull some trick out of sheer ingratitude, just to make his point. And if he didn't have them on hand, he would devise the means of destruction, chaos, and all kinds of suffering to get his way ... I believe this is so and I'm prepared to vouch for it, because it seems to me that the meaning of man's life consists in proving to himself every minute that he's a man and not a piano key. And man will keep proving it and paying for it with his own skin; he will turn into a troglodyte if need be. And, since this is so, I cannot help rejoicing that things are still the way they are and that, for the time being, nobody knows worth a damn what determines our desires. (Dostoyevsky 1961: 114–115)

The difficulty in universalising Dostoyevsky's 'man from the cellar' is that he is a man alone – marginal, resentful and misanthropic. The human need to be more than just an inert instrument on which others play their tunes – to be also the one who calls the tune – is more than a need for individual identity; it is a fundamental aspect of sociality. And though human beings often expect some degree of reciprocity in their relation to the extra-human world, this expectation all but governs relations with other human beings. We seek, as a matter of course, for reciprocal balance, not only between ourselves and others but between being subject to the *actions* of others, and being subjects who realise, in turn, our own capacity to act on them. This struggle to sustain and consummate one's being in relation to others is never more urgent than when we are robbed of the right to speak and act, or the capacity to act is unequally apportioned. Many ethnographers will know the erosion of self-confidence, the disorientation and despair, the acute vulnerability and vague paranoia to which one falls prey during the first few weeks of fieldwork, as one endures an eclipse of everything one knows, all that one has, and all that defines who one is.

A singularly compelling example of this losing struggle for being is Sartre's (1963) of Jean Genet's early childhood. A foundling, whose early years are spent in a Reformatory at Mettray, Genet is placed with a foster family of Morvan peasants when he is seven. He is already in the habit of pilfering, though 'innocently' and unreflectively, until one day in his tenth year he is discovered with his hand in the kitchen drawer, and loudly denounced as 'a thief'. Perhaps in his acts of petty theft, the child has been searching for the love and attention of which he had been deprived. But at the very instant his foster mother declares, 'You're a thief', his inchoate desires count for nothing; he is now reduced to this single word, this one overwhelming identity, this

stigma, this fate. Yet, this moment proves to be his real 'birth' and confirmation – the moment in which he 'came to himself'. His innocence
lost, his sense of self subverted by the word 'thief', Genet now cynically
decides to embrace this definition, and resist the external identification
by living it through in his own terms. At first he is confounded by the
label, and gropes blindly toward a way of being himself, but gradually
he discovers ways of bringing himself into being as 'the prince of
thieves', as a poet, as his own man. Later, he will write of this childhood moment of truth, 'I decided to be what crime made of me' (Sartre
1963: 17–48), a decision which, for Sartre, discloses the essence of
our humanity. 'We are not lumps of clay, and what is important is not
what people make of us but what we ourselves make of what they have
made us,' he writes, adding, 'since [Genet] cannot escape fatality, he
will be his own fatality' (ibid: 49).

This strategy for reclaiming or choosing one's own being in the face
of forces that diminish and demean one's humanity is often undra-
matic and unremarked. One thinks, for instance, of petty acts of sabo-
tage or malingering among manual workers who have no investment
in the corporation that hires their labour, and has the power to fire
them at will. One thinks of school children in overcrowded classrooms,
subverting routines, dodging lessons and flaunting their contempt for
the 'system'. One thinks of psychiatric care-workers and paramedics,
worn down by the indifference, abuse and degradation of those to
whom they minister help, regaining a sense of themselves and of their
worth by sharing with colleagues mocking and derisive anecdotes
about their clients. And one thinks of plantation slaves, subtly turning
the tables on their masters by subtly parodying their manners of walking, dancing, dressing, singing.

A South Carolina slave in the 1840s explained such oppositional
practices in these words:

> us slaves watch the white folk's parties when the guests danced a minute
> and then paraded in a grand march. Then we'd do it too, but we used to
> mock 'em, every step. Sometimes the white folks notices it but they seemed
> to like it. I guess they thought we couldn't dance any better. (Pierson 1976:
> 166–180)

In similar situations, tactics of distancing, narrative irony, parodic per-
formance and gallows humour abound. These are what Scott calls
'weapons of the weak' (1985), and Sartre refers to as 'provocative
impotence' (1987: 174), launched when the enemy is already the victor. 'When resistance is impossible, the vanquished party reacts with
an aggressive show of the passivity to which he has been reduced, and
arrogantly takes on himself what the other did to him' (ibid: 174). This

was how Genet reacted to being called 'a thief', and how many African intellectuals resisted colonial rule.[2]

> ... the African ... colonized, exploited, treated as a 'negro' by the racist colonizers, took up the notions and words those colonizers used to think about him and to signify him. He 'gathered them from the mud,' a black poet has said, 'in order to wear them with pride.' Negro, yes, and dirty nigger, if you like; but by tearing your words, your concepts, away from you and applying them to myself in full sovereignty, by laying claim to that nature you scorn but whose originality you cannot avoid recognizing, I recapture the initiative, I dare to think about myself, I personalize myself against you, and I become that permanent indignity – the self-conscious *other*. Thus was born the notion of 'negritude.' (ibid: 174–175)

Rather than subvert the words of the overseer, one may subvert his *time*. Zack Jakamarra spoke to me in this vein, recounting the period in the late 1940s when he worked off and on for whites at The Granites goldmine in Central Australia's Tanami desert.

After explaining to me how the white bosses did hardly any work themselves, relying on *yapa* (Aboriginal people) to do all the hard labour, Zack said: '*Yapa* people bin working hard, too many people, working for nothing, only tucker. And no blankets.' But like other men of his generation, Zack did not see himself as a victim, and spoke laughingly of how they used to outwit the whites, stealing amalgam from the battery plates, filching food from the store. While they took full advantage of what whites had to offer – flour, sugar and tea – they kept their own counsel, and determined their own timetables, heading off into the desert from time to time to hunt native cat, possum and goanna, and perform ceremony, always coming and going, Zack insisted, in their own good time, and riling the whites by going 'walkabout'. 'We never tell 'im, "Well I'm going now." We never say it that way. We just walk off the job. "Come on, we go!" Might be two of my mates. Working at that job. "Right, keep a little tucker!" Go on now, walk around somewhere, walk rouuuuuuund. Then we go back. *Kardiya* (whitefellas) say, "Let 'im come! Billy can! Bring 'im down. Fill 'im up, m*angari* (food). Making damper now. Sit down there now".'

Losses and Gains

Pierre Bourdieu writes that 'the social world gives what is rarest, recognition, consideration, in other words, quite simply, reasons for being' (2000: 240). But these reasons for being are, he notes, unequally distributed, so that while the lives of some people are recognised, valued and fostered, the lives of others are regarded as less worthwhile, and often written off. But this 'social world' of which Bourdieu speaks extends far beyond the world of persons, since people universally think of human being as distributed into the world of plants, animals and things. Among the Kuranko, for example, person-hood (*morgoye*) may be an attribute of people, ancestors, totemic animals, God and even plants, while antisocial people may lack it entirely. In other words, being is not restricted to *human* being (Jackson 1982: 17–18). It is also useful to make a distinction between hierarchical and horizontal dimensions of social interaction. Thus, the powers of the gods or the state are often seen as 'higher' powers that bestow the wherewithal of life only when 'lesser mortals' submit to them, giving the respect they are due, paying the tithes they demand, offering the sacrifices that feed and placate them.[3]

Among equals and contemporaries, however, there may be more forthright negotiation, and a more ferocious battle of wits and of wills. Nonetheless, the same logic obtains in both cases. Because being is both scarce and unequally distributed, one person's loss of being will tend to be interpreted as another's gain. Maori notions of *mana* and *tupu* exemplify this. While *tupu* is 'an expression of the nature of things and of human beings as unfolded from within' (Johansen 1954: 85), *mana* expresses the way in which being is realised and redistributed in the course of a person's interactions with the environment and with others. Like the Greek *dumanis*, *mana* implies 'power in action' (Marsden 1975: 194). Thus, while an insult reduces or weakens (*mate*) one's honour and repute, avenging the insult recovers it – though at the other's expense. *Tupu* (coming into existence) and *mate* (fading away) are thus likened to the waxing and waning of the moon, the lighting and dying of a fire, or a tree that is alive and a tree that has been felled. In a war between Mango and Whatihua, many of Whatihua's men were killed and Whatihua himself taken prisoner. Mango then shamed the captive chief by pissing on his bowed head. As a result Whatihua's spiritual power and charisma (*mana*) was taken by Mango (*ko te rironga tenei o te mana o Whatihua i a Mango*). Yet, in Whatihua's social death, his whole *hapu* lost *mana*, since the being of a chief is fused with the being of the land, as well as the being of those whose lives and livelihoods are invested in that land (ibid: 86). Hence the saying, 'It is hard to flee before the enemy ..., it is a sign that the *mana* and name (i.e., renown) of the tribe are destroyed by the blows of the weapons of the victorious tribe' (ibid: 88).

This sense that one's own fate is tied reciprocally to the fate of others, and that one person's fortune entails another's misfortune, is not simply an artefact of culture, peculiar to Maori thought, but a universal mode of intersubjective reason whose roots lie in the child's relation of give and take with its carer and in the unequal and variable distribution of the symbolic goods that give us life (Schieffelen 1990: ch.6). But as Maori ethnography makes clear, in calculating what constitutes a just apportionment of love, wealth, health or wellbeing, and deciding on stratagems to regain whatever has been wrongfully taken away, people everywhere make reference not only to their own individual need to be loved, rich, recognised, powerful or well, but to the history of the group, class, nation or collectivity with which they identify. This is why it is seldom possible to disentangle personal from political grievances, to draw clear distinctions between the quest for personal wellbeing and the quest for political autonomy, or to separate the narratives of the nation from personal lifestories. As we saw in chapter 3, an identical logic underwrites both personal and collective struggles for being. Inasmuch as one, or one's own, has suffered loss of life, livelihood or lifeworld, this loss can only be made good by symbolically taking something back from the person or group that is allegedly responsible for one's own misfortune, or else symbolically expunging that other from oneself.

If Life is Not Like a Box of Chocolates, Perhaps it May be Compared to a Pot of Soup

'Mama always said life was like a box of chocolates, never know what you're gonna get,' said Forrest Gump (1994). His mother also said, 'You have to do the best with what God gave you.' My own experience is that people seldom *live* as fatalistically as this, though this is a familiar enough way that people speak about events in retrospect, trying to come to terms with their limited capacity for comprehending or controlling their own fate. But if life is not like a box of chocolates, perhaps it may be compared with a pot of soup. It is a mix we work on constantly, making do with limited culinary skills and the ingredients that happen to be on hand as we try to achieve something that nourishes and satisfies. I am speaking here, not of the struggle to renegotiate the distribution of being in relation to the 'powers that be', nor even in relation to others, but within ourselves, in our immediate lives. I am speaking of the intimate and often trivial ways human beings create a sense that life is worth living, and celebrating it, despite the fact that, as Robert Burns famously put it, 'The best laid schemes o' mice an' men/ Gang aft a-gley,/ An' lea'e us nought but grief an' pain,/ For promised joy'.

Though Bourdieu (1977:178) is at pains to point out that his term 'symbolic capital' covers such things as fair words, smiles, small gestures, and mundane pleasures, it seems to me important that a distinction is drawn between actions that 'appear' to depend mainly on our environment, and what it affords us, and actions that' seem' to arise from our own native capacities. My interest here is in the ways people effectively redistribute being within the most intimate spaces of their lives, and imaginatively, practically and socially negotiate new relationships between external constraints and inner potentialities. I think for instance of those lines that Malcolm Lowry wrote (1963) when he and his first wife were living in British Columbia, and that so beautifully conjure up the miracle of conjugal love.

> Sitting in the sun at noon with the furiously
> Smoking shadow of the shack chimney –
> Eagles drive downwind in one,
> Terns blow backward,
> A new kind of tobacco at eleven,
> And my love returning on the four o'clock bus
> - My God, why have you given this to us?

I also have in mind a photo I took in Firawa thirty three years ago, of a couple on their house porch, the woman winding cotton thread onto a bobbin as her husband holds a spindle of raw cotton, teasing it out between his finger tips as a single twist of yarn. These images endure, despite decay and mortality. The *jeli* couple in my photo dead these many years. The tragedy of Lowry's marriages and the terrible alter-cations, the broken gin bottle in an upstairs room, the night of his death in 1957, his grave in Ripe, Sussex, not far from where a white horse is cut in chalk on the downs and where, in summer, the ripening barleycorn grazes you softly as you walk the flinty paths, and gather blood-red poppies from the gamboge grain. And I am remembering a passage from Anne-Line Dalsgård's ethnography of a *favela* in Recife, northeast Brazil, where she describes how women iron clothes, clean house, keep fit and 'improve' their lives and dwellings, despite grinding poverty, violence and the burden of raising a family. Sonia, for example, who dreamed of being something more than a *pé de chinelo* (a heel-less shoe, i.e., poor), and one day 'succumbed to temptation' and bought a pair of high-heeled shoes from a vendor who came to her door. Later that day, she realised that she had paid twice as much as the town prices for the cheap plastic shoes, and her broad feet, 'accustomed to the freedom of the *chinelo*' would not fit the new ones. On the day of the party to which she was to wear the heeled shoes, she had to remove them before even reaching the bus stop (Dalsgård 2000: 111–112).

Though revolutions may not be born of such small gestures toward opening up a space in which to live, life consists in them. This is why an anthropology that simply describes categorical modes of being –

male/female, elder/younger, oppressor/oppressed – fails to do justice to those miniscule details of everyday life that determine how a person's lot is actually lived. Once, in the Kuranko village of Kamadugu Sukurela, I talked to a group of women about the difficulties of their lives. One of these women, whose name was Sinkari Yegbe Kargbo, was married to Duwa Marah, a generous, amiable and gentle man with whom I had a particularly close relationship. Sinkari Yegbe was especially forthcoming on the question of marriage. 'Men pay too much bridewealth for us,' she said, 'so they have complete control over us, and every right to determine what we do. You cannot cook unless your husband gives you rice. You cannot go to market unless he gives you money. And if someone promises you something and fails to deliver, you have no redress, there is nothing that a woman can do.' Many years before, after her initiation, Sinkari Yegbe had married a man she did not love. She could not get used to being among strangers in the small farming hamlet where she was obliged to live after her marriage. She ran away with a young lover. For this she was put in the stocks. After her release, she returned to her natal village of Sukurela where she found support with her age-mates (who had warned her of the difficulties of adjusting to life in a bush hamlet), and where finally her father – though not her mother – accepted her decision to marry a man of her own choice. Knowing that many Kuranko women stoically adjusted to arranged marriages, and had to endure indifferent or abusive husbands, I was keen to know what Sinkari Yegbe had to say about women who did not 'run away' (*sumburi*, elopement). 'If a husband is overbearing, she could still go on *sumburi*. Sometimes it is just to pay the husband back (*talsare*, payback, i.e., revenge), sometimes it is because of love. But if her husband maltreats her, and uses force, she will have no alternative but to run away. Love should go and come back.' Later, Sinkari Yegbe told me that women use their wiles to get around men – malingering, cooking unappetising food, pretending to have their periods in order to dodge domestic chores and telling comic stories about the doltishness of men and the cleverness of their wives. As Mary Douglas pointed out, jokes have a 'subversive effect on the dominant structure of ideas', the joke 'breaks down control' (1968: 364).

It has been a recurring theme of this book that playing with words, objects and images, ludically or otherwise, changes our experience of the situations in which we find ourselves, and that these transformations in how we see the world involve subtle changes in the way we feel that being is distributed. Though I have been at pains not to judge such modes of action, not to see them as merely magical, or bereft of any power to change the world for the better, any human action has political potential. Thus, the desire for greater autonomy to which Sinkari Yegbe alluded may lead increasing numbers of Kuranko woman to

decide against circumcising their daughters, as in the case of Fatu
Marah mentioned in the previous chapter. Moreover, in her study of a
favela in Recife, to which I referred briefly above, Anne-Line Dalsgård
(2000) documents the ways in which large numbers of poor women
are electing to undergo sterilization by tubal ligation as a way of gain-
ing greater autonomy and recognition, and thereby breaking out of
the cycle of poverty and violence that dooms them to *a classe fraca* (the
weak class). And everywhere, people try to migrate from 'hopeless' circumstances to more 'hopeful' ones (Hage 2003), seeking to increase
their life chances and improve their lot – a phenomena that has the
potential to pluralise and revolutionise the world. These are all matters
of trading off losses against possible gains, working out a balance
between one's own capacities/desires and the promises or potentialities of the world.

Being and Belonging

There is another sense of being that seems to arise unbidden, which is
neither struggled for nor even 'possessed', as though it were in the
nature of things – an 'it' whose presence precludes the 'I' and even the
'we', yet seems to encompass all. Such moments of grace are gifted,
one might say. At such times the extra-human world, the world of others and of oneself appear to merge – as if the infinite being of the world
and our own finite being were one. After all the notebooks have been
filled, interpretations ventured and books published, these are the
moments that remain, transcending the boundaries of space and time.

Late one afternoon in the dry season of 1970, I was walking out of
Firawa alone. The laterite path had been trodden by generations of
bare feet. Brakes of elephant grass, flattened by fire, lay on either side.
Apart from the stitch of cicadas and the repeated call of a suluku bird,
the landscape was silent, though in the late afternoon light it was
glowing, as if it had absorbed the heat of the sun all day and was now
returning it against the coming night. As I rounded the hill, I glanced
up at the tawny grass and contorted lophira trees that covered it. It
was then that I glimpsed what I thought was a man – or rather his rus-
set tunic – moving slightly in the long grass. It was like Rousseau's
painting of the man tussling with a leopard, though there was no leopard. The moment was magical. The softness of the light. The appari-
tion of the man. The warmth that emanated from the path. The
strength and hope of youth that flowed through me. And the deep
sense of happiness that welled up as I became aware that I was doing
what I had always dreamed of doing, and that by nightfall I would
reach the river where I left my vehicle ten days before, and would drive

the remaining miles to Kabala and lie that night in the arms of someone I loved.

Twenty years later, I was with my second wife, Francine, in Central
Australia, travelling with Warlpiri friends near a place called Wapur-
tali, known by whites as Mount Singleton. Paddy Jupurrula, a painter
of some repute, sat beside me, silently indicating which way I should
turn whenever the track forked. I had only to watch the slight waver-
ing or flick of his flat hand to turn the steering wheel and remain on
course. There was no talk. The only sound was of saplings, spinifex
grass and anthills scraping the chassis of our Toyota.

When the track petered out, we began the laborious process of
bush-bashing – twisting and turning to avoid gulches and mulga
thickets – but moving steadily and quietly toward the range. Finally we
reached the wide floodout around Braitlings Bore, and the sandy bed of
a creek that led to Yirntardamururu.

We walked the last few kilometers, straggling out under the blue
shadows of the range. Jangala told me that as a young man he had
worked for Braitling. Braitling was a hard taskmaster. People did not
remain camped for long at the station. They hunted around Pikilyi
(Vaughan Springs), and foraged as far north as Jila – for ngurlu (grass
seed), yawakiyi (bush currants), yakajirri (bush plum) and yarla
(yams). Yirntardamururu was the main camp, the permanent water,
to which people from far and wide gravitated in the summer months.
They hunted in winter, in small bands – perhaps ten men and their
wives and children, two or three young men, five old people.

'This place my father,' Jupurrula explained. 'That Japanangka' –
and he indicated the younger man by pointing with his chin – 'my
wife's brother ... he's *kurdungurlu* for this place.' Jupurrula picked up
some grindstone shards, as if to confirm what he had said.

There were deep pools of water in the creek, with granite outcrops
and boulders all around. Jupurrula reminded me that this was also a
site on the marlu-jarra (two kangaroo) dreaming track that came
down through the centre of Australia from Gurintiji country in the
north, and ran on south via Nyirrpi to Uluru and Katajulu. The two
kangaroos had brought men's business into Warlpiri country. Here,
he told me, is where they camped for two or three weeks. And sure
enough, there in the rock were the kidney-shaped impressions left by
two kangaroos sleeping on their sides. Not far away he showed me
another *kurruwarri* – a sign, a mark, a vestige of the dreaming: a perfect circle of white limestone inlaid in the granite.

It was mid-afternoon when we headed back to Jila. Skin burned by
the sun, chafed by the wind, grazed by sharp branches and grimed
with soot, I steered the vehicle along the old tracks that Jangala now
remembered. In the back of the vehicle, the women spoke to Francine

of their elation at having visited a place they had not seen for twenty years – a place close to Ngurdipatu (place of many birds), also on the two-kangaroo track, where they had been born. But now they wanted to hunt.

Again we stopped, and the women disappeared into the grasslands, while the men walked about inspecting the brick-red earth for the spoor of animals.

I sat down in the shade of a mulga tree.

When Japanangka joined me without speaking, I thought of saying something, but it did not seem to be required. So I allowed myself to hear only the insects trilling in the grass, the blood pulsing in my head.

Then Japanangka pointed skyward. He had heard the murmur of an aircraft, seen its aluminium glint 35,000 feet above us in the clear blue sky. 'Going to Europe,' Japanangka said. 'Singapore'.

Suddenly I had this heightened sense of the difference between earth and ether – of how at peace I felt, sitting there with Japanangka, cross-legged on the ground, without the slightest desire to be in the airplane, to be anywhere else. Maybe it was because I was getting older. Jupurrurla had spoken to me two days before about the homesickness people feel when they are far from their own country, their yearning to return there to die ... and it is a theme reiterated in myths that describe how ancestors, wearied by travel and by the work of creating new country, pined for their places of origin and returned home, through the air or underground, there to sink back into the earth again, into a state of nascence, of pure potentiality. Certainly I had rarely felt more at peace within myself in any other period of fieldwork. No ambition for fame or fortune possessed me; not even a desire for knowledge – which was, all too often, ephemeral, abstract and chimerical anyway. As the airplane grew smaller and smaller in the northern sky, I felt that I was at last where I had always longed to be, a grassy plain under a cloudless sky, with people for whom being-in-the-world was defined through the metaphor of sitting on the ground, of being with others, closed circles and soft lines imprinted with the point of an index finger in the red dirt.

Notes

1. In extremis, people may give up on life. In the Nazi death camps such people were known as 'Muslims' because of their impassivity and fatalism. They 'died as men before their bodies died' (the line is from W.H. Auden's poem *The Shield of Achilles*). Yet others clung to hope, or found means of improving their chances of survival, degrading though these often were. Robbed of the power to act, people retained what Victor Frankl (1992) called 'the last freedom' – the freedom to 'choose one's attitude,' to construe one's situation in a way that made it more bearable.

2. I analyse self-deprecating first-contact myths in *Minima Ethnographica* (Jackson 1998: 108–124), and Fritz Kramer also provides insights into the 'mimetic' logic of these 'mythologemes' of cultural difference in *The Red Fez* (1993: 18–30).
3. Metaphors of power as cannibalism or vampirism (i.e. as extreme forms of greed and selfish consumption) are the product of a profound logic. One of the most compelling discussions of this theme is to be found in Michel Serres' *Statues* (1989), where he draws parallels between the explosion of the spaceshuttle *Challenger* at Cape Canaveral on 28 January 1986 and the ancient Carthaginians' practice of enclosing animals and children in a gigantic brass statue of the god Baal and incinerating them as a sacrifice to the deity. Serres' insights into this violent logic of asymmetrical power relations may be applied to colonial history and the radical inequality in today's world between rich and poor, for despite the marginalisation and disparagement of those who lack politico-economic power, it is their vital being – in the form of raw energy, labour, libido, land and natural resources – that sustains the being of the rich, who would otherwise suffer entropy, impotence and collapse.

BIBLIOGRAPHY

Abu-Lughod, Lila. 1991. 'Writing against Culture'. In Fox, Richard (ed.), *Recapturing Anthropology: Working in the Present*. Sante Fe: School of American Research Press, pp. 137–162.

_____ 1993. *Writing Women's Worlds: Bedouin Stories*. Berkeley: University of California Press.

Adams, John. 1851. 'Discourses on Davila'. In *Works of John Adams*, vol 6. Boston.

Adorno, Theodor. 1973. *Negative Dialectics* (trans. Ashton, E.B.). New York: Continuum.

_____ 1978. *Minima moralia: Reflections from Damaged Life* (trans. E.F.N. Jephcott). London: Verso.

_____ 1998. *Critical Models: Interventions and Catchwords* (trans. Henry Pickford). New York: Columbia University Press.

Ahearn, Laura M. 2001. 'Language and Agency'. In *Annual Review of Anthropology* 30, pp.109–137.

Appadurai, Arjun (ed.). 1986. *The Social Life of Things: Commodities in Cultural Perspective*. Cambridge: Cambridge University Press.

Archibald, Steven and Paul Richards. 2002. 'Converts to Human Rights? Popular Debate about War and Justice in Rural Central Sierra Leone', *Africa*, 72(3): 339–367.

Arendt, Hannah. 1958. *The Human Condition*. Chicago: Chicago University Press.

_____ 1963. *On Revolution*. New York: Viking Press.

_____ 1967. *The Origins of Totalitarianism*. New Edition. London: George Allen and Unwin.

_____ 1969. 'Reflections on Violence', *New York Review of Books*, 27 February 1969.

_____ 1971. *The Life of the Mind*. San Diego and New York: Harcourt Brace.

_____ 1982a. *On Revolution*. New York: Viking.

_____ 1982b. *Lectures on Kant's Political Philosophy* (ed. Ronald Beiner) Chicago: Chicago University Press.

Aristotle. 1952. *The Works of Aristotle, Vol. 12: Select Fragments* (translated under the editorship of Sir David Ross). Oxford: Clarendon Press.

Aronsson, Inga-Lill. 2002. *Negotiating Involuntary Resettlement: A Study of Local Bargaining during the Construction of the Zimapán Dam.* Occasional Papers 17, Department of Cultural Anthropology and Ethnology. Uppsala: Uppsala Universitet.

Austin, J.L. 1962. *How to do Things with Words.* Oxford: Clarendon Press.

Bakhtin, Mikhail. 1984a. *Rabelais and His World,* (trans. Hélène Iswolsky). Bloomington: Indiana University Press.

_____ 1984b. *Problems in Doestoevsky's Poetics,* (trans. Caryl Emerson). Minneapolis: University of Minnesota Press.

Baldwin, James and Margaret Mead. 1971. *A Rap on Race.* London: Michael Joseph.

Barley, Stephen R. 1988. 'The Social Construction of a Machine: Ritual, Superstition, Magical Thinking and Other Pragmatic Responses to Running a CT Scanner'. In Lock, Margaret, and Gordon, Deborah (eds) *Biomedicine Examined.* Dortrecht: Kluwer, pp. 497–539.

Bateson, Gregory. 1958. *Naven.* Stanford: Stanford University Press.

_____ 1973. *Steps to an Ecology of Mind.* Frogmore: Paladin.

Bauman, Zygmunt. 1998. *Globalization: The Human Consequences.* Cambridge: Polity Press.

Bech, Henning. 1997. *When Men Meet: Homosexuality and Modernity* (trans. Teresa Mesquit and Tim Davies). Cambridge: Polity Press.

Beck, Ulrich. 1999. *World Risk Society.* Cambridge: Polity Press.

Becker, Ernst. 1973. *The Denial of Death.* New York: Free Press.

Berger, John. 1976. *A Fortunate Man: the Story of a Country Doctor.* London: Writers and Readers Publishing Cooperative.

Bergson, Henri. 1911. *Laughter: An Essay on the Meaning of the Comic.* London: Macmillan.

Best, Elsdon. 1959. *The Maori School of Learning.* Dominion Museum Monograph 6. Wellington: Government Printer.

Bettelheim, Bruno. 1959. 'Joey: a "Mechanical Boy"', *Scientific American,* 200(3): 117–126.

Biebuyck, Daniel. 1973. *Lega Culture: Art, Initiation, and Moral Philosophy among a Central African People.* Berkeley: University of California Press.

Bird, Charles. 1976. 'Poetry in the Mande: Its Form and Meaning', *Poetics,* 5(2): 89–100.

Bledisloe, Caroline. 1992. 'The Cultural Transformation of Western Education in Sierra Leone', *Africa* 62(2): 182–202.

Bloom, Leslie Rebecca. 1992. '"How Can We Know the Dancer from the Dance?": Discourses of the Self-body', *Human Studies,* 15: 313–334.

Bode, Barbara. 1990. *Destruction and Creation in the Andes.* New York: Paragon.

Bolinger, Dwight and David A. Sears. 1981. *Aspects of Language.* New York: Harcourt Brace Jovanovich.

Boltanski, Luc. 1999. *Distant Suffering: Morality, Media and Politics* (trans. Graham Burchell). Cambridge: Cambridge University Press.

Bourdieu, Pierre. 1977. *Outline of a Theory of Practice* (trans. Richard Nice). Cambridge: Cambridge University Press.

_____ 1990a. *The Logic of Practice* (trans. Richard Nice). Stanford: Stanford University Press.

_____ 1990b. *In Other Words: Essays towards a Reflexive Sociology*, (trans. Matthew Adamson). Stanford: Stanford University Press.

_____ et al. 1993. *La misère du monde*. Paris: Seuil.

_____ 1998. *Acts of Resistance: Against the New Myths of Our Time*. Cambridge: Polity Press.

_____ 2000. *Pascalian Meditations* (trans. Richard Nice). Cambridge: Polity Press.

_____ 2001. *Masculine Domination* (trans. Richard Nice). Stanford: Stanford University Press.

Bowlby, John. 1971. *Attachment and Loss, 1: Attachment*. Harmondsworth: Penguin.

_____ 1975. *Attachment and Loss, 2: Separation and Anger*. Harmondsworth: Penguin.

Bruner, Jerome. 1990. *Acts of Meaning*. Cambridge, Mass.: Harvard University Press.

Buck-Morss, Susan. 1977. *The Origin of Negative Dialectics: Theodore W. Adorno, Walter Benjamin, and the Frankfurt Institute*. Hassocks (Sussex): Harvester Press.

Buñuel, Luis. 1985. *My Last Breath* (trans. Abigail Israel). London: Fontana.

Burridge, Kenelm. 1969. *Tangu Traditions*. Oxford: Clarendon.

Calame-Griaule, Geneviève. 1965. *Ethnologie et langage: la parole chez les Dogon*. Paris: Gallimard.

Carroll, Rory. 2003. 'Seven put on Trial for Atrocities in Sierra Leone', *Guardian*, 11 March 2003: 6.

Cendrars, Blaise. 1945. *L'homme foudroyé*. Paris: Denoël.

_____ (n.d.). Blaise Cendrars vous parle. Entretien premier, and entretien cinquième. In *Oeuvres complètes*, vol 8, Paris: Denoël.

Cendrars, Miriam. 1992. 'Interview with Frédéric Ferney, Boulogne-sur-Seine, 21 December 1992'. In Frédéric Ferney, *Blaise Cendrars*, Paris: Éditions François Bourin.

Clausewitz, Carl von. 1982. *On War*, Anatol Rapoport (ed.). Harmondsworth: Penguin.

Comaroff, Jean and Comaroff, John L. 1999. 'Occult Economies and the Violence of Abstraction: Notes from the South African Postcolony', *American Ethnologist* 26(2): 279–303.

Coombs, H.C. 1978. *Kulinma: Listening to Aboriginal Australians*. Canberra.

Cornwall, Rupert. 2001. 'Americans Face Giving up Their Treasured Freedoms', *Independent*, 13 September 2001: 7.

Cram, Fiona. 2001. 'Maori and Genetic Engineering'. Report published by International Research Institute for Maori and Indigenous Education, Auckland University.

Dalsgård, Anne-Line. 2000. *Matters of Life and Longing: Female Sterilisation in Northeast Brazil*. Copenhagen: Institute of Anthropology.

D'Andrade, Roy. 1995. 'Moral Models in Anthropology', *Current Anthropology* 36(1): 399–408.

Dangarembga, Tsitsi. 2001. *Nervous Conditions*. London: the Women's Press.

Daniel, E. Valentine. 1996. *Charred Lullabies: Chapters in an Anthropography of Violence*. Princeton: Princeton University Press.

Das, Veena. 1995. *Critical Events: An Anthropological Perspective on Contemporary India*. Delhi: Oxford University Press.

Davidson, Donald. 1980. *Essays on Actions and Events*. London: Oxford University Press.

De Certeau, Michel. 1984. *The Practice of Everyday Life* (trans. Steven Rendall). Berkeley: University of California Press.

DeLillo, Don. 2003. *Cosmopolis*. London: Picador.

Desjarlais, Robert. 1996. 'Struggling Along'. In Jackson, Michael (ed.) *Things as they Are: New Directions in Phenomenological Anthropology*. Bloomington: Indiana University Press, pp. 70–93.

Devereux, George. 1953. 'Why Oedipus Killed Laius: A Note on the Complementary Oedipus Complex in Greek Drama', *The International Journal of Psychoanalysis* 34: 132–141.

——— 1967. *From Anxiety to Method in the Behavioural Sciences*. The Hague: Mouton.

Devisch, René. 1995. 'Frenzy, Violence, and Ethical Renewal in Kinshasa', *Public Culture* 7(3): 593–629.

——— 2003. 'Maleficent Fetishes and the Sensual Order of the Uncanny in South-west Congo'. In Kapferer, Bruce (ed.) *Beyond Rationalism: Rethinking Magic, Witchcraft and Sorcery*. New York/Oxford: Berghahn.

De Waal, Alex. 1997. *Famine Crimes: Politics and the Disaster Relief Industry in Africa*. African Rights and the International African Institute in association with James Currey (Oxford) and Indiana University Press (Bloomington).

Dewes, Koro te Kapunga. 1975. 'The Case for Oral Arts'. In King, Michael (ed.) *Te ao hurihuri: The World Moves On*. Wellington: Hicks Smith, pp. 55–85.

Dewey, John. 1929. *Experience and Nature*. London: Allen and Unwin.

——— 1980. *The Quest for Certainty: A Study of the Relation of Knowledge and Action*. New York: Perigree Books.

Dickens, Charles. 2003. *Bleak House*. Harmondsworth: Penguin Books.

Disch, Lisa Jane. 1994. *Hannah Arendt and the Limits of Philosophy*. Ithaca and London: Cornell University Press.

Dostoyevsky, Fyodor. 1961. *Notes from Underground* (trans. Andrew MacAndrew). New York: Signet.

Douglas, Mary. 1966. *Purity and Danger: An Analysis of Concepts of Pollution and Taboo*. Harmondsworth: Penguin Books.

——— 1968. 'The Social Control of Cognition: Some Factors in Joke Perception', *Man*, New Series 3(3): 361–376.

Downey, Gary Lee. 1998. *The Machine in Me: An Anthropologist Sits among Computer Engineers*. New York and London: Routledge.

Election violence. http://www/sierra-leone.org/sinews.html.

Evans-Pritchard, E.E. 1934. 'Zande Therapeutics'. In Evans-Pritchard, E.E., Firth, Raymond and Malinowski, Bronislaw (eds) *Essays Presented to C.G. Seligman*. London: Kegan Paul, Trench, Trubner & Co, pp. 49–61.

Fadiman, Anne. 1997. *The Spirit Catches You and You Fall Down: A Hmong Child, Her American Doctors, and the Collision of Two Cultures.* New York: Farrar, Straus and Giroux.

Fanon, Frantz. 1968. *The Wretched of the Earth.* New York: Grove Press.

Farmer, Paul. 2001. *Infections and Inequalities: The Modern Plagues.* Updated Edition. Berkeley: University of California Press.

Faulkner, William. 1967. *The Unvanquished.* Harmondsworth: Penguin Books.

Feldman, Allen. 1991. *Formations of Violation: The narrative of the Body and Political Terror in Northern Ireland.* Chicago: Chicago University Press.

Ferme, Mariane. 1998. 'The Violence of Numbers: Consensus, Competition, and the Negotiation of Disputes in Sierra Leone', *Cahiers d'Études Africaines,* 150–152, (2–4): 555–580.

_____ 2001a. *The Underneath of Things: Violence, History, and the Everyday in Sierra Leone.* Berkeley: University of California Press.

_____ 2001b. 'La figure du chasseur et les chasseurs-milicens dans le conflit Sierra-Léonais', *Politique Africaine* 82: 119–132.

Fernandez, James. 1982. *Bwiti: An Ethnography of the Religious Imagination in Africa.* Princeton: Princeton University Press.

Ferney, Frédéric. 1993. *Blaise Cendrars.* Paris: Editions François Bourin.

Feyerabend, Paul. 2000. 'Letter to the Reader', *London Review of Books* 22 June 2000: 28.

Forrest Gump. 1994. Paramount Pictures.

Forsberg, Anna, Bäckman, Lars and Möller, Anders. 2000. 'Experiencing Liver Transplantation: A Phenomenological Approach', *Journal of Advanced Nursing* 32(332): 327–334.

Fortes, Meyer. 1955. 'Names among the Tallensi of the Gold Coast', *Afrikanistische Studien,* Deutsche Akad. d. Wissenschaften zu Berlin, Institut f. Orientforschung 26.

_____ 1987. *Religion, Morality and the Person: Essays on Tallensi Religion,* (ed. Jack Goody). Cambridge: Cambridge University Press.

Foucault, Michel. 1978. *The History of Sexuality, Vol.1: An Introduction.* New York: Pantheon.

_____ 1983. 'The Subject and Power'. Afterword to *Michael Foucault: Beyond Structuralism and Hermeneutics,* by Hubert L. Dreyfus and Paul Rabinow. 2nd Edition. Chicago: Chicago University Press.

Fox, Renée C. and Swazey, Judith P. 1972. *The Courage to Fail: A Social View of Organ Transplants and Dialysis.* Chicago: Chicago University Press.

Frankl, Victor. 1992. *Man's Search for Ultimate Meaning.* Boston: Beacon Press.

Freud, Sigmund. 1950. *Totem and Taboo.* London: Routledge & Kegan Paul.

_____ 1957. *Standard Edition of the Complete Psychological Works of Sigmund Freud,* (trans. and ed. James Strachey). London: Hogarth Press.

Fromm, Erich. 1973. *The Crisis in Psychoanalysis: Essays on Freud, Marx and Social Psychology.* Harmondsworth: Penguin Books.

Fukuyama, Francis. 1992. *The End of History and the Last Man.* Harmondsworth: Penguin Books.

Fuller, Buckminster. 1970. 'Total Thinking'. In Meller, James (ed.) *The Buckminster Fuller Reader.* London: Jonathan Cape, pp. 297–314.

Gausset, Quentin. 2001. 'AIDS and Cultural Practices in Africa: The Case of the Tonga (Zambia)', *Social Science and Medicine* 52: 509–518.

Geertz, Clifford. 1973. *The Interpretation of Cultures*. New York: Basic Books.

Gell, Alfred. 1975. *Metamorphosis of the Cassowaries: Umeda Society, Language and Ritual*. London School of Economics Monographs in Social Anthropology No.51. London: Athlone.

_____ 1979. 'The Umeda Language Poem', *Canberra Anthropology* 1(1): 44–62.

Geschiere, Peter. 1997. *The Modernity of Witchcraft: Politics and the Occult in Postcolonial Africa*, (trans. Peter Geschiere and Janet Roitman). Charlottesville: University Press of Virginia.

Gibson, James J. 1979. *The Ecological Approach to Visual Perception*. Boston: Houghton-Mifflin.

Girard, René. 1965. *Deceit, Desire and the Novel: Self and Other in Literary Structure*, (trans. Yvonne Freccero). Baltimore: Johns Hopkins Press.

_____ 1977. *Violence and the Sacred*, (trans. Patrick Gregory). Baltimore: Johns Hopkins University Press.

Gluckman, Max. 1956. *Custom and Conflict in Africa*. Oxford: Blackwell.

_____ 1958. *Analysis of a Social Situation in Modern Zululand*. Rhodes Livingtone Papers, no. 28. Manchester: Manchester University Press.

Golberine, Willie. 1989. 'Pauvre petite Marilyn bis'. *Paris Match*, August 1989.

Goldberg, Michael and David Handelman. 1987. 'Is Michael Jackson for Real?' *Rolling Stone*, 24 September 1987, pp. 36, 38, 39, 71–74.

Goody, Jack. 1962. *Death, Property and the Ancestors: A Study of the LoDagaa of West Africa*. London: Tavistock.

Gorz, André. 1989. *The Traitor*, (trans. Richard Howard). London: Verso.

Gould, Stephen Jay. 1997. 'Evolution: The Pleasures of Pluralism', *New York Review of Books*, 26 June 1997.

Gray, Chris Hables. (ed.) 1995. *The Cyborg Handbook*. New York and London: Routledge.

Guha, Ranajit. 1987. *Elementary Aspects of Peasant Insurgency in Colonial India*. Delhi: Oxford University Press.

Habermas, Jürgen. 1998. *On the Pragmatic of Communication*, (ed. Maeve Cooke). Cambridge (Mass.): MIT Press.

Hage, Ghassan. 1998. *White Nation: Fantasies of White Supremacy in a Multicultural Society*. Annandale: Pluto Press.

_____ 2002. 'The Differential Intensities of Social Reality: Migration, Participation, Guilt'. In Hage, Ghassan (ed.) *Arab-Australians Today*. Melbourne: Melbourne University Press, pp. 192–205.

_____ 2003. *Against Paranoid Nationalism: Searching for Hope in a Shrinking World*. London: Merlin.

Haraway, Donna. 1991. *Simians, Cyborgs, and Women: the Reinvention of Nature*. New York: Routledge.

Hegel, G.W.F. 1971. *Philosophy of Mind*, (trans. William Wallace). Oxford: Clarendon Press.

Heidegger, Martin. 1975a. 'The Origin of the Work of Art'. In *Poetry, Language, and Thought*, (trans. Albert Hofstader). New York: Harper and Row.

_____ 1975b. 'Building Dwelling Thinking'. In *Poetry, Language, and Thought*, (trans. Albert Hofstader). New York: Harper and Row.

_____ 1977. 'The Question Concerning Technology'. In *Martin Heidegger: Basic Writings*, (ed. David Krell). New York: Harper and Row.

Herzfeld, Michael. 1985. *The Poetics of Manhood: Contest and Identity in a Cretan Mountain Village*. Princeton: Princeton University Press.

_____ 1992. *The Social Production of Indifference: Exploring the Symbolic Roots of Western Bureaucracy*. New York: Berg.

_____ 1997. *Cultural Intimacy: Social Poetics in the Nation-state*. New York: Routledge.

Hooper, John. 2002. 'A Cog without Whom September 11 Would Not Have Succeeded', *Guardian*, 30 August 2002

Hopkins, Janet. 1998. *Biographical objects: How Things Tell the Stories of People's Lives*. New York and London: Routledge.

Hornborg, Alf. 2001. 'Symbolic Technologies: Machines and the Marxian Notion of Fetishism', *Anthropological Theory* 1(4).

Houseman, Michael and Severi, Carlo. 1998. *Naven or the Other Self: A Relational Approach to Ritual*, (trans. Michael Fineberg). Leiden, Boston, Köln: Brill.

Huizinga, Johan. 1970. *Homo ludens: A Study of the Play Element in Culture*. London: Paladin.

Husserl, Edmund. 1962. *Ideas: General Introduction to Pure Phenomenology*. (trans. J.N. Findlay). London: Routledge & Kegan Paul.

_____ 1967. 'The Thesis of the Natural Standpoint and its Suspension'. In Kockelmanns, J.J. (ed.) *Phenomenology: The Philosophy of Edmund Husserl and Its Interpretation*. Garden City: Doubleday.

Ihde, Don. 1979. *Technics and Praxis*. Boston Studies in the Philosophy of Science, Vol 24, (ed. Robert S. Cohen and Marx W. Wartofksy). Dortrecht: Reidel.

Ingold, Tim. 1997. 'Eight Themes in the Anthropology of Technology', *Social Analysis* 41(1): 106–138.

Ironside, Virginia. 2001. 'Dilemmas', *Independent* 3 May 2001: 15.

Jackson, Michael. 1975. 'Literacy, Communications and Social Change: A Study of the Meaning and Effect of Literacy in Early Nineteenth Century New Zealand'. In Kawharu, I.H. (ed.) *Conflict and Compromise: Essays on the Maori since Colonisation*. Wellington: Reed, pp. 27–54.

_____ 1977. *The Kuranko: Dimensions of Social Reality in a West African Society*. London: Hurst.

_____ 1982. *Allegories of the Wilderness: Ethics and Ambiguity in Kuranko Narratives*. Bloomington: Indiana University Press.

_____ 1983. 'Knowledge of the Body', *Man* 18: 327–345.

_____ 1989. *Paths toward a Clearing: Radical Empiricism and Ethnographic Inquiry*. Bloomington: Indiana University Press.

_____ 1995. *At Home in the World*. Durham: Duke University Press.

_____ 1998. *Minima Ethnographica: Intersubjectivity and the Anthropological Project*. Chicago: University of Chicago Press.

_____ 2002a. *The Politics of Storytelling: Violence, Transgression, and Intersubjectivity*. Copenhagen: Museum Tusculanum Press.

_____ 2002b. 'The Exterminating Angel: Reflections on Violence and Intersubjective Reason', *European Journal of Anthropology* 39: 137–148.

_____ 2000c. Biotechnology and the Critique of Globalisation. *Ethnos*, 67(2): 141–154.

_____ 2002d. 'Familiar and Foreign Bodies: A Phenomenological Exploration of the Human-technology Interface', *Journal of the Royal Anthropological Institute*, 8(2): 333–346.

_____ 2003. 'The Politics of Reconciliation: Reflections on the Postwar in Sierra Leone'. In Frykman, Jonas and Gilje, Nils (eds) *Being There: New Perspectives on Phenomenology in the Analysis of Culture*. Lund: Nordic Academic Press, pp. 95–105.

_____ 2004. *In Sierra Leone*. Durham: Duke University Press

_____ and Karp, Ivan. (eds) 1990. *Personhood and Agency: The Experience of Self and Other in African Cultures*. Uppsala Studies in Cultural Anthropology, 14. Stockholm: Almqvist and Wiksell.

Jackson, Moana. 2001. 'An Exquisite Politeness: the Royal Commission on Genetic Modification and the Redefining of the Treaty of Waitangi'. http://www.madge.net.nz/blind/articles/treaty.asp

Jakobson, R. 1960. 'Closing Statement: Linguistics and Poetics'. In Sebeok, T. (ed.) *Style in Language*. Cambridge (Mass.): MIT Press.

James, William. 1912. *Essays in Radical Empiricism*. New York: Longmans, Green & Co.

_____ 1950. *The Principles of Psychology*, Vol. 2. New York: Dover.

_____ 1978. *Pragmatism*. Cambridge (Mass.): Harvard University Press.

Jaspers, Karl. 1967. *Philosophical Faith and Revelation*, (trans. E.B. Ashton). New York.

Johansen, J. Prytz. 1954. *The Maori and His Religion in Its Non-ritualistic Aspects*. Copenhagen: Ejnar Munksgaard.

Johnson, Joyce. 1983. *Minor Characters: A Beat Memoir*. London: Virago.

Karp, Ivan. 1990. See Jackson, Michael, and Karp, Ivan.

Kazantzakis, Nikos. 1961. *Zorba the Greek*. London: Faber and Faber.

Keane, Webb. 1997. *Signs of Recognition: Powers and Hazards of Representation in an Indonesian Society*. Berkeley: University of California Press.

Kleinman, Arthur. 1995. *Writing at the Margin: Discourse between Anthropology and Medicine*. Berkeley: University of California Press.

_____ 2000. 'The Violences of Everyday Life: The Multiple Forms and Dynamics of Social Violence'. In Das, Veena, Kleinman, Arthur, Ramphele, Mamphela and Reynolds, Pamela (eds) *Violence and Subjectivity*. Berkeley: University of California Press, pp. 226–241.

_____ and Kleinman, Joan. 1996. 'Suffering and Its Professional Transformation: Toward an Ethnography of Interpersonal Experience'. In Jackson, Michael (ed.) *Things as They Are: New Directions in Phenomenological Anthropology*. Bloomington: Indiana University Press pp. 169–195.

_____ and Kleinman, Joan. 1997. 'The Appeal of Experience; the Dismay of Images: Cultural Appropriations of Suffering in Our Times'. In Kleinman, Arthur, Das, Veena and Lock, Margaret (eds) *Social Suffering*. Berkeley: California University Press.

Kramer, Fritz. 1993. *The Red Fez: Art and Spirit Possession in Africa*, (trans. Malcolm Green). New York: Verso.

Kroeber, A.L. 1917. 'The Superorganic', *American Anthropologist* 19: 163–213.

Krog, Antje. 1999. *Country of My skull*. London: Jonathan Cape.

Kurkiala, Mikael. 2003. 'Interpreting Honour Killings: The Story of Fadime Sahindal (1975-2002) in the Swedish Press', *Anthropology Today* 19 (1): 6–7.

Laing, Alexander Gordon. 1825. *Travels in the Timanee, Kooranko and Soolima Countries*. London: John Murray.

Laing, R.D. 1971. *Knots*. Harmondsworth: Penguin Books.

Lancaster, Roger. 1992. *Life is Hard: Machismo, Danger, and the Intimacy of Power in Nicaragua*. Berkeley: University of California Press.

Langer, Lawrence. 1997. 'The Alarmed Vision: Social Suffering and Holocaust Atrocity'. In Kleinman, Arthur, Das, Veena and Lock, Margaret (eds) *Social Suffering*. Berkeley: University of California Press, pp. 47–65.

Larreta, Enriquez Rodriguez. 2002. *"Gold is Illusion": The Garimpeiros of Tapajós Valley in the Brazilian Amazonia*. Stockholm: Stockholm Studies in Social Anthropology, 50.

Lattas, Andrew. 1998. *Cultures of Secrecy: Reinventing Race in Bush Kaliai Cargo Cults*. Madison: University of Wisconsin Press.

Leach, E.R. 1966. *Rethinking Anthropology*. London: The Athlone Press.

Leach, Melissa. 2000. 'New Shapes to Shift: War, Parks and the Hunting Person in Modern West Africa', *Journal of the Royal Anthropological Institute* 6(4): 577–595.

Leder, Drew. 1990. *The Absent Body*. Chicago: University of Chicago Press.

Leeming, David. 1994. *James Baldwin: A Biography*. New York: Henry Holt.

Lemonnier, Pierre. 1992. 'Elements for an Anthropology of Technology', Anthropology papers, Museum of Anthropology, University of Michigan, No.88. Ann Arbor: Michigan.

Levi, Primo. 1989. *The Drowned and the Saved*, (trans. Raymond Rosenthal). New York: Vintage.

Levinson, Bradley A.U. 2001. *We Are All Equal: Student Culture and Identity at a Mexican Secondary School 1988–1988*. Durham: Duke University Press.

Lévi-Strauss, Claude. 1963. *Structural Anthropology* Vol. 1, (trans.Claire Jacobson and Brooke Grundfest Schoepf). New York: Basic Books.

_____ 1964. *Totemism*, (trans. Rodney Needham). London: Merlin Press.

_____ 1966. *The Savage Mind*. London: Weidenfeld and Nicolson.

_____ 1973. *Tristes tropiques*, (trans. John and Doreen Weightman). Jonathan Cape: London.

_____ 1985. *The View from Afar*, (trans. Joachim Neugroschel and Phoebe Hoss). New York: Basic Books.

_____ 1990. *The Naked Man*. Vol. 4 of Mythologiques, (trans. John and Doreen Weightman). Chicago: Chicago University Press.

Lienhardt, Godfrey. 1961. *Divinity and Experience: The Religion of the Dinka*. Oxford: Clarendon Press.

Lindquist, Galina. 2000. 'In Search of the Magical Flow: Magic and Market in Contemporary Russia', *Urban Anthropology* 29(4): 315–357.

Lippert, Barbara. 1988. 'Megastars of the 80's (Ronald Reagan and Michael Jackson)', *Washington Post*, 28 August 28 1988, vol.111, col. 1: B1.

Lorimer, Francine. 2003a. 'The Smith Children Go Out to School – and Come Home Again: Place-making among Kuku-Yalanji Children in Southeast Cape York, Australia'. In Olwig, Karen F. and Gulløv, E. (eds) *Children's Paces: Cross-cultural Perspectives*. London: Routledge, pp. 58–76.

Lorimer, Francine. 2003b. 'Stories of Strangers around a Fire'. In Frykman, Jonas and Gilje, Nils (eds) *Being There: New Perspectives on Phenomenology in the Analysis of Culture*. Lund: Nordic Academic Press, pp. 107–127.

Lowry, Malcolm. 1963. *Selected Poems*. San Francisco: City Lights.

Lundin, Susanne. 1999. 'The Boundless Body: Cultural Perspectives on Xeno-transplantation', *Ethos: Journal of Anthropology, National Museum of Ethnography*, Stockholm 64(1): 5–31.

McNaughton, Patrick R. 1988. *The Mande Blacksmiths: Knowledge, Power, and Art in West Africa*. Bloomington: Indiana University Press.

Malinowski, Bronislaw. 1922. *Argonauts of the Western Pacific: An Account of Native Enterprise and Adventure in the Archipelagoes of Melanesian New Guinea*. London: Routledge & Kegan Paul.

_____ 1929. *The Sexual Lives of Savages: An Ethnographic Account of Courtship, Marriage, and Family Life among the Natives of the Trobriand Islands*. London: Routledge & Kegan Paul.

_____ 1965a. *Coral Gardens and Their Magic, Vol. 1, Soil-tilling and Agricultural Rites of the Trobriand Islands*. Bloomington: Indiana University Press.

_____ 1965b. *Coral Gardens and Their Magic, Vol. 2, The Language of Magic and Gardening*. Bloomington: Indiana University Press.

Malkki, Liisa. 1995. *Purity and Exile: Violence, Memory, and National Cosmology among Hutu Refugees in Tanzania*. Chicago: University of Chicago Press.

_____ 1997. 'News and Culture: Transitory Phenomena and the Fieldwork Tradition'. In Gupta, Akhil and Ferguson, James (eds) *Anthropological Locations: Boundaries and Grounds of a Field Science*. Berkeley: University of California Press, pp. 86–101.

Marquard, Odo. 1991. *In Defense of the Accidental: Philosophical Studies*, (trans. Robert M. Wallace). Oxford: Oxford University Press.

Marsden, Maori. 1975. 'God, Man and the Universe: A Maori View'. In King, Michael (ed.) *Te ao hurihuri: The World Moves On*. Wellington: Hicks Smith.

Marshall, Andrew. 2001. 'Fear is the dominant emotion now', *Independent*, 15 September 2001:11.

Marx, Karl. 1961. *Economic and Philosophic Manuscripts of 1844*. Moscow: Foreign Languages Publishing House.

_____ 1964. *Pre-capitalist Economic Formations*, (trans. J. Cohen). London: Lawrence and Wishart.

_____ and Engels, Frederick. 1976. 'The German Ideology', (trans. C. Dutt). In *Karl Marx-Frederick Engels: Collected Works*, Vol. 5. Moscow: Progress Publishers, pp. 19–608.

Mauss, Marcel. 1954. *The Gift: Forms and Functions of Exchange in Archaic Societies*, (trans. Ian Cunnison). London: Cohen and West.

Mead, Margaret. 1971. See Baldwin, James, and Mead, Margaret.

Meikle, James. 2000. 'Soya Gene Find Fuels Doubts on GM Crops', *Guardian*, 31 May 2000: 1.

Merleau-Ponty, Maurice. 1965. *The Structure of Behaviour*, (trans. A.L. Fisher). London: Methuen.

_____ 1962. *The Phenomenology of Perception*, (trans. Colin Smith). London: Routledge and Kegan Paul.

_____ 1964. *Sense and Non-sense*, (trans. Hubert L. Dreyfus and Patricia Allen Dreyfus). Evanston: Northwestern University Press.

_____ 1968. *The Visible and the Invisible (followed by working notes)*, (ed. Claude Lefort, trans. Alphonso Lingis). Evanston: Northwestern University Press.

Miller, Daniel. 1991. *Material Culture and Mass Consumption*. Oxford: Basil Blackwell.

Monk, Ray. 1990. *Ludwig Wittgenstein: The Duty of Genius*. New York: The Free Press.

Moore, Sally Falk. 1987. 'Explaining the Present: Theoretical Dilemmas in Processual Anthropology', *American Ethnologist* 14(4): 727–751.

Motion, Andrew. 1997. *Keats*. Chicago: University of Chicago Press.

Myers, Fred. 1986. *Pintupi Country, Pintupi Self: Sentiment, Place, and Politics among Western Desert Aborigines*. Washington, D.C.: Smithsonian Institution Press.

Nietzsche, Friedrich. 1996. *On the Genealogy of Morals*, (trans. Douglas Smith). Oxford: Oxford University Press.

Nordstrom, Caroline. 1997. *A Different Kind of War Story*. Philadelphia: University of Pennsylvania Press.

Nossack, Hans Erich. 1972. *Interview mit dem tode*. Frankfurt am Main.

Oakeshott, Michael. 1991. *Rationalism in Politics and Other Essays*. New and Expanded Edition. Indianapolis: Liberty Press.

O'Kane, Maggie. 2001. 'Last Stand in the Ghetto of Hate', *Guardian*, Saturday, 8 September 8 2001: 1–2.

Onians, Richard Broxton. 1951. *The Origins of European Thought*. Cambridge: Cambridge University Press.

Pandya, Vishvajit. (n.d.) 'Making of the Other: Vignettes of Violence in Andamese Culture', Unpublished paper, Department of Anthropology, Victoria University of Wellington.

Papagaroufali, Eleni. 1996. 'Xenotransplantation and Transgression: Immoral Stories about Human-animal Relations in the West'. In Descola, Philippe and Pálsson, Gísli (eds) *Nature and Society: Anthropological Perspectives*. London: Routledge, pp. 240–255.

Parliamentary Commissioner for the Environment. 2000. *Caught in the Headlights: New Zealanders' Reflections on Possums, Control Options and Genetic Engineering*. Wellington: Office of the Parliamentary Commissioner for the Environment.

Parr, C.J. 1961. 'A Missionary Library. Printed Attempts to Instruct the Maori, 1815–1845', *Journal of the Polynesian Society* 70(4): 429–450.

Peters, Krijn and Richards, Paul. 1998. 'Why We Fight: Voices of Youth Combatants in Sierra Leone', *Africa* 68(2): 83–210.

Pfaffenberger, Bryan. 1988a. 'The Social Meaning of the Personal Computer: or, Why the Personal Computer Revolution was no Revolution', *Anthropological Quarterly* 61(1): 39–47.

———— 1988b. 'Fetishised Objects and Humanised Nature: Towards an Anthropology of Technology', *Man* 23(2): 236–252.

———— 1992. 'Social Anthropology of Technology', *Annual Review of Anthropology* 21: 491–516.

Pierson, William D. 1976. 'Puttin' Down ol Massa: African Satire in the New World', *Research in African Literatures* 7(2): 166–180.

Piot, Charles. 1999. *Remotely Global: Village Modernity in West Africa*. Chicago: Chicago University Press.

Povrzanovic, Maja. 1997. 'Identities in War: Embodiments of Violence and Places of Belonging', *Ethnologia Europaea* 27: 153–162.

Price, Daisy. 2001. 'A Family Affair', *Independent* 23 April 2001: 18.

Rabinow, Paul. 1996. *Essays on the Anthropology of Reason*. Princeton, New Jersey: Princeton University Press.

Radcliffe-Brown, A.R. 1964. *The Andaman Islanders*. New York: Free Press.

Rapport, Nigel. 2003. *I am Dynamite: An Alternative Anthropology of Power*. London: Routledge.

Rawls, John. 1971. *A Theory of Justice*. Cambridge (Mass.): Belknap Press of Harvard University.

Rheinberger, Hans-Jörg. 2000. 'Beyond Nature and Culture: Modes of Reasoning in the Age of Molecular Biology and Medicine'. In Lock, Margaret, Young, Alan and Cambrosio, Alberto (eds) *Living and Working with the New Medical Technologies: Intersections of Inquiry*, Cambridge: Cambridge University Press, pp. 19–30.

Richards, Audrey. 1982. *Chisungu: A Girl's Initiation Ceremony among the Bemba of Zambia*. London: Routledge.

Richards, Paul. 1985. *Indigenous Agricultural Revolution: Ecology and Food Production in West Africa*. London: Hutchinson.

———— 1996. *Fighting for the Rainforest: War, Youth and Resources in Sierra Leone*. London: International African Institute.

———— 1998. See Peters, Krijn and Richards, Paul.

———— 2002. See Archibald, Steven, and Richards, Paul.

Ricoeur, Paul. 1992. *Oneself as Another*, (trans. Kathleen Blamey). Chicago: University of Chicago Press.

Rigby, Peter. 1968. 'Gogo Rituals of Purification'. In Leach, E.R. (ed.) *Dialectic in Practical Religion*. Cambridge Papers in Social Anthropology 5, Cambridge: Cambridge University Press, pp.153–178.

Rorty, Richard. 1979. *Philosophy and the Mirror of Nature*. Princeton: Princeton University Press.

———— 1982. *Consequences of Pragmatism*. Minneapolis: Minnesota University Press.

———— 1989. *Contingency, Irony, and Solidarity*. Cambridge: Cambridge University Press.

Rousseau, Jean-Jacques. 1992. 'Discourse on the Origin of Inequality', (trans. Donald A. Cress). London: Hackett.

Rousset, David. 1947. *Les jours de notre mort*. Paris.

Royal Commission on Genetic Modification. 2001. http://www/gmcommission.govt.nz/

Rupert, James. 1999. 'Machete Terror Stalks Sierra Leone', *Guardian*, 3 January 1999: 12.

Russell, Bertrand. 1967. *The Autobiography of Bertrand Russell 1872–1914*. New York: Atlantic-Little, Brown.

Said, Edward. 1994. *Representations of the Intellectual: The 1993 Reith Lectures*. New York: Pantheon Books.

Sahlins, Marshall. 1968. 'On the Sociology of Primitive Exchange'. In Banton, Michael (ed.) *The Relevance of Models for Social Anthropology*. London: Tavistock.

_____ 1972. *Stone Age Economics*. Chicago and New York: Aldine-Atherton.

_____ 2002. 'An Empire of a Certain Kind', *Social Analysis* 46(1): 95–103.

Said, Edward W. 1994. *Representations of the Intellectual: The 1993 Reith Lectures*. New York: Pantheon.

Salmond, Anne. 2000. 'Maori and Modernity: Ruatara's Dying'. In Cohen, Anthony P. (ed.) *Signifying Identities: Anthropological Perspectives on Boundaries and Contested Values*. Routledge: London, pp. 37–58.

Samson, Steven. 2003. 'From Reconciliation to Coexistence', *Public Culture* 15(1): 79–184.

Sartre, Jean-Paul. 1948. *The Emotions*. New York: Philosophical Library.

_____ 1956. *Being and Nothingness: An Essay on Phenomenological Ontology*, (trans. Hazel Barnes). New York: Philosophical Library.

_____ 1963. *Saint Genet: Actor and Martyr*, (trans. Bernard Frechtman). New York: George Braziller.

_____ 1964. 'L'artiste et sa conscience', Preface to a book of this title by René Leibowitz, 1950, *Situations 4*.

_____ 1968. *Search for a Method*, (trans. Hazel Barnes). New York: Vintage.

_____ 1969. 'Itinerary of a Thought', *New Left Review* 58: 43–66.

_____ 1973. *Existentialism and Humanism*, (trans. Philip Mairet). London: Methuen.

_____ 1974. *Beyond Existentialism and Marxism*, (trans. John Matthews). London: Verso.

_____ 1976. *Critique of Dialectical Reason*, (trans. Alan Sheridan-Smith). London: Verso.

_____ 1987. *The Family Idiot: Gustave Flaubert 1821–1857*. Vol. 2, (trans. Carol Cosman). Chicago: University of Chicago Press.

_____ 1989. 'Of Rats and Men', Foreword to *The Traitor*, by André Gorz. London: Verso.

Schama, Simon. 2002. 'The Dead and the Guilty', *Guardian*, 11 September 2002: 1

Scheper-Hughes, Nancy. 1992. *Death without Weeping: The Violence of Everyday Life in Brazil*. Berkeley: University of California Press.

_____ 1995. 'The Primacy of the Ethical: Propositions for a Militant Anthropology', *Current Anthropology* 36(1): 409–420.

_____ 1996. 'Theft of Life: The Globalization of Organ-stealing Rumours', *Anthropology Today* 12(3): 3–11.

Schieffelen, Bambia. B. 1990. *The Give and Take of Everyday Life: Language Socialization of Kaluli Children*. Cambridge: Cambridge University Press.

Schiller, F.C.S. 1934. *Must Philosophers Disagree?* London: Macmillan.

Schulkind, Jeanne. 1978. 'Introduction' to Virginia Woolf's *Moments of Being: Unpublished Autobiographical Writings*. London: Triad Grafton.

Schutz, Alfred. 1967. *The Phenomenology of the Social World*, (trans. George Walsh and Frederick Lehnert). London: Heinemann.

_____ and Thomas Luckmann. 1989. *The Structures of the Life-world*, Vol. 2, (trans. Richard M. Zaner and David J. Parent). Evanston, Ill.: Northwestern University Press.

Scott, Belinda. 1994. 'Probation for Knife-wielding Park Drinker', *Cairns Post*, 18 June 1994: 21.

Scott, James C. 1985. *Weapons of the Weak: Everyday Forms of Peasant Resistance*. New Haven: Yale University Press.

Searle, J.R. 1969. *Speech Acts: An Essay in the Philosophy of Language*. Cambridge: Cambridge University Press.

Sears, David .A. 1981. See Bolinger, Dwight and Sears, David A.

Sebald, W.G. 2001. *Austerlitz*. London: Hamish Hamilton.

_____ 2003. *On the Natural History of Destruction*, (trans. Anthea Bell). London: Hamish Hamilton.

Selvini, Mara Palazzoli. 1974. *Self-starvation: From the Intrapsychic to the Transpersonal Approach to Anorexia Nervosa*, (trans. Arnold Pomerans). Sussex: Chaucer Publishing.

Sen, Amartya. 1988. *The Standard of Living*, (ed. Geoffrey Hawthorn). Cambridge: Cambridge University Press.

Sennett, Richard. 1977. *The Fall of Public Man*. Cambridge: Cambridge University Press.

Serres, Michel. 1989. *Statues: le second livre des fondations*. Paris: Flammarion.

_____ with Latour, Bruno. 1995. *Conversations on Science, Culture, and Time*, (trans. Roxanne Lapidus). Ann Arbor: University of Michigan Press.

Severi, Carlo. 1993. 'Talking about Souls: The Pragmatic Construction of Meaning in Cuna Ritual Language'. In Boyer, Pascal (ed.) *Cognitive Aspects of Religious Symbolism*. Cambridge: Cambridge University Press, pp. 165–181.

_____ 1998. See Houseman, Michael and Severi, Carlo.

Sharp, Lesley A. 1995. 'Organ Transplantation as a Transformative Experience: Anthropological Insights into the Restructuring of the Self', *Medical Anthropology Quarterly* 9(3): 57–389.

Shaw, Rosalind. 1997. 'The Production of Witchcraft/witchcraft as Production: Memory, Modernity, and the Slave Trade in Sierra Leone', *American Ethnologist* 24(4): 856–876.

_____ 2002. *Memories of the Slave Trade: Ritual and Historical Imagination in Sierra Leone*. Chicago: Chicago University Press.

_____ 2003. 'Robert Kaplan and "Juju Journalism" in Sierra Leone's Rebel War: The Primitivizing of an African Conflict'. In Meyer, Birgit and Pels, Peter (eds) *Magic and Modernity: Interfaces of Revelation and Concealment*. Stanford: Stanford University Press, pp. 81–102.

Shelley, Mary. 1985. *Frankenstein*. Harmondsworth: Penguin.

Simon, Linda. 1998. *Genuine Reality: A Life of William James*. New York: Harcourt Brace & Co.

Sontag, Susan. 2003. 'The Power of Principle, Adapted from a Speech at the Presentation of the Rothko Chapel Oscar Romero Award to Ishai Menuchin, Chairman of Yesh Gvul', *Guardian*, 26 April 2003.

Staal, F. 1979. 'The Meaninglessness of Ritual', *Numen* 1 (26): 2–22,

_____ 1989. *Rules without Meaning: Ritual, Mantras and the Human Sciences*. New York: Peter Lang.

Strathern, Marilyn. 1992. *After Nature: English Kinship in the Late Twentieth Century*. Cambridge: Cambridge University Press.

Suchman, Lucy A. 1987. *Plans and Situated Actions: The Problem of Human-machine Communication*. Cambridge: Cambridge University Press.

Tamari, Tal. 1995. 'Linguistic Evidence for the History of West African "Castes"', In Conrad, David C. and Frank, Barbara E. (eds) *Status and Identity in West Africa: nyamakalaw of Mande*. Bloomington: Indiana University Press, pp. 61–85.

Tambiah, S.J. 1968. 'The Magical Power of Words', *Man* 3(2): 175–208.

Taylor, Richard. 1868. *The Past and pPresent, or, New Zealand, with Its Prospects for the Future*. Wanganui: Macintosh and Jones.

Thomas, Regina. 2003. 'Frankly Speaking', *Concord Times* 8 January 2003: 5.

Tjørnhøj-Thomsen, Tine. (in press). 'Close Encounters with Infertility and Procreative Technology'. In Jenkins, Richard, Jessen, Hanne, and Steffen, Vibeke (eds) *Matters of Life and Death: The Control of Uncertainty and the Uncertainty of Control*. Copenhagen: Museum Tusculanum Press.

Trankell, Ing-Britt. 2001. 'Songs of Our Spirits: Memory and Conflict in a Cambodian Cham Community', Unpublished Conference Paper, AAS, Chicago.

Tremlett, Gils, and Bendern, Paul de. 2003. 'Fear Grips Algeria as Quake Kills 1,000 Algerians', *Guardian*, 23 May 2003.

Turner, Victor. 1970. *The Forest of Symbols*. Ithaca: Cornell University Press.

Uchendu, Victor. 1965. *The Igbo of Southeast Nigeria*. New York: Holt, Rinehart and Winston.

Usborne, David. 2001a. 'Hopes of Finding Survivors among the Rubble and Metal Fade', *Independent*, 13 September 2001: 4.

_____ 2001b. 'Deadly Spores, Crazy Scares: A World on the Edge of Panic', *Independent*, 16 October 2001: 3.

Van Gennep, Arnold. 1960. *The Rites of Passage*, (trans. Monika B. Vizedom and Gabrielle L. Caffee). London: Routledge & Kegan Paul.

Van Gogh, Vincent. 1963. *The Letters of Vincent Van Gogh*, (Selected, edited, and introduced by Mark Roskill). London: Collins.

Vasagar, Jeeven. 2001. 'Poverty and Envy Fuel Racism in Burnley', *Guardian Weekly*, 5–11 July 2001: 12.

Von Sturmer, John. 1981. 'Talking with Aborigines', *Australian Institute of Aboriginal Studies Newsletter* 15: 3–30.

Walter, Natasha. 2003. 'Terror at Dol Dol', *Guardian G2*, 23 May 2003: 2–3.

Weems, Janice and Patterson, Ellen Tate. 1989. 'Coping with Uncertainty and Ambivalence While Awaiting a Cadaveric Renal Transplant', *ANNA Journal* 16(1): 27–31.

Weiner, James. 1991. *The Empty Place: Poetry, Space and Being among the Foi of Papua New Guinea*. Bloomington: Indiana University Press.

Whitehead, Alfred North. 1947. *Adventures of Ideas*. Cambridge: Cambridge University Press.

Winnicott, D.W. 1974. *Playing and Reality*. Harmondsworth: Penguin Books.

Wiredu, Kwasi. 1996. *Cultural Universals and Particulars: An African Perspective*. Bloomington: Indiana University Press.

Wittgenstein, Ludwig. 1953. *Philosophical Investigations*, (trans. G. E. M. Anscombe). Oxford: Blackwell.

_____ 1961. *Tractatus Logico-philosophicus*, (trans. D.F. Pears and B.F. McGuiness). London: Routledge & Kegan Paul.

Woolf, Virginia. 1977. *To the Lighthouse*. London: Triad Grafton.

Wright, Harrison M. 1959. *New Zealand, 1769–1840: Early Years of Western Contact*. Cambridge (Mass.): Harvard University Press.

Young, Allan. 1995. *The Harmony of Illusions: Inventing Post-traumatic Stress Disorder*. Princeton: Princeton University Press.

Zahan, Dominique. 1974. *The Bambara*. Leiden: E.J. Brill.

_____ 1979. 'The Religion, Spirituality and Thought of Traditional Africa', (trans. K.E. Martin and L.M. Martin). Chicago: Chicago University Press.

Zizek, Slavoj. 1991. *Looking Awry: An Introduction to Jacques Lacan through Popular Culture*. Cambridge (Mass.): MIT Press.

INDEX

biopower, 120. *See also*
   biotechnology
biosociality, 120, 140
biotechnology: and globalisation,
   111–125; impact among Maori,
   122–123
Bledisloe, Caroline, 74n.15
Boltanski, Luc, 144, 150, 154
Bourdieu, Pierre, x, xxviii, 14, 19,
   63, 111, 112, 121, 148, 185;
   on conatus, xx, xxii; on the feel
   for the game, xxiii; on habitus,
   xx–xxiv; on the illusio, xx, xxii,
   xxii–xxv; on the logic of
   practice, 36; on marginality,
   xxxiin.12; on ritual action, 93,
   95; on symbolic capital,
   xxxiin.18, 50n.6, 74n.14, 187
Buñuel, Luis, 40
Burridge, Kenelm, 117

C
cargo cults, 117
Cendrars, Blaise, 155–156
Cendrars, Miriam, 155–156
comparison, comparative method,
   30–32
culture: critique of, xii, xiv, xxxn.2,
   103; as potentiality, 103
Cuna, 83–84

D
Dalsgaard, Anne-Line, 188–189
Daniel, E. Valentine, 155
Das, Veena, 42, 73n.8, 152, 160
de Certeau, Michel, 16, 19–20
Devereux, George, 116, 129–130,
   141n.2, 181
Devisch, René, xvii, xxiv, 110n.7
Dewey, John, xxix
Dinka, 95, 110n.2
Dogon, 62
Dostoyevsky, Fyodor, 183
Douglas, Mary, 106
Downey, Gary Lee, 128, 131–132,
   137

E
ethics, 2; ethical ambiguity, 12
events, xxv–xxviii, xxix, 1–2,
   11–14; as abstract particulars,
   13; and aftereffects, 11–14;
   irreducibility of, 14; and stories,
   11
evolutionary biology, xii
exchange. *See* reciprocity
existential anthropology, xxviii,
   32n.1. *See also* being
existential imperatives, x, xxii, 90,
   103, 181–192
existential loss, 138
existential values, 64–65
existentialism: and existential
   anthropology, xi–xii. *See also*
   existential anthropology
experience, xxviii, 153, 165; and
   episteme, 35

F
Fanon, Franz, 39, 73n.9
Feldman, Allen, 54, 72–73n.2
Ferme, Mariane, 53, 72n.1, 73n.8
Fernandez, James, xix
Feyerabend, Paul, 14
Foi, 105
Fortes, Meyer, xxvi, 78
Foucault, Michel, 90, 119, 151
Freud, Sigmund, 106, 110n.1

G
Gausset, Quentin, 176
Geertz, Clifford, xxvi
Gell, Alfred, 87–88
Gibson, James, xxxin.6
Girard, René, 35, 44
globalisation: existential critique of,
   111–125
Gluckman, Max, xxvi, 61, 73n.10,
   129
Gogo (Tanzania), 38–39, 47
Goody, Jack, 105
Guha, Ranajit, 60